BACTERIAL LENSES

BACTERIAL LENSES

DAVID MEDINA CRUZ

NEW DEGREE PRESS

COPYRIGHT © 2020 DAVID MEDINA CRUZ

BACTERIAL LENSES

ISBN   978-1-63676-535-8   *Paperback*
        978-1-63676-081-0   *Kindle Ebook*
        978-1-63676-082-7   *Ebook*

DEDICATION

*To all those invisible friends who have kept me company
during long nights in the lab, who have inspired this
idea but will never read about it, and without whom
this book would have been finished years earlier*

TABLE OF CONTENTS

ACKNOWLEDGMENT   11

CHAPTER 0.   INTRODUCTION   13

CHAPTER 1.   BACTERIA AS THE ORIGIN OF LIFE   21

CHAPTER 2.   TERRAFORMING THE BACTERIAL WORLD   33

CHAPTER 3.   A SPARK OF COMPLEXITY IN
A UNICELLULAR WORLD   45

CHAPTER 4.   TOGETHER, FORWARD, FOREVER   59

CHAPTER 5.   JUST A LITTLE PUSH   73

CHAPTER 6.   THE BIRTH AND RISE OF INFECTION   87

CHAPTER 7.   WHAT LIES BENEATH THE ENDLESS SAND   101

CHAPTER 8.   GOD'S WRATH, HUMANITY'S AGONY   115

CHAPTER 9.   THE WHISPER THAT KILLED THE WORLD   129

CHAPTER 10.   SUNKEN HOPES IN THE SHORES OF
DESPAIR   143

CHAPTER 11.   SAND TO THE NAKED EYE   157

CHAPTER 12.   CONTROL AND CONTAINMENT   169

CHAPTER 13.   DEATH IN THE TIME OF CHOLERA   183

CHAPTER 14.   THE GOLDEN BULLET   197

CHAPTER 15.   WHAT DOES NOT KILL YOU MAKES
THEM STRONGER   211

CHAPTER 16.   INVISIBLE VOICES   225

CHAPTER 17. THE STONE THAT WE THROW
            OVER THE SKY   237
CHAPTER 18. WHAT'S LEFT   251
CHAPTER 19. TO BE WHAT WE CHOOSE TO BECOME   265

APPENDIX   279

"Fall in love with some activity, and do it! Nobody ever figures out what life is all about, and it doesn't matter. Explore the world. Nearly everything is really interesting if you go into it deeply enough."

—RICHARD P. FEYNMAN

ACKNOWLEDGMENT

First, I would like to thank my family. Mom and Dad, thanks for being as supportive as a six-hour time difference and a too-busy-to-answer son allows. Special thanks to you, Mom, for continually pushing me toward a writing career that we both knew wasn't mine but was fun.

Special thanks to Ada, for always being there and holding back your desire to kill me when I was repeatedly telling you to read my drafts—this book would not be what it is without you, as would I. And of course, thank you, Phoenix, for your feedback, although I know you will not even try to read this book, which is okay, buddy.

I would also like to thank the family that I chose, my dear friends on both sides of the Atlantic. I truly appreciate the support and help because both our short time together and the great distance that separates us have made us better.

Special thanks to all my interviewees—I am so sorry to have been centuries and decades late to our meetings. Still, I promise you that I have done my best to take the history you have written and make it accessible to those who will read this book. It would have been a pleasure to meet you, almost as much as reading about all you have lived through.

Of course, I give huge thanks to all on the New Degree Press and the Creator Institute team, and especially to Eric Koester. I appreciate your efforts to catch my attention by writing a book despite a full agenda of things to be done, most of which are still pending while this book is not. That is passion—one that you all transmitted to me.

I'd also like to gratefully acknowledge Junjiang Chen, Alfredo Cabañero, Veer Shah, Laurie Bishop, Franscico Hermida, Darshi Shah, Francisco Espejo, Jorge Luis Cholula Diaz, Eric Koester once again, and many more all over Europe, especially Spain, who preordered the book and helped make it what it is today.

Furthermore, I would like to thank all those who will see this book on a shelf (virtually or not) and decide to buy it, and to those who will just use it as a way to fill the empty space in their library. An everlasting thanks to you all, for reading it, or just trying. That does and will mean a lot to me, and I hope you enjoy it just a third of what I wrote these words.

Which is a lot, like what you are about to start reading.

CHAPTER 0

INTRODUCTION

———

"The ending is nearer than you think, and it is already written. All that we have left to choose is the correct moment to begin."
—ALAN MOORE, V FOR VENDETTA

What are you?

What does it mean to be you?

You are human.

But what does it mean to be human?

You are a highly intelligent primate whose kind has become the dominant species on Earth. You have a brain, a complex one, unlike anything else out there, capable of wonders whose boundaries are only set by the limitless imagination trapped inside its biological case. You can walk upright, fashion tools, and find things to satisfy your cravings, needs, and desires. You can have a social life. You can love and hate, be afraid, angry, or feel sadness, joy, and surprise.

You are a builder and a destroyer, or both at the same time. You can change the world around you, the people within it, and shape them both.

You can be a good person, a bad one, a horrible one. You can be human, a villain, a hero, or a monster who knows how to play a human. You can be sane in the right situation or mad in the wrong one. You can fit in any spectrum or create your own. You are capable of making mistakes and then learning from them or completely forgetting about them.

You have the privilege of existence and the singular ability to appreciate it.

You are.

Now, what are you really?

Look deep down. Atomically speaking, you are 99 percent oxygen, carbon, hydrogen, nitrogen, calcium, and phosphorus. All of those building blocks are necessary for you to be alive. However, these elements are not life by themselves.

Now, combine all the elements, shape them, and add "the spark," also known as the complex biochemical and metabolic machinery that is behind life. What do you have? The life within you. Cells: the smallest structural and functional building block of your existence. The cell has a life cycle, can undergo metabolism, grow, adapt to the environment, and respond to it. It can reproduce and make more of itself—thousands of clones, and eventually millions over time—by duplicating its genetic material.

After thousands of cycles of mitosis, more and more cells are exposed to the environment and everything that is changing within it. Then, the cell evolves. It becomes *you*. However, it is not alone. You are not a single cell, at least not anymore; you are more than one, more than two, dozens, hundreds, millions, and even billions. You are around thirty trillion cells, human ones. Your cells.

Then, you are thirty-nine trillion bacterial cells.[1]

Bacteria: microscopic unicellular microorganisms that have adapted and colonized every corner of the planet. Even you. They have reached places that we have discovered and those we do not even know about, from the deepest recesses of the ocean to the frozen lakes of Antarctica. They shaped the planet and all life within it long before any other organisms even existed.

Then, we appeared, and with us, the thirty-nine trillion. Bacteria and us, humans and them. Bacterial cells all over, within, coming in, out, and throughout you. They grow, reproduce, and die with you. Continuously. Some of them can double their population every twenty minutes. The whole life of a single organism inside you in just a few minutes. In a second, more bacterial cells live and die in your body than the number of people who have and will ever exist on this planet.

Thirty-nine trillion. An endless ecosystem thriving in every corner of your body. Some of them are happy, others cannot

---

1   Ron Sender, Shai Fuchs, and Ron Milo, "Revised Estimates for the Number of Human and Bacteria Cells in the Body," *PLOS Biology* 14, no. 8 (August 2016): e1002533.

hide their hate, and enough of them want to kill you. However, luckily, the vast majority of bacteria around feel safe with the home you are giving them.

The good ones are in symbiosis. You are the fruit of it; you are symbiosis. You need them; they need you. You will not exist without them; they will without you. Over eons of coevolution, bacteria have done all they could to help your ancestors (as you will learn throughout this book), from the single cell that eventually gave rise to the first mammals to those who raised you. They have done it, and they continue to do it because that is what they do; that is what you are.

You are alive because you contain life. You have a true ecosystem within you, and it is not human. The microbial universe that you bear inside is in homeostasis with your immune system, a defense mechanism whose action has been greatly shaped by bacteria.

From the moment that you are born, bacteria arrive and settle similarly as you do in the cities that we build. They create and destroy in the same way that you do. However, they do it within you. You are their fortress, their city, a place to call home. They might stay forever, be long gone, or stay for a few nights and give you a bad dream.

You are more bacteria than human. You are now what you are because once they were what they were supposed to be. Your genetic material, the core of your existence, has about a thousand genes similar to those of bacteria. The information encoded in those genes is so vital for you that evolution has left them untouched.

Over your entire history, there were many times in which you needed them. They helped you and left a mark. For instance, your ancestors were exposed to bacteria by weird accidents like the infection of egg or sperm cells.[2] This happened so many times that indeed you might just be the product of an accident. You may just be something that was not supposed to be. But it was.

You are theirs. Since the very beginning, watching and intervening. They have had a word in everything. Do you want to know why you age so quickly, why you have such a large appetite, why you behave in the way you do or why that lovely elderly couple in your neighborhood started forgetting their keys one day and your name not long after that?

Your past, present, and future are bacterial.

Bacteria have played a dominant role in human history. They have given you industrial wonders like fermentation and catastrophic pandemics like the Black Death.

Widespread epidemics have reduced the human population in some areas of the world by more than one-third. More armies were defeated by typhus, dysentery, and other bacterial infections than by humans' own desire to kill one another.

Bacteria have killed more people than will ever live, and the funny thing is that you cannot do anything about it. But we

---

2   Madeline Drexler and Institute of Medicine (US). *What You Need to Know About Infectious Disease* (Washington DC: National Academies Press, 2010).

have tried. Modern advancements in medicine, the development of bacterial vaccines, and the discovery of antibiotics have significantly reduced the incidence of bacterial diseases, such as pneumonia and tuberculosis. You have thrown countless weapons against them, and in doing so, you just have rushed the inevitable: the appearance of resistance.

Bacteria have not disappeared as infectious agents nor will they. They continue to evolve, creating increasingly virulent strains and acquiring resistance to whatever we create to fight them. You can slow them down but never stop them. Bacteria are not going to cease doing what they do, like it or not. Because if bacteria disappear, so do you.

Now, stop. Change your perception. Look at the world in front of you through bacterial lenses. No more human ones. Do so, and you will be able to learn from the past, adapt to the present, and anticipate a future of a constantly changing world that is not yours, but theirs—the bacterial world.

Like everyone else, I was once new to this world. During my childhood, bacteria were nothing else than those invisible things that might make me sick if I did not wash my hands or if I did not get my coat when going out to play with my friends in the winter. They were no more than a whisper in a thin hair full of many other things. However, everything changed when I got to college, where I had the chance to enjoy what would be my first of many experiences with microbiology. I remember the passion in the words of my professor, and suddenly, something that seemed odd and irrelevant to me became a pivotal key on my journey to understand the world that surrounded me.

It was then that I decided to pursue a career in microbiology. Sadly, my hands were tied as I was still a chemistry major at the time. Still, I had the intention. I took as many courses as possible that would allow me to face these microorganisms with such a vivid obsession that I often found myself theorizing about the thermodynamics of metabolic reactions inside the membranes of Gram-negative bacteria when I should have been studying them in a chemical engineering setting. Of course, it did not help my grades.

However, everything worked out in the end. I eventually had the chance to join a microbiology-related laboratory where I could research real problems involving the bacterial world. It was astonishing to learn about all that they could do and how much we could learn from them. It was then that I knew that my work at this lab was what I truly enjoyed, so I started to pursue a life of my liking.

After a few adventures in Europe, I came to the US as a master's student. After completing my defense, I decided to stay for my PhD in a nanotechnology lab. Although highly oriented toward material science, I was lucky to have the support of my advisor, who gave me the green light to work on the projects that I wanted. Since then, I have been developing nanomaterials for the treatment of diseases caused by bacterial infections, continually learning from them and broadening the horizons of my own knowledge.

Over all these years, the only thing that I have truly learned is how small we are when compared to bacteria in every aspect of our existence. However, not many people are aware of or share the same feeling. This void of knowledge has often led to huge problems, such as the constant rise in antimicrobial resistance to antibiotics that throw us to the post-antibiotic era.

I am keen to believe that by revising our long-lasting relationship with these microorganisms, we will be able to give some light to a future whose path might be darker than we are inclined to think. By understanding the impact that bacteria have had in our own development as humans, we might discover some interesting facts about our ultimate goal as a species.

This book is intended to be a quick and introductory view of everything that has happened on our planet from its formation to the moment you got your hands on this piece of paper from the perspective of those microorganisms, which have shaped every corner of reality. I hope that you will be able to look at the world with different eyes after you finish it.

CHAPTER 1

BACTERIA AS THE ORIGIN OF LIFE

"It was one thing to declare that we had not yet discovered the trace of a beginning, and another to deny that the Earth ever had a beginning."

—JOHN PLAYFAIR

Have you ever thought about what the beginning of everything looked like? What about right before? Some people believe that the universe was an infinite stretch of an ultra-hot and dense material that remained steady for as long as we could count. Others believe that everything was contained in the volume of an extremely hot peach.[3] Honestly, there might not be any point to even wondering about it. As Stephen Hawking once said, whatever was or happened before the beginning does not matter, as events were unmeasurable

---

3   Steven Weinberg, *The First Three Minutes: A Modern View of the Origin of the Universe* (New York: Basic Books, 1993), 127.

and undefined.[4] Therefore, where reality fades, imagination sparks.

Imagine yourself at the top of a cliff in the middle of nowhere. It is a warm summer night. Everything is dark, with no lights at all. There is a field, the endless firmament, and you, nothing much. You look at the sky, staring at it. Suddenly, a distant explosion lights the horizon, and as quickly as it came, it fades. Then, something unusual starts moving around, changing its shape in front of your eyes. It seems like a massive cloud of gas and dust, a continually moving piece of chaotic matter. In astronomical terms, we should call it a nebula.[5]

Everything might have begun there, just like that, on a summer night 4.5 billion years ago. The nebula that you are looking at now begins showing signs of a contraction that has been triggered by the gigantic shock wave from the previous and now distant explosion. The nebula suddenly starts to rotate, moving fast, accelerating at a kind of scary speed. Particles of cosmic dust start to collide, crash, and break, creating a symphony whose echoes are lost in time.

Now, some pretty interesting physical parameters that you might have read about in college, such as perturbations of angular momentum, gravity, and inertia, start taking place. If we put all those in an equation, the physical outcome might

---

4   Rachel Feltman, "Stephen Hawking Thinks He Knows What Happened before the Beginning of Time," *Popular Science*, March 2, 2018.

5   J.A. Chalmers and B. Chalmers, "XXXVII. The Expanding Universe—an Alternative View," *The London, Edinburgh, and Dublin Philosophical Magazine and Journal of Science* 19, no. 126 (February 1935): 436–46.

be what lies in front of your eyes: a nebula that quickly flattened into a protoplanetary disk perpendicular to its axis of rotation, full of colliding particles and small clusters of rock.[6] Variable perturbations due to collisions of other large debris start creating kilometer-sized large bodies of mass that orbit the center of the disc. Chaos builds in its wake.

The center of the nebula now collapses, producing an incredibly massive amount of heat that you can quickly feel despite the distance. Then, nuclear fusion of hydrogen into helium begins, and everything becomes so hot that it does not even make any sense to measure how much. After more contraction, in a tiny section of the giant disc, a star ignites and evolves into the Sun. At the same time, countless events just like this are happening everywhere out there.

In the meantime, in the outermost section of the nebula, gravity causes matter to condense.[7] Quickly, the disk begins separating into smaller rings in a process known as runaway accretion.[8] The consequence is grand, with larger fragments of dust and debris clumping together to form planets of different sizes. And so, among the limitless number of planets, there we have it: the Earth.

6   G. P. Kuiper, "On the Origin of the Solar System," *Proceedings of the National Academy of Sciences* 37, no. 1 (January 1951): 1–14.

7   K. Tsiganis et al., "Origin of the Orbital Architecture of the Giant Planets of the Solar System," *Nature* 435, no. 7041 (May 2005): 459–61.

8   Brian D. Metzger, Roman R. Rafikov, and Konstantin V. Bochkarev, "Global Models of Runaway Accretion in White Dwarf Debris Discs," *Monthly Notices of the Royal Astronomical Society* 423, no. 1 (June 2012): 505–28.

It's focusing our attention right there—on a planet that is nothing like you would know. No cities are crawling with people wandering around, nor forests full of wildlife to watch. There are no clouds in a blue sky, nor beautiful and calm sunsets to enjoy. Indeed, after taking a closer look, everything is moving; everything is still chaos.

Dust is jumping around, volcanic outgassing rising above a continually twisting and cracking mass of matter. It is not your first choice for a holiday trip, so with nothing more to see here, we need to move around ten million years forward. Sadly, the view does not improve much. The surface of the planet does not stand still. It continuously moves, collapses, shrinks, and swells and, more importantly, grows.

The Earth is somewhat closer to a sphere now, but it still lacks a clear distinction between core and surface. The extreme heat melts the heavy metals from the crust. Silicates start to float around because of their light density, while the heavy metals quickly start sinking. This is what we call the iron catastrophe that resulted in the separation of a primitive mantle and a metallic core, producing the layered structure of Earth and setting up the formation of the magnetic field.[9] Suddenly, there is a kind of solid crust that we could call "floor." Moving another ten million years forward, everything seems to settle down a bit. Over this time, the crust solidifies.

____

9   H. St C. O'Neill, "The Origin of the Moon and the Early History of the Earth-A Chemical Model. Part 2: The Earth," *Geochimica et Cosmochimica Acta* 55, no. 4 (April 1, 1991): 1159–72.

And that's it—we have the primitive Earth.[10] Still strange, but closer to what you would call home.

Now, the problem is not within the surface but the sky. A relatively small protoplanetary object, which has been approaching Earth all this time, finally hits the surface, ejecting part of the newly created mantle and crust into space. A few million years later, all that material that was released from the collision has compacted and stabilized in a process similar to the one happening on Earth not far from us. And just like that, we have the Moon.[11] Now the sky will not be such a boring place to stare at, will it?

However, this massive collision is not the end, as there are small celestial bodies quickly following the same path toward the surface of the Earth. They start landing and making huge craters all over the place. We call this the Late Heavy Bombardment, which took place around 4.4 billion years ago. Some of these celestial bodies, especially comets, carried water and other chemical compounds from distant places all over the universe.[12] Still, everything is so hot that it vaporized upon contact.

---

10   Jon Wade and B. J. Wood, "Core Formation and the Oxidation State of the Earth," *Earth and Planetary Science Letters* 236, no. 1–2 (July 2005): 78–95.

11   Robin M. Canup and Erik Asphaug, "Origin of the Moon in a Giant Impact near the End of the Earth's Formation," *Nature* 412, no. 6848 (August 2001): 708–12.

12   R. Gomes et al., "Origin of the Cataclysmic Late Heavy Bombardment Period of the Terrestrial Planets," *Nature* 435, no. 7041 (May 2005): 466–69.

The next few million years are characterized by constant geological chaos: volcanoes, earthquakes, and lava floating everywhere. When everything seems lost to this crude reality, something starts happening. More accurately, something starts falling: rain, but more specifically, a rainfall like no other that does not stop when the surface of the planet begins to flood.

But where did this water came from? Apparently, it was there from the very beginning and had a meteoritic source.[13] However, most of it was lost during the Moon-forming impact. The impact left a massive layer of debris that condensed within two thousand years, leaving behind tons of carbon dioxide in the atmosphere, along with hydrogen and water vapor.[14] Liquid water oceans may have existed despite the surface temperature of 230°C due to the increased pressure of the atmosphere. As the cooling continued, most carbon dioxide was removed from the atmosphere by subduction and dissolution in ocean water. Eventually, this movement of water led to different cycles that ended with a massive rain.

Then, four billion years ago, everything that can be seen is covered by water—an ocean just formed in front of you,

---

13   T. Albertsson, D. Semenov, and Th Henning, "Chemodynamical Deuterium Fractionation in the Early Solar Nebula: The Origin of Water on Earth and in Asteroids and Comets," *Astrophysical Journal* 784, no. 1 (March 2014): 39.

14   Matija Ćuk and Sarah T. Stewart, "Making the Moon from a Fast-Spinning Earth: A Giant Impact Followed by Resonant Despinning," *Science* 338, no. 6110 (November 2012): 1047–52.

which seems to be extremely calm.[15] Still, under the surface, volcanoes continue to rise, some of them resisting sinkage, with an unstoppable release of dark and dense fumes that can be seen from everywhere. For a while, all stays the same. It might be a bit boring, being the only living thing on the whole planet, don't you think? The problem is that we are not looking in the right direction. Not at all.

Let us be clear about something: There is no oxygen gas on the planet, which means no ozone. Therefore, there is not any layer to block the deadly ultraviolet light that comes from the Sun. Consequently, life, by any means, could not have survived on the surface of the planet at this time. With such a lack of life-friendly space on the surface, the right place for anything to happen is underwater. If we take a close look underneath the ocean and go closer to the bottom, you will find yourself around hydrothermal vents, fissures on the seabed from which heated, sulfide mineral-rich waters spew up from the still-pretty-hot core.[16]

Once underwater, we will see plenty of things moving around. While dust, debris, and other inorganic particles in a fluid move following a random Brownian motion, there are tiny filaments, knobs, and tubes whose movement seems to have a purpose. These not-randomly moving objects are

---

15 A. H. Delsemme, "Cometary Origin of Carbon, Nitrogen and Water on the Earth," *Origins of Life and Evolution of the Biosphere* 21, no. 5–6 (September 1991): 279–98.

16 John A. Baross and Sarah E. Hoffman, "Submarine Hydrothermal Vents and Associated Gradient Environments as Sites for the Origin and Evolution of Life," *Origins of Life and Evolution of the Biosphere* 15, no. 4 (December 1985): 327–45.

approaching small clusters of other things—let us call them nutrients—which suddenly disappear. Then, they move again. Have you ever asked yourself where we come from? The answer might be in simple tiny things eating other even tinier things.

This primordial and unnamed form of life had come to our time, but not as they were. Due to unknown reasons, they ended buried under tons of sediments and rocks where the heat and pressure triggered a release of hydrogen and oxygen from their tissue, leaving behind the element of life, carbon. This process, called carbonization, yielded a detailed carbon impression of the organism that remained hidden in sedimentary rocks for millions of years, until someone found these pseudo-skeletons in the Eastern Shore of the Hudson Bay, close to Quebec, in Canada.[17]

That someone was Dr. Dominic Papineau, a professor at the University College London (UCL), in the United Kingdom, discovered them.[18] Where there was water before, Dominic found quartz layers compressed on top of each other within what is called a Nuvvuagittuq Supracrustal Belt (NSB), a

---

17 Maria Magdalena Titirici, Axel Funke, and Andrea Kruse, "Hydrothermal Carbonization of Biomass." in *Recent Advances in Thermochemical Conversion of Biomass,* ed. Rajeev K. Sukumaran (Amsterdam: Elsevier Inc., 2015), 325–52.

18 Matthew S. Dodd et al., "Evidence for Early Life in Earth's Oldest Hydrothermal Vent Precipitates," *Nature* 543, no. 7643 (March 2017): 60–64.

sequence of the oldest volcanic and sedimentary rocks known to science.[19]

"I thought to myself that we have got it, we have got the oldest fossils on the planet," Dr. Papineau mentioned in an interview to BBC News on 2017. "It relates to our origins. For intelligent life to evolve to a level of consciousness, to a point where it traces back its history to understand its origin."[20]

Although Dominic and his colleagues vigorously defend their conclusions and are confident that their findings will stand the test of time, not everyone in the scientific community agreed with them. For instance, in 2019, a paper came out and explained that the tubes and filaments with the same shape and chemical makeup as those that were living underwater a few billion years back could be produced abiotically (meaning in the absence of life) by the use of a simple chemical experiment (chemical gardens), which may form naturally in some hydrothermal settings. On the other hand, other researchers believe that the rocks where the fossilized materials were found are younger than what has been claimed.[21]

Therefore, to date, if we want to meet the well-established and direct oldest evidence of life on the planet, we have to

---

19 Nicolas Dauphas et al., "Identification of Chemical Sedimentary Protoliths Using Iron Isotopes in the > 3750 Ma Nuvvuagittuq Supracrustal Belt, Canada," *Earth and Planetary Science Letters* 254, no. 3–4 (February 2007): 358–76.

20 Pallab Ghosh, "Earliest Evidence of Life on Earth 'found' ", *BBC news, Science & Environment*, March 1, 2017.

21 Sean McMahon, "Earth's Earliest and Deepest Purported Fossils May Be Iron-Mineralized Chemical Gardens," *Proceedings of the Royal Society B: Biological Sciences* 286, no. 1916 (December 2019): 2019-2410.

travel to Western Australia. In particular, we have to go to the Pilbara Craton, one of the oldest crusts identified on the Earth. Here, Dr. Raphael Baumgartner, a scientist from the University of New South Wales in Australia, and other researchers were looking for such pieces of evidence on Apex Chert rocks (a type of mineral formation).

They discovered some irregular shapes that were dated to 3.4 billion years back.[22] After some analysis, the team concluded that these rocks once contained microorganisms.[23] Baumgartner was clear about his findings: "We have found smoking-gun evidence for some of the earliest life on Earth. There are no convincing organic matter or microbial remains older than ours." Since their discovery, they have been studying the oldest direct evidence of life on Earth, a snapshot of the microbial world that ruled the planet before ours.

But what do we call them? The fossilized materials that were found are said to show remnants of stromatolites (from modern Latin *stroma*, meaning covering). Stromatolites are identified as layered mounds, columns, and sheet-like sedimentary rocks that were initially formed by the growth of microorganisms that were yet able to survive and thrive in

---

22 Carl Zimmer, "How and Where Did Life on Earth Arise," *Science* 309, no. 5731 (July 2005): 89.

23 Raphael J. Baumgartner et al., "Nano-Porous Pyrite and Organic Matter in 3.5-Billion-Year-Old Stromatolites Record Primordial Life," *Geology* 47, no. 11 (November 2019): 1039–43.

such an environment as extreme as the one offered by Earth at the moment.[24]

Stromatolites can be seen as the fingerprint of a particular type of microorganism that ruled the world back then: bacteria. However, not just any kind of bacteria—cyanobacteria.[25] As the oldest known forms of life, it might be surprising for you to think that cyanobacteria are still around us. However, they are, and they have become one of the largest and most important groups of bacteria on Earth.

As the American writer, Bill Bryson wrote in *In a Sunburned Country* in 2000, "It's not the sight of Stromatolites that makes them exciting. It's the idea of them."[26] Stromatolites are a consequence of life, most likely of the oldest sign of it on this planet. The growth of cyanobacteria, combined with photosynthesis, crated the characteristic shape of these fingerprints from the past.

When these bacteria grow, they use up the carbon dioxide in the surrounding water, which causes calcium carbonate (a pretty common salt on our planet) to precipitate and solidify from its dissolved state in water. Afterward, cyanobacteria make a sticky material, similar to glue, that captures calcium carbonate and forms a crust over the microorganism, which

---

24 Andrew H. Knoll, "Paleobiological Perspectives on Early Microbial Evolution," *Cold Spring Harbor Perspectives in Biology* 7, no. 7 (July 2015): 1–17.

25 James F. Kasting and Janet L. Siefert, "Life and the Evolution of Earth's Atmosphere," *Science* 296, no. 5570 (May 2002): 1066–68.

26 Bill. Bryson, *In a Sunburned Country* (Portland: Broadway Books, 2000), 102.

continues to grow around and through the crusty layer. This process continues forming layer after layer, leading to the characteristic tubular shape that we eventually found millions of years after.[27]

Why are they so important? Cyanobacteria were the oldest living organisms to inhabit this planet during a time when life was not welcome anywhere but in the deepest sides of the ocean. Stromatolites are more than an old fossil—they are proof that bacteria were there; they existed and survived despite the deadly surface that was regularly hit by cosmic rocks and ultraviolet radiation.

They are the remaining ashes of an old match that lit a fire that triggered the transformation of the planet from a lifeless piece of rock to the biosphere we enjoy today. We must understand that by just living, cyanobacteria changed the planet forever, setting the scene for the origin of a more diverse and purposeful life of which we humans are a part. However, such a gigantic transition did have more than a few pitfalls which have threatened the loss of everything on more than one occasion.

27 Kevin Lepot et al., "Microbially Influenced Formation of 2,724-Million-Year-Old Stromatolites," *Nature Geoscience* 1, no. 2 (February 2008): 118–21.

CHAPTER 2

TERRAFORMING THE BACTERIAL WORLD

"It is not the strongest or the most intelligent who will survive, but those who can best manage change."

—LEON C. MEGGINSON

In the last chapter, we left a primitive Earth with conditions that were far from what is imaginable today, loaded with plenty of simple and strange microscopic creatures. It now becomes difficult to imagine how we went from there to what we have today: a beautiful planet thriving with a complex mixture of almost endless kinds of life forms. How? The answer is purely chemical, and what lies beyond is far better than all that was left behind.

Around four billion years ago, deep down in the oceans, hydrothermal vents were like lighthouses in a dark and lifeless planet. In these settings, seawater encountered minerals from the planet's crust, triggering chemical reactions that created a warm and mineral-rich environment containing variable amounts of hydrogen (H).

All these elements provided a sustained source of energy that facilitated chemical reactions that led the synthesis of organic compounds often used as nutrients for different microscopic entities.[28] With populations exponentially increasing in size, some of these individuals around started to move far from their hometowns, exploring areas closer to the surface. However, they were still confined to the water, but not for long.

As we already know, the surface of the planet was not yet habitable due to a lack of life-friendly breathable gases. Besides, the Sun was constantly throwing deadly ultraviolet radiation that could not be stopped by an atmosphere like the one we have today.

Indeed, there were two other atmospheres before the current one. The first one was part of that nebula whose contraction created the solar system, composed of light elements like hydrogen and helium (He).[29] The intensive wind, solar storms, and heat caused these elements to be driven off, soon gone forever into the cosmic oblivion.

Then, when the Moon was created, a release of volatile gases from the surface happened. These compounds created the

28 Holger W. Jannasch, "Microbial Processes at Deep Sea Hydrothermal Vents," in *Hydrothermal Processes at Seafloor Spreading Centers*, ed. Peter A. Rona (New York: Springer US, 1983), 677–709.

29 Kevin Zahnle, Laura Schaefer, and Bruce Fegley, "Earth's Earliest Atmospheres.," *Cold Spring Harbor Perspectives in Biology* 2, no. 10 (October 2010): a004895.

second atmosphere, fed by volcanic fumes mostly composed of water vapor, carbon dioxide, sulfur dioxide, and hydrogen sulfide. These gases quickly increased the density of this new atmosphere. Within a few million years, the air on the planet became tremendously rich in greenhouse gases but weak in oxygen.[30]

The transition from the second to the third and current atmosphere started sometime around 3.8 billion years ago when bacteria abandoned the water and started to conquer the surface.[31] Just as Columbus did with America, the bacterial world prepared an explorer to reach the surface. Its name was LUA, a simple acronym for the Last Universal Ancestor.[32] Sadly, unlike Columbus, LUA never reached a destiny but prepared everything so that the bacterial world could jump to this unknown land.

If you're wondering what LUA might have looked like, that is up to you. Just think about all these small life forms swimming around a hydrothermal vent while underwater, and pick one of them, the one that you most like.[33] That is LUA,

---

30 L. V. Berkner and L. C. Marshall, "Limitation on Oxygen Concentration in a Primitive Planetary Atmosphere," *Journal of the Atmospheric Sciences* 23, no. 2 (March 1966): 133–43.

31 Norio Kitadai and Shigenori Maruyama, "Origins of Building Blocks of Life: A Review," *Geoscience Frontiers* 9, no. 4 (July 2018): 1117–53.

32 Patrick Forterre et al., "The Nature of the Last Universal Ancestor and the Root of the Tree of Life, Still Open Questions," *BioSystems* 28, no. 1–3 (January 1992): 15–32.

33 Massimo Di Giulio, "The Universal Ancestor Lived in a Thermophilic or Hyperthermophilic Environment," *Journal of Theoretical Biology* 203, no. 3 (April 2000): 203–13.

the one who survived, the one microorganism who stood out among the others.

What LUA did was indeed remarkable. It survived an Earth characterized by the sudden rise of water temperature, the depletion of nutrients in the environment, and the quick appearance of larger organisms that were trying to engulf smaller ones and make them an excellent dessert. LUA did what it did because it was armed with an extraordinary array of evolutionary advantages.

For instance, we know that LUA was similar to a single pro-karyote cell, lacking a nucleus, but with a cell membrane and probably ribosomes (tiny bio-machines that make pro-teins). LUA might have been able to use DNA as its genetic code, RNA for information transfer and protein synthesis, and enzymes to catalyze reactions.[34] Besides, it was able to absorb food from the surroundings and most likely used fermentation to break down the chemical bones within the nutrients to generate energy. Then, this energy was used to grow and reproduce.[35]

For the first time in the whole story of life, we can truly speak of something that is 100 percent alive. Sadly, LUA was lim-ited to its development, confined underwater. However, soon

---

34 W. Ford Doolittle, "The Nature of the Universal Ancestor and the Evo-lution of the Proteome," *Current Opinion in Structural Biology* 10, no. 3 (June 2000): 355–58.

35 Carl Woese, "The Universal Ancestor," *Proceedings of the National Acad-emy of Sciences of the United States of America* 95, no. 12 (June 1998): 6854–59.

after, one of the descendants of LUA stepped its non-literal feet onto the surface.[36]

Now before explaining what happened there, let me just stop here for a second and explain a concept that is going to be extremely important: photosynthesis. Jokes aside, it is time to give some light to the matter. Nowadays, most of the life that covers the surface of the planet depends directly or indirectly on photosynthesis. From your vegetarian food to the inhabitants of any green space within your city or park, to that green thing in the corner of your house that might slowly turn brownish if you stop watering it.

All of them and the organisms that they support depend on this phenomenon that was discovered by a Dutch-British physician and scientist named Jan Ingenhousz.[37] In 1730, Jan saw that green plants released bubbles of oxygen in the presence of sunlight, but the bubbles stopped when it was dark. He also noticed that at that point, plants began to emit some carbon dioxide. Simply speaking, this is photosynthesis.

Photosynthesis has, indeed, two forms. The most common is oxygenic photosynthesis, which turns carbon dioxide, water, and sunlight into nutrients. It captures the energy of the

---

36 Arthur L. Koch, "Development and Diversification of the Last Universal Ancestor," *Journal of Theoretical Biology* 168, no. 3 (June 1994): 269–80.

37 Howard Gest, "Bicentenary Homage to Dr Jan Ingen-Housz, MD (1730-1799), Pioneer of Photosynthesis Research," *Photosynthesis Research* 63, no. 2 (February 2000): 183–90.

Sun within energy-rich molecules, which then provide the organism enough power to make carbohydrates.[38]

The other side of the coin is anoxygenic photosynthesis, used by some bacteria.[39] In this process, light energy is captured and converted to energy-rich molecules. So far, the process is the same. However, there is no production of oxygen, which means that water is not required. Instead, hydrogen sulfide is employed, and elemental sulfur (S) produced.[40] Nowadays, this type of photosynthesis is only seen in extremophile organisms and restricted to unhospitable environments such as hot springs and hydrothermal vents.

These settings were widely available in the primitive Earth that was, generally speaking, a hell of an environment at that time, which is the reason why these extremophile organisms thrived. Because of such a population, they were the first ones to reach the surface, armed with a whole range of metabolic and evolutionary adaptations coming from their ancestor LUA, which they had to test on the surface if wanted to survive.[41] As soon as these bacteria reached land, they did a simple thing that commenced the beginning of the end of

---

38   Nathan Nelson and Adam Ben-Shem, "The Complex Architecture of Oxygenic Photosynthesis," *Nature Reviews Molecular Cell Biology* 5, no. 12 (December 2004): 971–82.

39   Y. Cohen, E. Padan, and M. Shilo, "Facultative Anoxygenic Photosynthesis in the Cyanobacterium Oscillatoria Limnetica," *Journal of Bacteriology* 123, no. 3 (September 1975): 855–61.

40   S Garlick, A Oren, and E Padan, "Occurrence of Facultative Anoxygenic Photosynthesis among Filamentous and Unicellular Cyanobacteria.," *Journal of Bacteriology* 129, no. 2 (February 1977): 623–29.

41   William Martin et al., "Hydrothermal Vents and the Origin of Life," *Nature Reviews Microbiology* 6, no. 11 (September 2008): 805–14.

the lifeless surface: They breathed, and they continued doing it for quite a long time.[42]

Among all these bacterial species, a new kind emerged from deep in the ocean. Unlike their predecessors, they were able to do the most common type of photosynthesis: oxygenic. This was something huge at that time, evolutionary speaking. Around 3.2 billion years ago, these bacteria were everywhere on the surface, producing massive amounts of oxygen.[43] We know them from before as cyanobacteria, a species that suddenly was dominating the whole planet.

The amount of oxygen in Earth increased by a magnitude of two to three just within a few million years, which, temporally speaking, is a huge jump. An almost oxygen-free atmosphere was now full of it. Completely full. The oxygen in this new atmosphere was exposed to and stimulated by solar ultraviolet radiation, which started releasing large amounts of ozone that was collected in a layer near the upper part of the atmosphere.[44]

This ozone layer absorbed—and still does—a significant amount of the ultraviolet radiation coming down from the Sun. Therefore, the bacterial cells were now shielded from

---

42   G. J. Olsen, C. R. Woese, and R. Overbeek, "The Winds of (Evolutionary) Change: Breathing New Life into Microbiology," *Journal of Bacteriology* 176, no. 1 (January 1994): 1-6.

43   James F. Kasting and Janet L. Siefert, "Life and the Evolution of Earth's Atmosphere," *Science* 296, no. 5570 (May 2002): 1066-68.

44   U. Kogelschatz, B. Eliasson, and M. Hirth, "Ozone Generation From Oxygen And Air: Discharge Physics And Reaction Mechanisms," *Ozone: Science & Engineering* 10, no. 4 (September 1988): 367–77.

high radiation that might have triggered significant levels of mutation. Consequently, these microorganisms were happily inhabiting, virtually every single corner of the planet. They thrived in what might be considered the "industrial revolution" of the microscopic world, and just like the human iteration of this story, real consequences surfaced for them.

Have you ever heard of that saying, "too much of a good thing?" It literally means that something beneficial might become harmful in large quantities or over an extended period of time. Well, that beneficial thing was oxygen. Why did it become harmful? Let's put it simply: Oxygen is toxic—pretty toxic. And that is how, ironically, bacteria almost signed their own death warrant by trying to just live.

It is now time to explain the story of how bacteria almost screwed up everything, also known as the Great Oxygenation Event, the first apocalypse, or the deadliest mass extinction that this planet has ever seen.[45]

As we know, at the beginning, the atmosphere was rich in carbon dioxide and other greenhouse gases. Water and iron-rich minerals on the surface acted like sponges, absorbing the small concentrations of oxygen present by default.[46] Everything was in equilibrium. Then, cyanobacteria arrived at the

---

45 Genming Luo et al., "Rapid Oxygenation of Earth's Atmosphere 2.33 Billion Years Ago," *Science Advances* 2, no. 5 (May 2016): e1600134.

46 Barry Knight, "A Review of the Corrosion of Iron from Terrestrial Sites and the Problem of Post-excavation Corrosion," *The Conservator* 14, no. 1 (January 1990): 37–43.

match. Better prepared and adapted, they started thriving, leaving literally tons of oxygen behind as they grew.[47]

What was the consequence? The composition of the atmosphere dramatically changed. There was plenty of oxygen building up in every centimeter of the ocean's surface and in every cubic millimeter of air. The water became saturated, as did the iron-rich minerals.[48] The unavoidable happened. All bacteria were literally breathing poison.

Murphy's law was not even invented by that time, but I am sure he would take the example right from this event. Bacterial species, whole populations, were literally dying, leaving billions, trillions of lifeless forms on the surface of the planet.

Now, have you ever heard that saying, "in life things can always go wrong?" Well, they did. The continuously increasing levels of oxygen led to the oxidation of atmospheric methane to carbon dioxide and water. The consequence was a significant weakening of the greenhouse effect of the Earth's atmosphere. This event triggered an extremely quick planetary cooling, which subsequently led to a series of ice ages.[49] Now I have to tell you: this was not like another bad

---

47 R. T. Brinkmann, "Dissociation of Water Vapor and Evolution of Oxygen in the Terrestrial Atmosphere," *Journal of Geophysical Research* 74, no. 23 (October 1969): 5355–68.

48 Woodward W. Fischer, James Hemp, and Joan Selverstone Valentine, "How Did Life Survive Earth's Great Oxygenation?," *Current Opinion in Chemical Biology* 31 (April 2016): 166-78.

49 Grant M. Young, "Precambrian Supercontinents, Glaciations, Atmospheric Oxygenation, Metazoan Evolution and an Impact That May Have Changed the Second Half of Earth History," *Geoscience Frontiers* 4, no. 3 (May 2013): 247–61.

winter in Boston. It was a massive glaciation event, a global ice age, where the term cold lost the realistic opportunity to be measured.[50]

You might be wondering, what was the consequence of such a series of catastrophic events? Putting it in a friendly, even poetic, way, what happened was a biological diversification. Those organisms that were not prepared died (nearly all of them), while the ones that could withstand the environmental adversities survived. Those last ones had a difficult decision from the evolutionary standpoint: adapt or die. And they adapted, starting to breathe what was killing them.

These bacterial survivors had to use oxygen in their own metabolism, something that was not common at the time.[51] They could combine it with some other molecules present in the environment, and release energy, tons of it. As their ancestors LUA did millions of years before underwater, they survived to withstand their presence on the surface. They grew faster, and they lived.

The chaos, the will to survive, and the extreme environmental conditions led to a significant and slight change within these cells, giving these organisms the means to obtain energy to exploit new, more complex settings all over the surface: from

---

50   I. N. Bindeman, A. Bekker, and D. O. Zakharov, "Oxygen Isotope Perspective on Crustal Evolution on Early Earth: A Record of Precambrian Shales with Emphasis on Paleoproterozoic Glaciations and Great Oxygenation Event," *Earth and Planetary Science Letters* 437 (March 2016): 101–13.

51   Jose Castresana and Matti Saraste, "Evolution of Energetic Metabolism: The Respiration-Early Hypothesis," *Trends in Biochemical Sciences* 20, no. 11 (November 1995): 443–48.

the top of constantly rising mountains to the deepest and darkest corners of caves.

The microscopic world almost perishes in its will to expand, and from the ashes of such utopia, a renewed bacterial kingdom was about to start ruling the planet, setting the stage for a real industrial revolution in the story of life.

CHAPTER 3

A SPARK OF COMPLEXITY IN A UNICELLULAR WORLD

"Life spirals laboriously upward to higher and even higher levels, paying for every step."

—LUDWIG VON BERTALANFFY

Often, when everything is lost, all that we need to survive is a spark of warmth in the middle of the winter that can remind us of the better times to come. Perhaps, that was all that life required to move ahead in a planet that was turning colder every year. Cyanobacteria, in their simple desire to live, triggered a massive extinction in which oxygen killed as much as 99 percent of all life on Earth.

Right after, the Huronian glaciation, the longest ice age that our planet has ever seen, arrived. The Earth was slowly turning into a giant snowball whose formation would have made life extinct entirely.[52] However, let me prove this wrong.

Indeed, microfossils, such as our already-known Stromatolites, proved that in shallow marine environments, life did not suffer any considerable perturbation.[53] Instead, many microorganisms developed an outstanding trophic complexity, leading to some advanced and unexpected evolutionary modifications.

In an icy and cold world, liquid water meant life. You know why? Imagine that you just put a swimming pool in your backyard. Sadly, it is the beginning of winter. One night you notice how the temperature has just gotten below freezing. Since the air changes its temperature faster than water, your swimming pool seems much warmer in the evening. So, although the wind is cold, the water is not freezing yet.

Just when you want to take a swim, you notice how the temperature continues to go down. Suddenly, the water at the very top of the pool, which is in direct contact with the cold air, quickly freezes. Since ice is less dense than water, the sheet of ice does not sink, even when you push it. The temperature continues going down, and you notice how the sheet of ice gets thicker.

---

52   Haoshu Tang and Yanjing Chen, "Global Glaciations and Atmospheric Change at ca. 2.3 Ga," *Geoscience Frontiers* 4, no. 5 (September 2013): 583–96.

53   Yasuhito Sekine et al., "Manganese Enrichment in the Gowganda Formation of the Huronian Supergroup: A Highly Oxidizing Shallow-Marine Environment after the Last Huronian Glaciation," *Earth and Planetary Science Letters* 307, no. 1–2 (July 2011): 201–10.

Still, the ice also acts as a barrier between the cold air and the warmer water underneath; as you may realize by now, when the layer of ice forms, it prevents the liquid water from becoming ice.[54] Now, this unusual property of water is what saved life in our primitive planet.

While some bacterial organisms survived in the deepest oceanic hydrothermal vents, reservoirs of anaerobic and low-oxygen life, photosynthetic bacteria could not go far from light, so they stayed closer to the surface and populated most of the superficial liquid environments.

Among all of them, the most widely available life reservoirs were pockets of water within and under the ice caps, similar to Lake Vostok.[55] This lake is the largest one in Antarctica, and its liquid water has been the host for a deeply unknown ecosystem under two miles of ice for around fifteen million years.

Additionally, temperatures predictions suggested that the equatorial sublimation would prevent tropical ice thickness from exceeding ten meters.[56] Since photosynthesis can take place under ice up to one hundred meters thick, photosynthetic bacteria were able to obtain energy when the sunlight

---

54 M. Akyurt, G. Zaki, and B. Habeebullah, "Freezing Phenomena in Ice-Water Systems," *Energy Conversion and Management* 43, no. 14 (October 2002): 1773–89.

55 Blaire Steven et al., "Microbial Ecology and Biodiversity in Permafrost," *Extremophiles* 10, no. 4 (August 2006): 259–67.

56 David L. Naftz and Mark E. Smith, "Ice Thickness, Ablation, and Other Glaciological Measurements on Upper Fremont Glacier, Wyoming," *Physical Geography* 14, no. 4 (1993): 404–14.

was hitting the surface and survive long and icy periods of time.[57]

Other places with abundant liquid water where life could prosper were areas with high levels of volcanism and geo-thermal activity that were full of thermal vents. These vents allowed water to remain liquid in small ponds with a con-stant flow of nutrients through the ice.[58] Such environments may have covered approximately 12 percent of the global sur-face area at that time.

At the end, with some struggle and thanks to the proper-ties of water, those microorganisms that emerged from the deepest part of the oceans did survive their self-provoked apocalypse. The Huronian glaciation ended somewhere around 2.1 billion years ago and was followed by a massive explosion of life.

Over this time, two new domains of life appeared: Archaea and Eukarya, meaning "ancient things" and "good kernel" from the Greek.[59] Now, how are they all different from the others? Similar to bacteria, Archaea do not have inte-rior membranes.[60] Although both have a cell wall and use

---

57   Kay Vopel and Ian Hawes, "Photosynthetic Performance of Benthic Microbial Mats in Lake Hoare, Antarctica," *Limnology and Oceanography* 51, no. 4 (July 2006): 1801–12.

58   Eric Gaidos et al., "A Viable Microbial Community in a Subglacial Volca-nic Crater Lake, Iceland," *Astrobiology* 4, no. 3 (September 2004): 327–44.

59   Simonetta Gribaldo and Celine Brochier-Armanet, "The Origin and Evolution of Archaea: A State of the Art," *Philosophical Transactions of the Royal Society B: Biological Sciences* 361, no. 1470 (June 2006): 1007–22.

60   G. Wächtershäuser, "From Pre-Cells to Eukarya — a Tale of Two Lipids," *Molecular Microbiology* 47, no. 1 (December 2002): 13–22.

flagella to move, Archaea's cell wall lacks peptidoglycan, a polymer consisting of sugars and amino acids that forms a layer outside the membrane of most bacteria.[61] On the other hand, Eukarya were composed of organisms whose cells had a nucleus enclosed within membranes, unlike prokaryotes and archaea, which have no membrane-bound organelles.

The decision of including these organisms in three separate domains did not come without problems and skepticism. As most prokaryotes do not have distinctive morphologies, fossil shapes cannot be used to identify them as Archaea and suggest a difference from bacteria, which introduces a problem in dating which domain was first to appear on the planet.[62]

However, the current consensus accepts that Bacteria, Archaea, and Eukaryotes represent separate lines of descent that diverged early on from an ancestral colony of organisms, potentially a thermophile microorganism. If demonstrated to be true, this claim would raise the possibility that lower temperatures were extreme environments for Archaea, meaning that they appeared later in time.[63]

Still, if something is subjected to constant analysis, that is the origin of Eukarya, those cells making up the building blocks of animal and plants, among other kingdoms. In 1966, an

61   Víctor Sojo, Andrew Pomiankowski, and Nick Lane, "A Bioenergetic Basis for Membrane Divergence in Archaea and Bacteria," ed. David Penny, *PLoS Biology* 12, no. 8 (August 2014): e1001926.

62   Philip Hunter, "Molecular Fossils Probe Life's Origins," *EMBO Reports* 14, no. 11 (November 2013): 964–67.

63   Madeline C. Weiss et al., "The Physiology and Habitat of the Last Universal Common Ancestor," *Nature Microbiology* 1, no. 9 (July 2016): 1–8.

American biologist and faculty member at Boston University at the time, Dr. Lynn Margulis, presented to the world "On the Origin of Mitosing Cells," a theoretical paper that was rejected by about fifteen scientific journals.

In that article, she developed the endosymbiotic theory to explain the origin of eukaryotes.[64] This theory states that such organisms may be the product of one cell engulfing another, one living within another, and evolving until the separate cells were no longer recognizable as such.[65]

This revolutionary theory shows that what moves evolution is not a competition, but cooperation—symbiosis. In her own words, "Life did not take over the world by combat, but by networking."[66] Lynn also stated that genetic variation takes place mainly through the transfer of nuclear information between bacterial and eukaryotic cells. Nowadays, it has become clear that the nuclear genes in eukaryotic cells, as well as the molecular machinery responsible for replication and expression, appear closely related to those in Archaea.

On the other hand, the metabolic organelles and genes responsible for many energy-harvesting processes had their

---

64 William F. Martin, Sriram Garg, and Verena Zimorski, "Endosymbiotic Theories for Eukaryote Origin," *Philosophical Transactions of the Royal Society B: Biological Sciences* 370, no. 1678 (September 2015): 20140330.

65 Verena Zimorski et al., "Endosymbiotic Theory for Organelle Origins," *Current Opinion in Microbiology* 22 (December 2014): 38-48.

66 Lynn Margulis, *Microcosmos: Four Billion Years of Microbial Evolution* (Berkeley: University of California Press 1997), 47.

origins in Bacteria.[67] In this evolutionary scenario, Archaea and Bacteria represent the only primary domains of life, and Eukarya later emerged from lineages within these groups.[68] Still, much remains to be clarified about how this relationship occurred, which continues to be an exciting field of discovery in biology.

Consequently, if we seek to understand the origin of complex life and the identity of the cells of which all of us are made, we have to once again look to bacteria for an answer. One of the most interesting stories around the theory is related to the creation of the mitochondria. Also known as the power-house of the cell, mitochondria are primarily responsible for converting air and nutrients into the energy that sustains life.

The tale of the origin of mitochondria starts with a bacterial cell that had evolved to metabolize oxygen.[69] This bacterium entered a larger prokaryotic cell, which lacked that capability. Perhaps the large cell attempted to digest the smaller one but failed. Maybe the smaller cell may have tried to parasitize the larger one but could not do it. In the end, the smaller cell survived inside the larger one. Using oxygen, the smaller

---

67 N. Iwabe et al., "Evolutionary Relationship of Archaebacteria, Eubacteria, and Eukaryotes Inferred from Phylogenetic Trees of Duplicated Genes," *Proceedings of the National Academy of Sciences of the United States of America* 86, no. 23 (December 1989): 9355–59.

68 David Alvarez-Ponce et al., "Gene Similarity Networks Provide Tools for Understanding Eukaryote Origins and Evolution," *Proceedings of the National Academy of Sciences of the United States of America* 110, no. 17 (April 2013): E1594–1603.

69 Michael W. Gray, Gertraud Burger, and B. Franz Lang, "The Origin and Early Evolution of Mitochondria," *Genome Biology* 2, no. 6 (June 2001): 1–5.

bacterium metabolized the larger cell's waste products and derived more energy, part of which was returned to the host for its entire use.

Experiencing such a rewarding effect, the bigger cell allowed the smaller one to stay and replicate inside. Over time, the larger cell acquired some genes from the smaller cell, and the two became dependent on each other. The larger cell could not survive without the energy produced by the smaller one, and this, in turn, could not survive without the raw materials provided by its host.[70] At this point in the story, the cell within a cell structure is now considered a single organism, and the smaller cell is classified as an organelle, which is, in this case, the mitochondrion.

Interestingly, a mitochondrion only arises from the division of another existing mitochondrion. They divide independently of the whole cell by a process that resembles binary fission in bacteria. Specifically, mitochondria are not formed from scratch (what is called *de novo*) by the eukaryotic cell; they reproduce within it and are distributed with the cytoplasm when a cell divides or two cells fuse.[71] Furthermore, mitochondria have their own DNA chromosome, which carries genes similar to ones found in primitive bacteria.[72] All

---

70 Michael W. Gray, Gertraud Burger, and B. Franz Lang, "Mitochondrial Evolution," *Science* 283, no. 5407 (March 1999): 1476-81.

71 Tsuneyoshi Kuroiwa et al., "The Division Apparatus of Plastids and Mitochondria," *International Review of Cytology* 181 (January 1998): 1–41.

72 R. R. Meyer and M. V. Simpson, "DNA Biosynthesis in Mitochondria: Partial Purification of a Distinct DNA Polymerase from Isolated Rat Liver Mitochondria.," *Proceedings of the National Academy of Sciences of the United States of America* 61, no. 1 (September 1968): 130–37.

these features support that mitochondria were once free-living prokaryotes that found better conditions inside another cell than out there in the world.

On the other hand, we have eukaryotic organisms that are photosynthetic (those who made plants, for instance). Their cells contain, in addition to the standard eukaryotic organelles, another kind of structures called plastids. When such cells are carrying out photosynthesis, their plastids are abundant in the pigment chlorophyll, which is involved in harvesting energy from light.[73] Photosynthetic plastids are called chloroplasts, and similar to mitochondria, their origin appears to be extremely related to endosymbiosis.[74] Lynn also stated that plastids were derived from cyanobacteria that lived inside the cells of an ancestral aerobic and heterotrophic eukaryote.[75]

Science has told us that chloroplasts have a circular DNA chromosome and ribosomes similar to those of cyanobacteria.[76] Moreover, plastids cannot live independently outside the host, and they are derived from the division of other plastids and never built from scratch.

73 R. G. Jensen and J. A. Bassham, "Photosynthesis by Isolated Chloroplasts.," *Proceedings of the National Academy of Sciences of the United States of America* 56, no. 4 (October 1966): 1095–1101.

74 Geoffrey Ian McFadden, "Primary and Secondary Endosymbiosis and the Origin of Plastids," *Journal of Phycology* 37, no. 6 (December 2001): 951–59.

75 Sven B. Gould, Ross F. Waller, and Geoffrey I. McFadden, "Plastid Evolution," *Annual Review of Plant Biology* 59, no. 1 (June 2008): 491–517.

76 *Arnold J. Bendich, "Circular Chloroplast Chromosomes: The Grand Illusion," Plant Cell (American Society of Plant Biologists) 16, no. 7 (July 2004): 1661-1666.*

These two synergies between evolution and symbiosis led to the origin of the complicated eukaryotic life that different animals, including us, plants, and other living organisms are made of. Over time, Archaea, Bacteria, and Eukarya continued to diversify, becoming more complex and better adapted to their environments, which were continually changing. Each domain repeatedly split into multiple lineages, triggering an explosive diversification.[77]

Around 1.1 billion years ago, the plant, animal, and fungi lines split, though they still existed as solitary cells.[78] It was then that something truly extraordinary happened. Some of these individual cells that were doing just okay living on their own started to aggregate into colonies looking for a competitive and collaborative advantage over other microorganisms.

Soon after, a division of labor and tasks started to take place.[79] For instance, those cells on the periphery of the colony might have started to assume different roles from those in the interior in terms of the collection of nutrients or defense against other microorganisms. In an individualized and solitary world, colonies started to proliferate with better chances for survival than those who remained alone.

---

77   C. R. Woese, O. Kandler, and M. L. Wheelis, "Towards a Natural System of Organisms: Proposal for the Domains Archaea, Bacteria, and Eucarya," *Proceedings of the National Academy of Sciences of the United States of America* 87, no. 12 (June 1990): 4576–79.

78   Carl R. Woese, "On the Evolution of Cells," *Proceedings of the National Academy of Sciences of the United States of America* 99, no. 13 (June 2002): 8742–47.

79   Jumpei F. Yamagishi, Nen Saito, and Kunihiko Kaneko, "Symbiotic Cell Differentiation and Cooperative Growth in Multicellular Aggregates," *PLoS Computational Biology* 12, no. 10 (October 2016): e1005042.

Then, around one billion years ago, these individual cells living in colonies transitioned to a truly multicellular organism, which was a huge advancement in terms of evolution; however, it is still under debate how exactly this happened.[80]

The first hypothesis states that the origin of multicellularity is related to a group of function-specific cells that were aggregated into a slug-like mass called a grex, which moved as a multicellular unit.[81] This is essentially what slime molds do.

A second hypothesis tells that a primitive cell underwent nucleus division. In doing so, it became a coenocyte, a multinucleated cell that did not physically separate in two or more. Then, a membrane formed around each nucleus, thereby resulting in a group of connected cells and the transition into an organism.

The third and last hypothesis explains that as a unicellular organism divided, daughter cells failed to separate, resulting in a conglomeration of identical cells in one organism, which could later develop specialized tissues, just as plants and animal embryos do.[82]

---

80 Bettina E. Schirrmeister, Alexandre Antonelli, and Homayoun C. Bagheri, "The Origin of Multicellularity in Cyanobacteria," *BMC Evolutionary Biology* 11, no. 1 (February 2011): 1–21.

81 Richard K. Grosberg and Richard R. Strathmann, "The Evolution of Multicellularity: A Minor Major Transition?," *Annual Review of Ecology, Evolution, and Systematics* 38, no. 1 (December 2007): 621–54.

82 Nicholas J. Butterfield, "Modes of Pre-Ediacaran Multicellularity," *Precambrian Research* 173, no. 1–4 (September 2009): 201–11.

These first multicellular organisms were simple and soft organisms lacking bone, shell, or other hard body parts. Then, the first genuinely multicellular plants emerged, and sometime around nine hundred million years ago, a right multicellularity entity had also evolved in the animal kingdom. At first, it probably resembled today's sponger living in aqueous environments.[83]

Single cells with increased size have a reduced surface-to-volume ratio, hence they have difficulty absorbing sufficient nutrients and transporting them throughout the cell. Multicellularity allowed primitive organisms to exceed the size limits typically imposed by diffusion.[84] Besides, they showed longer lifespans, as they continued living when individual cells died.[85]

Nowadays, complex life forms, such as ourselves, are the consequence of multicellularity, a product of the cooperative efforts of our microorganisms' ancestors to adapt better to a constantly evolving world. Then, it might seem obvious for you to think that the transition between both stages was something that had to happen. Life moved from something simple to a complex and multifunctional organism. But was it like that? Although multicellularity can be seen as an advance in the desired evolutive path, nowadays, this is under debate.

83   Richard E. Michod et al., "Life-History Evolution and the Origin of Multicellularity," *Journal of Theoretical Biology* 239, no. 2 (March 2006): 257–72.

84   Karl J. Niklas, "The Evolutionary-Developmental Origins of Multicellularity," *American Journal of Botany* 101, no. 1 (January 2014): 6–25.

85   R. E. Michod and D. Roze, "Cooperation and Conflict in the Evolution of Multicellularity," *Heredity* 86 no. 1 (January 2001): 1-7.

As of today, the vast majority of life forms are single cellular, and even in terms of biomass, single cellular entities are far more successful than any other complex living organism.[86] Therefore, evolution did not erase unicellular life, and that has to be because of a very good reason. Rather than seeing traits such as longer lifespans and greater size as an advantage, evolution might have seen these only as examples of diversity, with associated tradeoffs.

In any case, within time, the division of labor was completed in all lines of multicellular organisms. Cells became more specialized and more dependent on each other. A better, larger, and more prepared life organism was ready to shine in all kingdoms. Then, evolution, in the pure sense of how we understand it, would have called for the disappearance of isolated cells, such as bacteria, which might have been seen as weaker and less adapted organisms. However, just as I did at the beginning of the chapter, let me prove this wrong.

---

86 Rick K. Grosberg and Richard R. Strathmann, "One Cell, Two Cell, Red Cell, Blue Cell: The Persistence of a Unicellular Stage in Multicellular Life Histories," *Trends in Ecology and Evolution* 13, no. 3 (March 1998): 112–16.

CHAPTER 4

TOGETHER, FORWARD, FOREVER

———

"You are not an encapsulated bag of skin dragging around a dreary little ego. You are an evolutionary wonder, a trillion cells singing together in a vast chorale, an organism-environment, a symbiosis of cell and soul."

—JEAN HOUSTON

Evolution has always been a fan of grand entrances and extremely dramatic exits. Dinosaurs have made us familiar with the latter; however, there have been other equally spectacular bursts of creation. Life explosions, the rise and fall of entire animal kingdoms, and the birth of relationships that drove evolution to where we are right now are related, in some way or another, to the world that came before ours, ruled by bacteria.

The whole architecture of the actual bio-diversification process has been subjected to the uninterrupted orchestration of microorganisms for millions of years. When entire ecosystems were turning to multicellularity and complexity, certain bacteria remained the same. However, despite such apparent motionless evolution, they were key components of all that came after, and so will they be for whatever comes after us.

I want you to remember that three billion years ago, the planet just had awakened and thawed from an extensive glaciation.[87] While the surface slowly became warmer, life started to flourish exponentially. Individual cells found clear advantages in becoming multicellular organisms, so they organized themselves into new three-dimensional structures that were able to better adapt and survive the environment and the presence of new predators.[88]

This particular shift toward a more complicated life organization was accompanied by what is called evolutionary radiation.[89] Unlike gamma or ultraviolet rays, evolutionary radiation is defined as an increase in taxonomic diversity caused by elevated rates of speciation. In simpler terms, it is an extremely fast diversification of a single organism into newer and more complex life forms. Evolutionary radiation only happens in really specific conditions. For instance, when a new habitat has opened up or is relatively isolated,

<hr>

87 Robert M. Hazen, *The Story of Earth : The First 4.5 Billion Years, from Stardust to Living Planet* (London: Penguin Books, 2013), 78.

88 Andrew H. Knoll, "The Multiple Origins of Complex Multicellularity," *Annual Review of Earth and Planetary Sciences* 39, no. 1 (May 2011): 217–39.

89 J. Todd Streelman and Patrick D. Danley, "The Stages of Vertebrate Evolutionary Radiation," *Trends in Ecology and Evolution* 18, no. 3 (March 2003): 126–31.

containing plenty of space.[90] Therefore, a thawing planet matched these conditions perfectly, probably better than any other moment in its history.

The first of these events was called the Avalon explosion, which happened around 575 million years ago.[91] Over this time, the first multicellular organisms started to populate the whole planet. These entities were truly enigmatic, with tubular and frond shapes, resembling mostly sessile bodies.[92] Sadly, most of them disappeared with the rapid increase in biodiversity of the next evolutionary radiation, the Cambrian explosion.[93]

One of the most widely accepted hypotheses suggests that by the beginning of the Cambrian explosion, multicellular organisms higher in the food chain caused the bacterial mats to mostly disappear. Therefore, if you are a small multicellular entity and a bigger and more evolved organism arrives and takes your food, you do not have much more choice than to peacefully fade into extinction.

90 Francine R. Abe and Bruce S. Lieberman, "Quantifying Morphological Change during an Evolutionary Radiation of Devonian Trilobites," *Paleobiology* 38, no. 2 (March 2012): 292–307.

91 Bing Shen et al., "The Avalon Explosion: Evolution of Ediacara Morphospace," *Science* 319, no. 5859 (January 2008): 81–84.

92 Dmitriy V. Grazhdankin et al., "Carbonate-Hosted Avalon-Type Fossils in Arctic Siberia," *Geology* 36, no. 10 (October 2008): 803–6.

93 Ed Landing et al., "Cambrian Evolutionary Radiation: Context, Correlation, and Chronostratigraphy-Overcoming Deficiencies of the First Appearance Datum (FAD) Concept," *Earth-Science Reviews* 123 (August 2013): 133–72.

Right after this, the Cambrian period truly began approximately 541 million years ago. Over this time, most major animals appeared in the fossil record, resulting in the divergence of most modern species: plants, animals, or insects, among others. Most of the living things that you can see around today, including the one in front of the mirror each morning, had their origin around this time.

Indeed, the Cambrian fauna is a complete wonder. The first discovered fossils from this time were the well-known trilobites. Just google "fossil," and you will see a bunch of them. These extinct marine arthropods are the earliest known of their kind.[94]

In 1859, Charles Darwin, in his book *On the Origin of Species*, discussed the inexplicable lack of earlier fossils as one of the main difficulties for his theory of descent with slow modification through natural selection.[95] The implications of his work show that the appearance of the Cambrian fauna, seemingly abruptly, without precursor, could not be done without a significant push. Whatever it was, it helped single-celled organisms make the leap to multicellular life forms. Now, what is this match, that instead of being consumed, has remained shinning to our days? What if bacteria drove the evolution of animals?

---

94 M. Gabriela Mángano et al., "Trilobites in Early Cambrian Tidal Flats and the Landward Expansion of the Cambrian Explosion," *Geology* 42, no. 2 (February 2014): 143–46,.

95 Koen B. Tanghe, "On *The Origin of Species* : The Story of Darwin's Title," *Notes and Records: The Royal Society Journal of the History of Science* 73, no. 1 (March 2019): 83–100.

To find an answer, we must meet a new friend with a kind-of-tricky name: Choanoflagellates, a group of free-living unicellular and colonial flagellate eukaryotes cells. Maybe oddly unfamiliar to you, they are considered to be the oldest living relatives of the animal kingdom, which emerged somewhere between six hundred and eight hundred million years ago.[96]

As old as they are, Choanoflagellates are nowadays still among us. They are present in a wide variety of marine and freshwater habitats, are abundant in polar waters, and occur at abyssal depths of the oceans and in the permafrost of Siberia.[97] Indeed, some of them have been retrieved from frozen soils approximately thirty-two thousand years old.

Sadly, they are not the most charismatic and beautiful creatures that you can imagine. Choanoflagellates consist of an oval blob equipped with a single tail-like flagellum that propels the organism through the water and also allows it to eat. The tail, thrashing back and forth, drives a current across a rigid, collar-like fringe of the cell membrane's thin strands.[98] The cell moves with a single desire: to eat. And its prey? Bacteria, which can get caught up in the current and stick to the collar to suddenly be engulfed by the hunter.

---

96 "Choanoflagellates and the Origin of Animal Multicellularity." *iBiology*, accessed July 12, 2020.

97 Daniel Stoupin et al., "Cryptic Diversity within the Choanoflagellate Morphospecies Complex Codosiga Botrytis — Phylogeny and Morphology of Ancient and Modern Isolates," *European Journal of Protistology* 48, no. 4 (November 2012): 263–73.

98 Helge Abildhauge Thomsen, "External Morphology of the Choanoflagellate Salpingoeca Gracilis James-Clark," *Journal of the Marine Biological Association of the United Kingdom* 57, no. 3 (August 1977): 629–34.

Indeed, Choanoflagellates have developed some interesting abilities to trap bacteria. For instance, a particular species can use silicon from seawater to deposit "matchstick-like" rods of silica onto surfaces, called strips, whose function is to enclose the cell and direct the flow of particle-containing water onto the collar, thereby trapping bacteria as they go through.[99]

However, the most brilliant feature of these organisms is their versatility. Choanoflagellates can live either as single cells or as multicellular colonies, and they switch between one state or the other depending on their conditions. Now, this becomes important. One of these conditions is nutrition. No one was sure why Choanoflagellates formed colonies, but one explanation might be an effective way of exploiting bacteria as a food source.[100] Instead of individual microorganisms rocketing around in search of bacteria to eat, they can form an efficient bacteria-eating death star that sits in the middle of its food source and chows down.[101]

Now, you may wonder whether bacteria could have triggered a swift change toward a multicellular lifestyle in these

---

99   Thomas Cavalier-Smith, "Origin of Animal Multicellularity: Precursors, Causes, Consequences—the Choanoflagellate/Sponge Transition, Neurogenesis and the Cambrian Explosion," *Philosophical Transactions of the Royal Society B: Biological Sciences* 372, no. 1713 (February 2017): 20150476.

100 William E. Kumler et al., "Does Formation of Multicellular Colonies by Choanoflagellates Affect Their Susceptibility to Capture by Passive Protozoan Predators?," *Journal of Eukaryotic Microbiology* 67, no. 5 (May 2020): 555–65.

101 Stephen R. Fairclough, Mark J. Dayel, and Nicole King, "Multicellular Development in a Choanoflagellate," *Current Biology* 20, no. 20 (October 2010): R875–76.

organisms. If so, bacteria might have played a crucial role in unleashing the era of complex animals. This hypothesis is not unusual at all.[102]

Let me now introduce you to Dr. Nicole King, a biologist at the University of California, Berkeley, who has been extensively studying the origins of animals and their link to the relationship between Choanoflagellates and bacteria. With this hypothesis, Nicole's team decided to study *Salpingoeca rosetta* (or *S. rosetta*), a particular species of Choanoflagellates.

This organism prepares to divide but stops short of splitting apart, leaving two daughter cells connected by a thin filament. The process repeats all over again, creating rosettes or spheres containing as many as fifty cells.[103] When King began studying *S. rosetta*, she could not get the cells to form colonies in the lab consistently. Simply, the conditions were not suitable for this process to happen. Something was blocking this pathway.

The breakthrough came in 2006 when one of her students was preparing a solution containing the organism for genome sequencing. The student doused a culture with antibiotics, which inhibit the proliferation of bacteria. *S. rosetta*, which

---

102 Arielle Woznica et al., "Bacterial Lipids Activate, Synergize, and Inhibit a Developmental Switch in Choanoflagellates," *Proceedings of the National Academy of Sciences of the United States of America* 113, no. 28 (July 2016): 7894–99.

103 Mark J. Dayel et al., "Cell Differentiation and Morphogenesis in the Colony-Forming Choanoflagellate Salpingoeca Rosetta," *Developmental Biology* 357, no. 1 (September 2011): 73–82.

was present in the media as single cells, suddenly bloomed into copious multicellular rosettes.

They collected the bacteria from this media and added them back into a lab culture of single-cell Choanoflagellates. They, too, formed colonies. The likely explanation for this phenomenon is that the antibiotic treatment inadvertently killed off one species of bacteria, allowing another that competes with it to rebound and thrive.[104]

When King's team looked to the trigger of the switch between single-cells and colonies, they found a compound produced by the bacteria, a previously unknown species of *Algoriphagus* that *S. rosetta* use as food.[105] *S. rosetta* seemed to interpret the compound as an indication that conditions are favorable for group living and successfully switched from unicellular to multicellular[106]

King hypothesizes that something similar could have happened more than six hundred million years ago when the last common ancestor of all animals started its fateful journey toward multicellularity: "I suspect that the progenitors of animals were able to become multicellular but could switch

104 Mark J. Dayel and Nicole King, "Prey Capture and Phagocytosis in the Choanoflagellate Salpingoeca Rosetta," *PLoS ONE* 9, no. 5 (May 2014): e95577.

105 Rosanna A. Alegado et al., "Complete Genome Sequence of Algoriphagus Sp. PR1, Bacterial Prey of a Colony-Forming Choanoflagellate," *Journal of Bacteriology* 193, no. 6 (March 2011): 1485–86.

106 Stephen R. Fairclough et al., "Premetazoan Genome Evolution and the Regulation of Cell Differentiation in the Choanoflagellate Salpingoeca Rosetta," *Genome Biology* 14, no. 2 (February 2013): 1–15.

back and forth based on environmental conditions."[107]
Indeed, this bacteria-organism relationship might have triggered most of the transitions between single and multicellular cell-based organisms.

Another strong hint that bacteria may have prompted that ancient transition to multicellularity is that many of today's simplest animals are governed by microbial messages. Corals, sea squirts, sponges, and tube worms all begin life as larvae floating in the water, and they too respond to compounds released by bacteria as signals to attach themselves to rocks or other surfaces and transition to new, more complex life forms.[108]

If this kind of relationship is so common among animals from the most ancient families, it seems plausible that the first animals were equally attuned to their bacterial neighbors. Furthermore, the breadth and significance of the animal-bacteria relationship goes far beyond the development of a handful of ancient aquatic creatures like sponges.

Nowadays, we know that bacteria are necessary for the development of organs in squid; others have found similar partnerships that shape the maturation of animal immune systems, such as the guts of zebrafish and mice, and even

---

107 Kat McGowan, "How Life Made the Leap From Single Cells to Multicellular Animals" *WIRED*, August 1, 2014.

108 Sebastian Fraune and Thomas C.G. Bosch, "Why Bacteria Matter in Animal Development and Evolution," *BioEssays* 32, no. 7 (July 2010): 571–80.

mammalian brains.[109] All these evolutionary adaptations and accomplishments cannot be understood without symbiosis between bacteria and their hosts.

Symbiosis is indeed a beautiful word with an almost-always beneficial meaning that comes from the Greek συμβίωσις, meaning "living together." If you would like to define symbiosis, it can be any type of close and long-term biological interaction between two different biological organisms.[110] The living creatures, each termed a "symbiont," may be of the same or different species.

The symbiosis between bacteria and their host is truly pleasant and often bizarre. One of the most relevant examples was found in the early 1970s, with the discovery of Paracatenula, a several-millimeters-long, mouth- and gut-less flatworm, which is found anywhere from tropical oceans to the Mediterranean.[111]

At this time, it was a mystery how the worms acquired their food without a mouth and gut. However, at the deep ocean hot vents, these worms live in symbiosis with intracellular bacteria that oxidize reduced sulfur compounds that can be found all over the place. The energy obtained in this chemical

---

109 Margaret J. McFall-Ngai, "Unseen Forces: The Influence of Bacteria on Animal Development," *Developmental Biology* 242, no. 1 (February 2002): 1–14.

110 Margulis and L., *Symbiosis in Cell Evolution: Life and Its Environment on the Early Earth* (New York: W. H. Freeman & Co, 1981), 144.

111 Harald Ronald Gruber-Vodicka et al., "Paracatenula, an Ancient Symbiosis between Thiotrophic Alphaproteobacteria and Catenulid Flatworms," *Proceedings of the National Academy of Sciences of the United States of America* 108, no. 29 (July 2011): 12078–83.

process is used by the symbionts to fix inorganic carbon into biomass, just like how plants use sunlight.[112]

Due to the high productivity of the symbionts, their hosts can derive all their nutrition from them. Interestingly, the bacteria live in specialized cells called bacteriocytes, which account for up to 50 percent of the total tissue of the worm. That is significantly more than in all other known symbioses between animals and bacteria. Based on the genetic sequencing of the bacteria, the scientists have roughly extrapolated the age of the symbiosis: around five hundred million years, which makes this relationship the oldest known animal-bacteria association.[113]

Another interesting example can be found in Trichoplax, a shapeless little blob that is considered one of the simplest animals. These organisms live in warm coastal waters around the world, where they graze on microscopic algae that cover sand and rocks. Trichoplax can also be found in almost any saltwater aquarium with corals.

Until the 1970s, it was not clear whether Trichoplax was even a proper, fully-grown animal or just the juvenile stage of a jellyfish. Only about a half a millimeter in diameter, these animals lack a mouth, gut, and any other organs, and are

---

112 Ulrich Dirks et al., "Bacterial Symbiosis Maintenance in the Asexually Reproducing and Regenerating Flatworm Paracatenula Galateia," *PLoS ONE* 7, no. 4 (April 2012): e34709.

113 Oliver Jäckle et al., "Chemosynthetic Symbiont with a Drastically Reduced Genome Serves as Primary Energy Storage in the Marine Flatworm Paracatenula," *Proceedings of the National Academy of Sciences of the United States of America* 116, no. 17 (April 2019): 8505–14.

made up of only six different kinds of cells. However, they are not as simple as they look. Trichoplax is the host of one of the most sophisticated symbioses with a highly unusual bacteria.[114] Indeed, the bacterial symbionts are very picky, as each one of them lives in only one type of host cell, avoiding contact with one another.

The first symbiont is named Grellia, which lives inside the endoplasmic reticulum (ER) of Trichoplax, a home that they never abandon. As you may know, the ER plays a central role in protein and membrane production. There are a few parasitic bacteria that imitate the structure of the ER to trick the hosts into thinking they are not harmful.[115] However, Grellia, although closely related to parasites, does not appear to be harmful to Trichoplax. It has genes that would allow it to steal energy from its host, but it does not use them. Apparently, Grellia just wants to live there, and its host is happy with that.

On the other hand, we have the second symbiont, Ruth-mannia, which belongs to a rare type of bacteria: the Margulisbacteria, the so-called "microbial dark matter," or microorganisms that biologists have found through sequencing, but are unable to be cultured.[116] This symbiont lives in

114 Harald R. Gruber-Vodicka et al., "Two Intracellular and Cell Type-Specific Bacterial Symbionts in the Placozoan Trichoplax H2," *Nature Microbiology* 4, no. 9 (September 2019): 1465–74.

115 Luca Galluzzi, Aurora Diotallevi, and Mauro Magnani, "Endoplasmic Reticulum Stress and Unfolded Protein Response in Infection by Intracellular Parasites," *Future Science OA* 3, no. 3 (August 2017): FSO198.

116 Corie Lok, "Mining the Microbial Dark Matter," *Nature* 522, no. 7556 (June 2015): 270–73.

cells that Trichoplax uses to digest its algal food. Ruthmannia appears only to eat the fats and other lipids of the algae and leaves the rest to its host. In return, Ruthmannia may provide Trichoplax with vitamins and amino acids that are produced after consumption of the algae.

So, at the end, maybe animals are not all that special, or at least, alone. After all, they would be nothing without their microbial friends. Indeed, life would be extremely different if that microbial push did not happen. Then, all things considered, it is possible to speculate. For instance, what if bacteria wanted multicellular life to happen?

Imagine bacteria continuously stressed by the presence of other single-cell microorganisms competing for both nutrients and space. Maybe the best way to survive was to push other species to change, instead of changing themselves. Perhaps, by doing so, bacteria found more stability and safety within these complex organisms, hence driving multicellular life to an end that allowed symbiosis to happen.

Hypotheses and ideas aside, bacteria should be considered an integral part of development and evolution, an essential piece of the puzzle that brings direction and, perhaps, intention to the chaotic, complex, and endless portrait of life.

CHAPTER 5

JUST A LITTLE PUSH

———

"Man still bears in his bodily frame the indelible stamp of his lowly origin."

—CHARLES DARWIN

Everything changes, and nothing ever stays the same. Why would life be different? Our still young Earth had to go through a few mass extinctions, glaciations, and evolutionary explosions to determine what life had to become, closing the doors for what it never was.[117] A chaotic animal diversification led to the rise and fall of monstrously huge two-feet land invertebrates, massive fifteen-pound parrots terrorizing New Zealand, weirdly shaped amphibians, and almost the whole cast of Jurassic Park.[118]

---

117 William A. Shear and Jarmila Kukalová-Peck, "The Ecology of Paleozoic Terrestrial Arthropods: The Fossil Evidence," *Canadian Journal of Zoology* 68, no. 9 (September 1990): 1807–34.

118 Trevor H. Worthy et al., "Evidence for a Giant Parrot from the Early Miocene of New Zealand," *Biology Letters* 15, no. 8 (August 2019): 20190467.

Among all that entropy, the microbial world had to shift from an isolated way of living to meaningful symbiotic relationships. This critical movement drove the evolution that shaped the future of those who contained them, including humankind.

Moving the clock, we end sixty-five million years ago somewhere in the middle of what is now modern North America. The land was inhabited with something similar to a two-foot long squirrel. On the other side of the world, China was plagued by a small lemur with the weight of a golf ball that spent most of its time gathering fruit from the top of a tree. *Plesiadapis* and *Archicebus,* respectively, were just living their lives without really knowing that one day they would be considered the oldest known primate-like mammals on the planet.[119] They also had a few cousins all over Eurasia and Africa, which places these mammals around the globe. The time of primates had finally arrived.[120]

Soon after, the tropical population of primates gave rise to the rest of the modern lineages—including the Great Apes—which were formed by humans, gorillas, and chimpanzees. Then, somewhere between eight and four million years ago,

---

119 David W. Krause, "Paleocene Primates from Western Canada," *Canadian Journal of Earth Sciences* 15, no. 8 (August 1978): 1250–71.

120 Marian Dagosto et al., "Estimating Body Size in Early Primates: The Case of Archicebus and Teilhardina," *Journal of Human Evolution* 115 (February 2018): 8–19.

first the gorillas, and then the chimpanzees, split off from the line leading to what you might consider primitive humans.[121]

However, let's not just jump right to that point, and let's talk about the different ways in which a wedding can be ruined. A box full of old rusty bones is probably not on your registry. Still, it was what happened to Australian anatomy professor Raymond Dart. He was adjusting the collar of his suit in preparation for a friend's ceremony when a box, shipped from a limestone quarry near Taung, in South Africa, arrived at his doorstep in Johannesburg in November 1924.

Raymond abandoned his task to check the contents of the package, ignoring the complaining of his wife and the groom, who was anxious to begin the ceremony. Inside the box, he found a fossilized mold of a brain and a matching child's skull partially buried in stone. Raymond quickly realized the significance of the finding, and a few months after, he published an article in *Nature* identifying a new species: *Australopithecus africanus*.[122] The 2.8-million-year-old Taung child, as Raymond called it, was the first member of the Australopithecus genus discovered, and it challenged contemporary ideas about human evolution.

Now, the Taung child was probably not a kid. The Australopithecus species was small, 1.2 to 1.4 meters in size. They lived

---

121 Maynard V. Olson and Ajit Varki, "Sequencing the Chimpanzee Genome: Insights into Human Evolution and Disease," *Nature Reviews Genetics* 4, no. 1 (January 2003): 20–28.

122 Phillip V. Tobias, "The Discovery of the Taung Skull of Australopithecus Africanus Dart and the Neglected Role of Professor R.B. Young," *Transactions of the Royal Society of South Africa* 61, no. 2 (January 2006): 131–38.

in eastern Africa around four million years ago, and soon after, they spread throughout the continent.[123] They represent the common ancestor of the genus Homo, which includes us.

Still, there were apparent differences. Australopithecus had a brain about 35 percent of the size of ours. Although their intelligence was likely no more sophisticated than that of modern apes, they were the first primate to walk on two feet. Besides, they were the first ones to fashion tools that were often used to carve animal carcasses to extract the meat from their prey.[124]

Their diet consisted mainly of raw meat.[125] Sadly, they had not yet discovered the culinary art of cooking, so they consumed the meat as it was extracted from the animals. This behavior probably caused one of the first direct and unwanted contacts of our ancestors with the bacterial world.

An analysis of a 1.5- to 2.8-million-year-old vertebrae of Australopithecus recovered in the Sterkfontein caves, near Johannesburg (South Africa), revealed signs of a bacterial infection that is usually contracted from eating meat or dairy. One of the researchers working on the study, Ruggero D'Anastasio, a paleoanthropologist at State University "Gabriele

---

123 T. D. White, D. C. Johanson, and W. H. Kimbel, "Australopithecus Africanus," in *New Interpretations of Ape and Human Ancestry*, ed. Russell L. Ciochon and Robert S. Corruccini (New York: Springer US, 1983), 721–80.

124 Matthew M. Skinner et al., "Human-like Hand Use in Australopithecus Africanus," *Science* 347, no. 6220 (January 2015): 395–99.

125 Matt Sponheimer and Julia A. Lee-Thorp, "Isotopic Evidence for the Diet of an Early Hominid, Australopithecus Africanus," *Science* 283, no. 5400 (January 1999): 368–70.

d'Annunzio" in Chieti, Italy, diagnosed the skeleton with a bacterial disease. "This is the most ancient case of an infectious disease in a hominin," he said in an interview in 2009.[126]

The disease in question was brucellosis, a highly contagious bacterial infection caused by the ingestion of unpasteurized milk or undercooked meat from infected animals. Unfortunately for our Australopithecus ancestors, they neither knew a guy named Pasteur nor thought of cooking their food. Hence, they developed a flu-like illness that they did not know how to cure.

Brucella, a Gram-negative bacterium, can reach the muscles and bones of their hosts and get to the spinal vertebrae, causing damage similar to the one found in the analyzed bones.[127] The ancient patients may have acquired brucellosis by eating fetal tissue from a similar animal, potentially another mammal, leading to death. However, the consequence in this particular case might not have been that bad, with the exception of the victims.

Now, try to imagine a small group of Australopithecus gathering around their deceased friend. They somehow realized that death was caused by that piece of raw meat. Researchers believe that Australopithecus often avoided skeletal-clinging

---

126 Ewen Callaway, "Ancient Bones Show Earliest 'human' Infection" *New Scientist*, August 5, 2009.

127 R. D'Anastasio et al., "Origin, Evolution and Paleoepidemiology of Brucellosis," *Epidemiology and Infection* 139, no. 1 (January 2011): 149–56.

meat as it was quickly contaminated by harmful bacteria.[128] Of course, they did not know about the cause, but the consequence of eating that meat was obvious. Instead, they consumed marrow (a fatty and soft vascular tissue inside bones) and brains. Why? By contrast, this meat is encased inside bones, retains low bacteria counts, and persists much longer without spoiling.[129]

Australopithecus did start to refine their dietary habits, consuming more marrow over time. Marrow is where blood cells are produced and is also high in fat, cholesterol, and numerous micronutrients. This precious resource, as some scientists believe, may have acted as a catalyst in the development of our distinctly large and complex brain. Therefore, by avoiding bacterial-contaminated meat, our ancestors found a way to become bigger and smarter over time.[130]

Sadly, about two million years ago, Australopithecus became extinct.[131] The reason is not extremely clear, but they might have vanished as a result of global climate cooling. Others

---

128 Ken Sayers and C. Owen Lovejoy, "Blood, Bulbs, and Bunodonts: On Evolutionary Ecology and the Diets of Ardipithecus, Australopithecus, and Early Homo," *Quarterly Review of Biology* 89, no. 4 (December 2014): 319–57.

129 David R. Braun, "Palaeoanthropology: Australopithecine Butchers," *Nature* 466, no. 7308 (August 2010): 828.

130 William R. Leonard and Marcia L. Robertson, "Evolutionary Perspectives on Human Nutrition: The Influence of Brain and Body Size on Diet and Metabolism," *American Journal of Human Biology* 6, no. 1 (January 1994): 77–88.

131 Andrew Du et al., "Statistical Estimates of Hominin Origination and Extinction Dates: A Case Study Examining the Australopithecus Anamensis–Afarensis Lineage," *Journal of Human Evolution* 138 (January 2020): 102688.

are keen to believe that they disappeared due to the pressure of growing populations of taller, better-looking, and smarter players: the genus Homo, the early humans.

Let us now jump a generation ahead. The earliest documented representative of the genus is Homo habilis, which evolved around 2.8 million years ago. Homo habilis was able to use stone tools, and their brains were about the same size as a chimpanzee's.[132] During the next million years, a process of rapid encephalization occurred. Soon after came the arrival of Homo erectus—the longest-lived hominin species—and Homo ergaster in the fossil record, whose cranial capacities doubled to 850 cm3. This number may not seem like much, but it means that each generation had about one hundred twenty-five thousand more neurons than the last, which is quite an accomplishment.[133]

These early humans became smarter and more curious. They were the first ones to leave Africa, spreading throughout the continent, Asia, and Europe between 1.3 to 1.8 million years ago. Then, the archaic Homo sapiens, the forerunner of anatomically modern humans, evolved in the Middle Paleolithic between four hundred thousand and two hundred fifty thousand years ago.

The transition to behavioral modernity with the development of symbolic culture, language, and specialized lithic

---

132 Bernard Wood, "Origin and Evolution of the Genus Homo," *Nature* 355, no. 6363 (February 1992): 783–90.

133 Simon Neubauer, Jean Jacques Hublin, and Philipp Gunz, "The Evolution of Modern Human Brain Shape," *Science Advances* 4, no. 1 (January 2018): eaao5961.

technology happened around fifty thousand years ago.[134] Then human history took place, and we wrote about it. After a few wars, the emergence of politics, the rise of arts, and a bunch of wonderful and disgraceful events, we arrive at the present day, where Homo sapiens is the only extant species of its genus.

However, let's not jump to conclusions and analyze the reasons why we are here and how intriguingly they are related to the presence of bacteria. First, let us begin with a simple statement that will not surprise you: Humans move. We love to move, discover, and always be in transition to somewhere else. Aspirations or the power of free will. Call it whatever you like.

The desire for nutrition, both in quality and quantity, drives us in an instinctual way. The climate and a few attempts of the cosmos to annihilate us were most likely the reasons that pushed our ancestors to discover new previously unexplored areas. Once there, they had to change what they ate and how they behaved.[135]

Then, those primitive humans started to aggregate in small societies that worked together and separated roles, something similar to what happened in the transition from individual cells to multicellular organisms, just on a bigger scale. In this creation of roles, hunting was the most desired job

---

134 S. H. Ambrose, "Paleolithic Technology and Human Evolution," *Science* 291, no. 5509 (March 2001): 1748–53.

135 Hillard Kaplan et al., "A Theory of Human Life History Evolution: Diet, Intelligence, and Longevity," *Evolutionary Anthropology: Issues, News, and Reviews* 9, no. 4 (January 2000): 156–85.

by that time, meaning that you were the one responsible for hunting the food for your people. Now, if you want to be a good hunter, you need good tools.

By the Middle Pleistocene (somewhere around seven hundred thousand years ago), stone-tool manufacturing and big-game hunting were widespread. Soon after, agricultural practices and the domestication of animals began, particularly dairy animals.[136] All this transition led to significant changes around and within us. Curiously, the latter is far more important but less visible than the former.

You may probably have heard the expression *"we are what we eat,"* but most likely, you did not hear that *"we are bacteria."* Indeed, we are mere vessels with a full living world inside us. As a by-product of the collision of both statements in the time of our ancestors, we have a continually evolving human microbiome inside us.[137]

What is this microbiome? Simply, the microbiome is the aggregate of all microbiota (bacteria, fungi, and viruses, among others) that reside on or within us. Indeed, we might be in front of the most sophisticated and useful tool that evolution has granted us. The human-bacteria symbiosis is such a complex relationship that many might argue that life cannot be sustained without them.

---

136 Samuel Bowles, "Warriors, Levelers, and the Role of Conflict in Human Social Evolution," *Science* 336, no. 6083 (May 2012): 876–79.

137 Andrew H. Moeller et al., "Rapid Changes in the Gut Microbiome during Human Evolution," *Proceedings of the National Academy of Sciences of the United States of America* 111, no. 46 (November 2014): 16431–35.

Truth be told, an important question arises among those who have devoted their lives to the study of the human microbiome: Did bacteria drive human evolution? Could these tiny microorganisms be responsible for what we are and how we got here?

Unfortunately, most of the answers are buried deep down on the planet, long awaiting our discovery. Nevertheless, we know that the human microbiome adapted quickly to new environmental conditions and that these adaptive microbes might have been critical for human success in a range of different ecosystems.[138]

When the first humans walked into new geographic areas, they confronted new food choices. Their adaptive microbiome made it possible to digest or detoxify the foods they were eating in that particular region. At the same time, bacteria increased our ancestors' ability to endure the presence of microorganisms to which they had never been exposed before and to defeat new diseases.[139]

When the first societies were created, the microbiome had an important role. The social sharing of microbes was the norm, leading to local microbial adaptations. One of the most relevant examples of this behavior comes with the human discovery of fermentation. This process allowed our ancestors to store food and stay in one place for a longer time.

---

138 Stephanie L. Schnorr et al., "Insights into Human Evolution from Ancient and Contemporary Microbiome Studies," *Current Opinion in Genetics and Development* 41 (December 2016): 14–26.

139 Emily R. Davenport et al., "The Human Microbiome in Evolution," *BMC Biology* 15, no. 1 (December 2017): 1–12.

Additionally, it enabled larger groups to live together, making stronger societies.[140] When groups of humans consumed food items together, microbes were shared and introduced to the consumers.

Consequently, we share 25 percent of our microbes with each other. Therefore, it makes sense to state that we strongly relied on them in our expansion throughout the planet, which allowed bacteria to became like a fingerprint of our existence.[141] For instance, several studies indicate that different aspects of the gut microbiota can distinguish human populations according to their histories and lifestyles, including diet.

One of the most incredible examples is found in the stomach-associated bacterium *Helicobacter pylori* (or *H. pylori*), which perfectly exemplifies coevolution between microbes and humans better than any other bacteria. Patterns of Homo sapiens migration out of Africa and across the globe can be traced from the bacterium diversity. Since *H. pylori* are mostly host-specific, different research articles showed that they have coevolved with humans at least since their joint exodus from Africa sixty thousand years ago and likely throughout their evolution.

---

140 Elisa Guerra-Doce, "The Origins of Inebriation: Archaeological Evidence of the Consumption of Fermented Beverages and Drugs in Prehistoric Eurasia," *Journal of Archaeological Method and Theory* 22, no. 3 (September 2015): 751–82.

141 Martin J Blaser, "Who Are We?," *EMBO Reports* 7, no. 10 (August 2006): 956–60.

H. pylori colonize our stomachs in childhood and persist throughout our entire lives, which implies a near-perfect adaptation to the human body and a perfectly developed ability to evade the human immune response.[142] The bacterium has become an essential part of our microbiome and defines our identity in a much better way than any ID ever will.

One important fact that we should be aware of is that despite half the world's population carrying *H. pylori*, only a small proportion develop ulcers or gastric cancer, a pathology for which the bacterium is mostly known. However, nowadays, the bacterium's presence has now gradually disappeared from some populations, including much of the US and western Europe.[143] What is the consequence? Other diseases are becoming much more prevalent: from gastroesophageal reflux disease, obesity, or type 2 diabetes, to atopic and allergic diseases, including asthma.

When reading about this, one cannot avoid wondering if there is a chance that the absence of *H. pylori* can be related to imbalances that contribute to diseases of modern life. This bacterium was with our ancestors from the very beginning, becoming a part of us. It should not be surprising that its disappearance might bring an obvious imbalance to the equation, as it should not be considered that the bacterium, like many others, is a direct source of what we are now.

---

142 John C. Atherton and Martin J. Blaser, "Coadaptation of Helicobacter Pylori and Humans: Ancient History, Modern Implications," *Journal of Clinical Investigation* 119, no. 9 (September 2009): 2475–87.

143 Martin J. Blaser, "Disappearing Microbiota: Helicobacter Pylori Protection against Esophageal Adenocarcinoma," *Cancer Prevention Research* 1, no. 5 (October 2008): 308–11.

However, relationships like one of the humans with *H. pylori* are not isolated. For instance, one of the reasons why we humans can have an omnivorous diet and eat as many vegetables as we want is related to our bacterial companions. Those mammals from which we evolved needed help to liberate sugars from the complex plant polysaccharides that they ate.

Different bacterial species that had enzymes needed for the breakdown of complex polysaccharides were quickly penetrating the hosts. Once there, the large animals had to use prolonged digestion times, which led to a subsequent enlargement of parts of the gut to retain microbes.[144] They needed them, so they changed. Bacteria gave them new powers but took the chance to change them from within.

It becomes easy to understand now that no living creature on this planet has been free of the relationship with bacteria. Those who have adapted and started symbiosis have evolved or stayed the same over millions of years, while those who did not have developed some of the most deadly diseases or were wiped out of existence.

If you look closer to nature, you can easily find both types of bonds with bacteria: symbiosis and pathogenesis. A constant fight between two opposing forces which are continually changing, seeking balance inside every living organism. Because in the end, everything is about balance. Now, it is time to focus. The human era is about to burst onto this planet, the sole witness of the rise of a new king in a world with no throne.

---

144 Burk A. Dehority, "Protozoa of the Digestive Tract of Herbivorous Mammals," *International Journal of Tropical Insect Science* 7, no. 03 (June 1986): 279–96.

CHAPTER 6

THE BIRTH AND RISE OF INFECTION

———

"It is perfectly true, as philosophers say, that life must be understood backward. But they forget the other proposition, that it must be lived forward."

—SØREN KIERKEGAARD

The time of the homo sapiens had finally arrived. Our primate-like past was just a distant memory in a history that now owns us. *We*, as individuals, changed. We started gathering, working together, learning from each other. Animals were now domesticated, and we welcomed them to our newly created settlements. The first societies had arrived.

In the very beginning, humans quickly moved away from rudimentary stone tools to more sophisticated versions, and at the same time they learned to master fire. Hunting was slowly substituted by agriculture and livestock, and houses were built close to valleys and rivers, where crops and animals could prosper. Our lifestyle completely changed; we settled down. For the first time in history, there was no need to move far away to seek resources—we were bringing them to us. The long night was over. The dawn of human civilization had just begun.

Despite of our transition toward a more sedentary life, this time was the witness of important journeys that brought the human race to all continents. Somewhere around ten thousand years ago, we were everywhere. The world was ours. *Or, at least, that was what we thought.*

Our expansion triggered the inevitable collision of two powerful entities: human and bacterial. The consequence of this crash was not sudden but had a tremendous impact on the development of our civilization.

When evolution brought us together and farther at the same time, we had contact with different people and environments, different bacterial settings. Then, something changed, not only around us but also within us—with *them.* Those tiny organisms that helped us so much along the way gave rise to some of the most worrisome diseases and pathologies that we had ever seen.[145]

Now, when did bacteria start to infect humans, seeking other than symbiosis? They were likely doing it as soon as the homo sapiens appeared on this planet. Thanks to the wonders of

---

145 Gabriel Trueba and Micah Dunthorn, "Many Neglected Tropical Diseases May Have Originated in the Paleolithic or before: New Insights from Genetics," *PLoS Neglected Tropical Diseases* 6, no. 3 (March 2012): e1393.

genetics and sequencing, we know that bacteria changed their behavior at the same time we did.

Paleolithic people had a hard life, and of course, a hard time being alive. Things such as cuts, bruises, broken bones—without antiseptics, proper facilities, or knowledge of germs—could kill you, often very painfully. Besides, nothing could stop whatever was sickening you from jumping to your neighbors, and from them to more people.

Before we started to share as a society, the fate of any bacterial disease was clear: You and your people get over it, or you do not. In any case, the disease's spreading died with you. But now, in the time of settlements, people were behaving in a way that was not much different from how we do now. They had to bring food to their families in another town after months of journeys; someone else was moving to a better village from a faraway one; or a stranger was just passing through to go from one settlement to another.[146]

The world started to become connected, bringing us closer together. Pathogenic bacteria used that to their advantage, quickly evolving and adapting to infect the best, most evolved and often not the smartest vector on the whole planet: us. As such, we enter the age of pathogenesis.

One of the most relevant cases plays around *Mycobacteria leprae* (or *M. leprae*) and its associated pathology, leprosy. This chronic infection of the skin and nerves reached humans

---

146 Mary C. Stiner and Steven L. Kuhn, "Changes in the 'connectedness' and Resilience of Paleolithic Societies in Mediterranean Ecosystems," *Human Ecology* 34, no. 5 (October 2006): 693–712.

at the very beginning of our existence, possibly in Africa during the Paleolithic period.[147] Recent genomic studies of common *M. leprae* strains have further traced it along global human dispersals during the past one hundred thousand years, meaning that leprosy most likely started their parasitic evolution in humans or early hominids millions of years ago.

This suggests that *M. leprae* are extraordinarily stable within their human hosts, a sign of adult parasitic life beginning far before the point that we left Africa. The bacteria have learned how to seek and hide with the immune system better than many other parasites, a consequence of probably being the oldest human-specific infection.[148]

Another example comes from the common bacteria that cause salmonellosis: *Salmonella enterica* (or *S. enterica*). Let us meet Felix M. Key, Alexander Herbig, and Johannes Krause of the Max Planck Institute for the Science of Human History. They have been looking at human remains recovered across Western Eurasia and reconstructed eight ancient as *S. enterica* genomes—all part of a related group within the much broader diversity of the modern bacteria. Their results illuminate what was likely a serious health concern in the past and reveal how this bacterial pathogen evolved over six thousand five hundred years.

147　Gabriel Trueba, "The Origin of Human Pathogens," in *Confronting Emerging Zoonoses: The One Health Paradigm*, ed. Lisa Conti (Tokyo: Springer Japan, 2014), 3–11.

148　Xiang Y. Han and Francisco J. Silva, "On the Age of Leprosy," *PLoS Neglected Tropical Diseases* 8, no. 2 (February 2014): e2544.

The presence of *S. enterica* in the teeth of ancient individuals suggested they were suffering from systemic disease at their time of death. They were able to determine that six Salmonella genomes recovered were the progenitors to a strain that infects humans explicitly but is rare today. Those ancient Salmonella, however, were probably not yet adapted to humans and instead infected humans and animals alike. This suggests once more that cultural practices and the birth of societies facilitated the emergence of those progenitors and, subsequently, human-specific diseases.

However, when talking about infectious bacteria that have a long relationship with humans, we have to talk about what might be considered our bacterial nemesis. This bacterium is responsible for as many as one billion deaths in the last two hundred years alone, but whose origins can be traced back as long as seventy-five thousand years ago.[149] Indeed, it is going to be a typical protagonist in the following chapters, and for no good reasons. We are talking of *Mycobacterium tuberculosis* and their perfect weapon: tuberculosis (TB).

If you think of its effects nowadays, TB is still one of the deadliest bacterial diseases in the world, despite our organized healthcare system. Knowing this, you may wonder: How did a devastating illness like TB not eradicate humankind in the time of our ancestors? The answer is linked to the research of Pere-Joan Cardona, Martí Català, and Clara Prats, a team of

---

149 Stewart T. Cole, "Comparative and Functional Genomics of the Mycobacterium Tuberculosis Complex," *Microbiology* 148, no. 10 (October 2002): 2919–28.

Spanish researchers at the Experimental Tuberculosis Unit at the Polytechnic University of Catalonia.[150]

As we know, fifty thousand years ago, our ancestors were nomadic hunters and gatherers who were organized in small tribes. Despite everything, they had relatively good health thanks to a lifestyle based on a varied diet, low work intensity, and moderate exercise. Consequently, their life expectancy was around thirty-three years. Then, TB arrived.

Cardona and colleagues suggested that early strains of TB began as latent infections that generally remained dormant and only occasionally killed only the weak, old, and young. Somewhere around forty-eight thousand years ago, however, modern lineages of the bacteria emerged that were far more deadly and could persist in a latent stage. Indeed, we now know that *Mycobacterium tuberculosis* is extremely good at hiding in a dormant stage within us, so good that nowadays, about a quarter of all humans are currently infected with latent TB.[151]

The researchers showed that TB could quickly kill off an entire nomadic tribe and spread to others. The population growth fell from 1 percent to only 0.003 percent, resulting in small groups that were infected, probably dying out.

<hr>

150 Pere Joan Cardona, Martí Català, and Clara Prats, "Origin of Tuberculosis in the Paleolithic Predicts Unprecedented Population Growth and Female Resistance," *Scientific Reports* 10, no. 1 (December 2020): 1–20,.

151 Martin Gengenbacher and Stefan H.E. Kaufmann, "Mycobacterium Tuberculosis: Success through Dormancy," *FEMS Microbiology Reviews* 36, no. 3 (May 2012): 514-32.

Therefore, with the constant increase of settlements, the disease could have brought humanity to the brink of extinction.

However, that never happened. But why? To overcome the deadly infection, humans underwent a massive population increase. Our numbers multiplied by twenty times in just a hundred years. Over the Paleolithic, the mortality rate during infancy was 50 percent. Therefore, women needed to have two surviving children just to keep the population (meaning four births). Then, when the more virulent strains of *Mycobacterium* appeared, women needed to have three surviving children (meaning six births) to just keep our existence. Such an extraordinary change in biological behavior was needed, and somehow, we did it.

Bacteria, once more, brought us to a new match where the only way to win was to change and to adapt. We had to raise more people and to come together and start growing our food, which gave us more stability and safety. The only chance for our ancestors to survive the ravages of TB was to increase fertility, and the best way to do this was probably to start farming and increasing food production while gathering in bigger settlements.

Around this same time, something critical happened: resistance and immunity. Those people who had been infected by earlier strains of the bacteria and survived became resistant to the disease. They were more prepared for new waves of infection, including not only TB but also other pathogens that were using animals as vectors to infect human beings.[152] Those who survived then turned their eyes to the field.

Twelve thousand years ago, a group of people who were gathered in large settlements around the Eastern Mediterranean and Western Asia started growing wild cereals closer to their homes. They were called the Natufian people. They settled in what today is the Palestinian city of Jericho, which may, therefore, be the longest continuously inhabited urban area on Earth.

The Natufian were the fathers of agriculture. A narrow range of plants, both wild and domesticated, which included wheat, millet, and spelt, was frequently employed in farming cycles. At the same time, dogs, sheep, and goats started to be an essential part of their settlements.[153] The expansion of their practices marks the origins of a truly outstanding event in our history: the Neolithic Revolution, which led to the appearance of the first cities.[154]

Examples of these include the Motza-mega site, about three miles to the west of Jerusalem, founded around ten thousand years ago, or Çatalhöyük, in Turkey, which contained eight thousand individuals. Humankind was now far gone from

---

152 Daniel Rock, "Tuberculosis: A Global Emergency," *Work* 8, no. 1 (January 1997): 93–105.

153 Ofer Bar-Yosef, "The Natufian Culture in the Levant, Threshold to the Origins of Agriculture," *Evolutionary Anthropology: Issues, News, and Reviews* 6, no. 5 (January 1998): 159–77.

154 Jacob L. Weisdorf, "From Foraging To Farming: Explaining The Neolithic Revolution," *Journal of Economic Surveys* 19, no. 4 (September 2005): 561–86.

our initial small settlements into authentic urban hells. People were living in very crowded conditions, with trash pits and animal pens right next to some of their homes. Besides, no sanitation systems and the lack of hygiene practices became a standard.

Nevertheless, what might seem a hell for us was a paradise for infectious diseases. Pathogens started to spread more rapidly than they had before. Genetic traces of diseases that jumped from the animal to the human population peaked among this time, with common names such as influenza, smallpox, and measles becoming real pains among societies.[155]

The Turkish Çatalhöyük has nowadays become a gold mine for those trying to find the origins of diseases in ancient cultures.[156] Dental pulp analysis has suggested that the city's inhabitants had a nutritionally deficient diet that was overly reliant on grains, which did not help them to become immunized to pathogens.[157]

Bacteria specialized in human-associated niches and underwent an intense transformation after the social and

---

155 Clark Spencer Larsen et al., "Bioarchaeology of Neolithic Çatalhöyük Reveals Fundamental Transitions in Health, Mobility, and Lifestyle in Early Farmers," *Proceedings of the National Academy of Sciences of the United States of America* 116, no. 26 (June 2019): 12615–23.

156 Marissa L. Ledger et al., "Parasite Infection at the Early Farming Community of Çatalhöyük," *Antiquity* 93, no. 369 (June 2019): 573–87.

157 Clark Spencer Larsen et al., "Bioarchaeology of Neolithic Çatalhöyük: Lives and Lifestyles of an Early Farming Society in Transition," *Journal of World Prehistory* 28, no. 1 (March 2015): 27–68.

demographic changes that took place with the first settlements.[158] However, subsequent generations of bacteria did find some resistance in accordance with natural selection.

As we mentioned before, the humans who first domesticated big mammals quickly built up immunities to diseases and had better chances of survival. Indeed, in their approximately ten thousand years of shared proximity with animals such as cows, Eurasians and Africans became more resistant to those diseases compared with the indigenous populations encountered outside these areas, with consequences that we will soon explore in this book.[159]

With different epidemics rampaging all over the newly created settlements, different healing practices started to appear. For instance, trepanations (making a hole through the skull to the surface of the brain) were often done around this time.[160] Such operations would have high rates of subsequent bacterial infections, but this was not the case; the reason why, it is speculated, is that these ancient cultures knew how to treat them.

One of the most relevant examples was found in the frozen body of Ötzi, or the Iceman, a five-thousand-year-old

158 Alex Mira, Ravindra Pushker, and Francisco Rodríguez-Valera, "The Neolithic Revolution of Bacterial Genomes," *Trends in Microbiology* 14, no. 5 (May 2006): 200–206.

159 Laura S. Weyrich, "Evolution of the Human Microbiome and Impacts on Human Health, Infectious Disease, and Hominid Evolution" in *Reticulate Evolution*, ed. Nathalie Gontier (New York: Springer, 2015), 231–53.

160 J. Weber and J. Wahl, "Neurosurgical Aspects of Trepanations from Neolithic Times," *International Journal of Osteoarchaeology* 16, no. 6 (November 2006): 536–45.

mummy from the Alps.[161] Researchers discovered a mushroom fastened to leather bands in his equipment, which the man may have used to calm inflammation or as an antibiotic. Furthermore, the skin of the Iceman has numerous linear carbon tattoos, presumably used for medicinal purposes.[162]

Despite some baby steps toward what we could call medicine, the Neolithic Revolution was hiding the worst pathogen yet to come. Around five thousand four hundred years ago, especially in Western Europe, many of these cities suddenly collapsed, and new ones were not built in the same areas. This time was known as the Neolithic Decline.

Nowadays, there are many hypotheses trying to explain why this happened. However, the massive burning of houses and rapid abandonment observed in mega-sites is a suitable explanation for the spread of infectious diseases. Furthermore, huge graveyards whose bodies were dated to have died in a short duration also helps to indicate an epidemic event.[163]

Scientists proposed that new and deadlier bacteria appeared on the scene and caused all this destruction and decline: *Yersinia pestis* (or *Y. pestis*). You might know this bacterium for an epidemic that it caused in the Middle Ages, but we

---

161 Q. Schiermeier and K. Stehle, "Frozen Body Offers Chance to Travel Back in Time," *Nature* 407, no. 6804 (October 2000): 550.

162 Walter F. Kean et al., "The Musculoskeletal Abnormalities of the Similaun Iceman ('otzi'): Clues to Chronic Pain and Possible Treatments," *Inflammopharmacology* 21, no. 1 (February 2013): 11–20.

163 Nicolás Rascovan et al., "Emergence and Spread of Basal Lineages of Yersinia Pestis during the Neolithic Decline," *Cell* 176, no. 1–2 (January 2019): 295-305.e10.

will talk about that later. Scientists concluded that during the decline of Neolithic populations in Europe, multiple lineages of *Y. pestis* branched and expanded throughout Eurasia, leading to what can be considered the first pandemic.

However, this did not stop us from moving forward, as we soon arrived at the early Bronze Age, a time of change, around three thousand years ago. People in Europe began to smelt copper and tin together to make bronze items and weapons, and pastoralism intensified, with goats, cattle, and sheep herding becoming ever more critical.[164]

Migrations happened more and more often, with people establishing trade and communication routes all over the known world.[165] Ancient DNA has revealed a quick infusion of new DNA in the population as soon as the Bronze Age began, flowing in from present-day Russia.

Such a change in our genome can only be linked to massive population replacement or mass migration. "During the emerging Bronze Age, we see a genetic turnover, with what we have coined 'steppe ancestry' coming in," said Professor Wolfgang Haak in an interview from *Horizon Magazine* in 2019.[166] He is an expert in ancient DNA at the Max Planck Institute for the Science of Human History in Jena, Germany.

---

164 Morten E. Allentoft et al., "Population Genomics of Bronze Age Eurasia," *Nature* 522, no. 7555 (June 2015): 167–72.

165 Peter de Barros Damgaard et al., "The First Horse Herders and the Impact of Early Bronze Age Steppe Expansions into Asia," *Science* 360, no. 6396 (June 2018): eaar7711.

166 Anthony King, "How Did the Plague Reshape Bronze Age Europe?" *Horizon: The EU Research & Innovation Magazine*, December 3, 2019.

"We see this different genetic profile before and after, but we can't explain how this came about." However, we can guess.

Prof. Haak is sequencing up to one thousand individuals from the period 4,000 to 3,000 BC to try to get a clearer picture of what happened. Data has shown that *Y. pestis* DNA was present in up to 8 percent of analyzed teeth from that time. All of this suggests that a plague epidemic rippled across early Bronze Age Europe.[167] However, this theory is still under debate.

What is clear now is that the cultural and societal changes that the Neolithic and subsequent Bronze Age witnessed supposed a real boom period for the emergence of bacterial diseases. Humankind completely mutated its lifestyle in a few thousand years, getting closer and more united, becoming the perfect vector for the spread of disease.

Consequently, more and more pathogens were adding to the match, and it was about time that the real star of the team appeared. Humanity was now arriving at a time where civilizations rose and fell seeking power and control, without noticing that something far worse than anything else was about to rise and whose fall was not yet to be written in time.

---

167 Simon Rasmussen et al., "Early Divergent Strains of Yersinia Pestis in Eurasia 5,000 Years Ago," *Cell* 163, no. 3 (October 2015): 571–82.

CHAPTER 7

WHAT LIES BENEATH THE ENDLESS SAND

"It is far more important to know what person the disease has, than what disease the person has."

—HIPPOCRATES

A newborn humanity was turning its eyes to more sophisticated settlements that grouped more people together each time. Society was growing, but no progress comes without a price. Diseases were spreading all over the old world. Cities became a source of illnesses with people crowding around, seeking stability that was taking its time to arrive. These hard times witnessed the rise of one of the most magnificent qualities of human nature: the tendency to fix ourselves.

Among the shadows of pandemics and infectious diseases, the first true civilizations started to create healers who aimed to treat and cure a growing number of patients while recording their practices. They told us that diseases could be treated, patients could be saved, and that bacteria could be fought.

Every story has a beginning, and this one is set in 5500 BC in the Nile Valley. Small tribes were inhabiting an area with plenty of water for crops and abundant food for animals. Among the many tribes, the Naqada people rose as a robust society. They had strong organization and a mighty army, and most importantly, dreams of greatness. In just a couple of hundred years, they were in control of every person and resource all over the valley.[168]

The Naqada culture has transcended to our days because of their writing symbols, strange characters that slowly turned into a full system of hieroglyphics that today we know as the ancient Egyptian language. In 3150 BC, Upper and Lower Egypt were unified under the first pharaoh of the First Dynasty, Narmer.[169] This event gave rise to one of the most influential and enigmatic cultures of the world: the Ancient Egyptian civilization, whose supremacy ended with its annexation by the Roman Empire on August 12, 30 BC.[170]

168 Izumi H. Takamiya, "Egyptian Pottery Distribution in A-Group Cemeteries, Lower Nubia: Towards an Understanding of Exchange Systems between the Naqada Culture and the A-Group Culture," *The Journal of Egyptian Archaeology* 90, no. 1 (December 2004): 35–62.

169 Robert J. Wenke, "The Evolution of Early Egyptian Civilization: Issues and Evidence," *Journal of World Prehistory* 5, no. 3 (September 1991): 279–329.

170 Paul Johnson, *The Civilization Of Ancient Egypt* (London: Weidenfeld & Nicholson, 1978).

Over almost three thousand years of domination of the valley, Egyptians created the foundation for sciences and technological practices that have arrived at our days. This happened because Egypt had an extremely well-organized economy and system of government. These factors, when added to a settled population and social conventions, as well as a relatively wealthy society, created a suitable environment for progress.[171]

Egyptian physicians, most of whom were also priests, started developing a vast array of treatments for different diseases. They did this as no one else did before, becoming the first culture to stand up and fight back those invisible enemies that were killing thousands. Unfortunately, most of their work will remain in the void of knowledge and history, under the sand on a mysterious land, waiting for someone to find it, and if not, remain lost forever.

One of the most valuable Egyptian's works had the luck to be found by Edwin Smith, an American Egyptologist. He was hanging around Luxor's market, in the ancient Thebes, when he found a papyrus in the stand of Mustafa Agha, a local dealer. After a generous amount of money, the papyrus ended up in his hands.[172] Unfortunately, Smith was not skilled enough to translate the manuscript, and it was forgotten until he died in 1906. His family gave the manuscript to the New York Historical Society, where James Henry Breasted,

---

171 Carole Reeves, *Egyptian Medicine* (London: Shire Books, 2008), 155.

172 Robert P Feldman and James T Goodrich, "The Edwin Smith Surgical Papyrus," *Child's Nervous System* 15, no. 6–7 (July 1999): 281–84.

another American Egyptologist, was able to translate and publish its content.[173]

The Edwin Smith papyrus, as it is known now, was dated around 1600 BC. However, it is accepted that the manuscript is a copy of an older papyrus from 3000 BC, speculating that the author was Imhotep, the polymath of the pharaoh Djoser.[174] These dates make the papyrus the oldest written report of something that we could call quasi-modern medicine.

The papyrus contains forty-eight cases of traumatic lesions, such as wounds, fractures, and dislocations in different parts of the body, along with their symptoms and how to follow up and make a good prognosis and treatment.[175] The degree of detail is extraordinary for that time, describing primary lesions as well as their subsequent evolution. With this knowledge, physicians could search for emerging complications, such as the development of secondary bacterial infections and inflammatory responses.[176] In several of the described cases, the presence of pus as a secondary and late

<hr>

173 Edmund S. Meltzer and Gonzalo M. Sanchez, *The Edwin Smith Papyrus: Updated Translation of the Trauma Treatise and Modern Medical Commentaries* (Nottingham: Lockwood Press, 2012), 227.

174 P. W. Brandt-Rauf and S. I. Brandt-Rauf, "History of Occupational Medicine: Relevance of Imhotep and the Edwin Smith Papyrus," *British Journal of Industrial Medicine* 44, no. 1 (January 1987): 68–70.

175 Iain S. Whitaker et al., "The Birth of Plastic Surgery: The Story of Nasal Reconstruction from the Edwin Smith Papyrus to the Twenty-First Century," *Plastic and Reconstructive Surgery* 120, no. 1 (July 2007): 327–36.

176 Marc Stiefel, Arlene Shaner, and Steven D. Schaefer, "The Edwin Smith Papyrus: The Birth of Analytical Thinking in Medicine and Otolaryngology," *The Laryngoscope* 116, no. 2 (February 2006): 182–88.

phenomenon is described and associated with an adverse prognosis.[177]

Egyptians did not know about the microbial world, but they identified some clear signs of systemic disease. Moreover, thanks to the Edwin Smith papyrus and several others found over the years, we know that even though they could not see microorganisms in the intestinal flora, they knew that the intestine contained some type of substance that could find a way through the blood vessels and intoxicate the body.[178]

Another fascinating manuscript is the Eber's papyrus, dated in 1400 BC, which was found between the legs of a mummy and sold to Smith in 1862. In the text, physicians recommend the use of honey and grease on open wounds as well as pus removal to promote wound healing.[179] Without knowing what was making them sick, Egyptians found a way to treat and cure the disease.

As such, Egyptian society was relatively healthy compared to other cultures at that time. However, not all the merit came from their physicians. What if I told you that Egyptians had access to a powerful antibiotic that was not discovered until the early 1950s? If you want to know more, the answer can

---

177 John Thorne Crissey and Lawrence Charles Parish, "Wound Healing: Development of the Basic Concepts," *Clinics in Dermatology* 2, no. 3 (July 1984): 1–7.

178 Walter W. Hamburger, "The Earliest Known Reference to the Heart and Circulation. The Edwin Smith Surgical Papyrus, circa 3,000 B.C.," *American Heart Journal* 17, no. 3 (March 1939): 259–74.

179 D Lynn Loriaux, "Diabetes and The Ebers Papyrus," *The Endocrinologist* 16, no. 2 (March 2006): 55–56.

be found in the work of an anthropologist, a professor, and a medicinal chemist; Dr. Armelagos, Professor C. White, and Dr. Nelson have been extracting tetracyclines (TCs), a powerful antibiotic, from hundreds of ancient Egyptian bones for years.[180]

They take the bones of old mummies and dissolve them in hydrofluoric acid, one of the strongest acids in the world. This process results in demineralization and release of compounds present in the structures. After analysis, they showed that three first-generation TCs were present in nearly all the bones. "We tend to associate drugs that cure diseases with modern medicine," Armelagos said in an interview conducted at Emory University in 2010.[181] "But it's becoming increasingly clear that this prehistoric population was using empirical evidence to develop therapeutic agents. I have no doubt that they knew what they were doing."

The presence of these TCs were not only artifacts. They found that 95 percent of the bones extracted had some form of TC, and 56 percent of these cases had bones whose composition was more than 5 percent of antibiotic. Such a concentration

---

180 Mark L. Nelson et al., "Brief Communication: Mass Spectroscopic Characterization of Tetracycline in the Skeletal Remains of an Ancient Population from Sudanese Nubia 350-550 CE," *American Journal of Physical Anthropology* 143, no. 1 (September 2010): 151–54.

181 Carol Clark, "Ancient Brewers Tapped Antibiotic Secrets," *eScienceCommons* (blog), *Emory University*, Agust 30, 2010.

of the drug would allow them not to show any signs of infections in the bone.[182]

However, how did they consume a modern-day antibiotic over two thousand years ago and in such high doses? For sure, they were not using pills or injections. Then, what was it? Let me give you a clue: Germany, pubs, hops. Not yet? Telling you that it is one of the most popular drinks in the world would help. The answer is beer. They had such a concentration of antibiotics in their bones because of beer—what a wonderful world Ancient Egypt was.[183]

Egyptians were already masters in the science of fermentation. Everything indicates that they might have produced the drug on purpose in their beers. The antibiotics might have been added to the beer during fermentation as a result of using barley plants, which have trace amounts of *Streptomyces*. This bacterium was added to the fermentation vessel.[184] The beer would have looked just like others, except it would have had floating golden lumps.

Around that time, it was common practice to inoculate a new batch of beer with 10 percent of the previous batch. Therefore,

---

182 Corey Maggiano et al., "Spectral and Photobleaching Analysis Using Confocal Laser Scanning Microscopy: A Comparison of Modern and Archaeological Bone Fluorescence," *Molecular and Cellular Probes* 20, no. 3–4 (June 2006): 154–62.

183 Ana María Rosso, "Beer and Wine in Antiquity: Beneficial Remedy or Punishment Imposed by the Gods?," *Acta Medico-Historica Adriatica : AMHA* 10, no. 2 (December 2012): 237–62.

184 Eric Seidlitz, Zeina Saikali, and Gurmit Singh, "Use of Tetracyclines for Bone Metastases," in *Bone Metastasis*, ed. Gurmit SinghShafaat and A. Rabbani (Totowa: Humana Press, 2005). 293–303.

the Streptomyces-containing beverage would be a continuous source of the bacteria from proceeding batches. This method would result in high enough concentrations of TCs that could have had medicinal effects and, consequently, be retained in the bone.

Besides, they likely used this beer to heal individuals with common bacterial pathologies, including urinary tract infections and small wounds.[185] This miraculous medical activity would not be free of consequences, as we will discuss later in this book. However, now, let us cheer for some antibiotic-rich ancient beer.

Ancient Egyptians had another hidden weapon to fight bacterial diseases that, indeed, looked pretty nice on them: We are talking about their eye makeup. What was unique about it? The cosmetic contained lead.[186] Bizarre enough, they added the heavy metal to their cosmetics on purpose, clearly unaware of the potential side-effects of such an activity.

The analytical chemist Philippe Walter and colleagues at the French National Centre for Scientific Research (CNRS) analyzed several samples of the Egyptians' black eyeliner in the Louvre's collection. After some experiments, they identified

---

185 Ryan Metcalfe, "Bread and Beer in Ancient Egyptian Medicine," in *Mummies, Magic and Medicine in Ancient Egypt*, ed. Campbell Price (Manchester: Manchester University Press, 2016), 157–68.

186 Zafar A. Mahmood, Iqbal Azhar, and S. W. Ahmed, "Kohl Use in Antiquity: Effects on the Eye," in *Toxicology in Antiquity*, ed. Philip Wexler (Amsterdam: Elsevier, 2018), 93–103.

two types of lead salt not found in nature, which means that they must have synthesized them.[187]

Making lead salts is a tricky and extremely delicate process that often takes weeks. Moreover, unlike other conventional makeup components, the salts are not glossy. So why did they bother? The answer as hidden in some ancient manuscripts: People were making lead salts as treatments for eye ailments, scars, and discolorations.

Now the question is, did they know about the toxic effects of lead back then? And if they knew, why use them? Maybe there was some health benefit. To study this hypothesis, the researchers added lead salts to human skin cells that were grown in a laboratory. The lead was shown to stress the cells, triggering the release of nitric oxide (NO) and other com-pounds involved in the body's immune response.[188]

The presence of NO can trigger biochemical processes that ultimately send macrophages (a type of immune cell) to the site of infection, where they engulf the bacteria in the area.[189] Although not likely, it is impossible to tell whether they knew

---

187 Issa Tapsoba et al., "Finding out Egyptian Gods' Secret Using Analytical Chemistry: Biomedical Properties of Egyptian Black Makeup Revealed by Amperometry at Single Cells," *Analytical Chemistry* 82, no. 2 (January 2010): 457-60.

188 Santi M. Mandal et al., "Kaajal Fights against Eye Pathogens and Is Safe for Eye Make-up: A Reinvestigation of an Ancient Practice," *Analyst* 138, no. 18 (September 2013): 5197–99.

189 P. Kirkham, "Oxidative Stress and Macrophage Function: A Failure to Resolve the Inflammatory Response," *Biochemical Society Transactions* 35, no. 2 (April 2007): 284–87.

about that or not. It might be all about balance, one whose ancient logic we may never uncover.

Skilled physicians, beers, and eye makeup aside, it seems like the arrival of the ancient Egyptian culture to the match would give some advantage to our ancestors in their fight with bacteria. However, pathogenic bacteria and diseases did not stop spreading. For instance, ancient remains in Upper Egypt, dated around 3400 BC, have suggested that our already well-known TB must have been endemic throughout the population at the origin of urban life.[190] Other work on the Early Dynastic period concluded that for two thousand five hundred years, the frequency of TB remained the same, becoming the first evidence for an extensive presence of bacterial disease in various ancient populations.[191]

However, something far worse was happening and spreading unnoticed. Two documents from that time—the Hearst and the London Medical papyruses—talked about an unusual epidemic that plagued Egypt. The pandemic, known as "one of the Asiatics," linked to foreigners from the Syria-Canaan-Transjordan area.[192]

190 B Ziskind and B Halioua, "Tuberculosis in Ancient Egypt.," *Revue Des Maladies Respiratoires* 24, no. 10 (December 2007): 1277–83.

191 A. R. Zink et al., "Molecular Study on Human Tuberculosis in Three Geographically Distinct and Time Delineated Populations from Ancient Egypt," *Epidemiology and Infection* 130, no. 2 (April 2003): 239–49.

192 Siro I. Trevisanato, "Did an Epidemic of Tularemia in Ancient Egypt Affect the Course of World History?," *Medical Hypotheses* 63, no. 5 (January 2004): 905–10.

The Hearst papyrus speaks of bodies turned into charcoal, the Egyptian god Seth repelling the Mediterranean Sea as well as the disease jumping from body to body. Although lethality was not explicitly mentioned in this papyrus, modern scholars have linked this disease to *Y. pestis* and its bubonic plague, while others think that it was more similar to typhus.[193] As we will learn later, *Y. pestis* often takes advantage of humans traveling along trade routes, and the expansion of these around Africa, Asia, and the Mediterranean would have allowed for a devastating epidemic.

With such exposure to diseases, more and more societies started to understand them: not the way they work, but how deadly they may become. Therefore, it was about time to have someone thinking about using such power to take advantage of others. With that in mind, it is time to meet the Hittites of Anatolia, whose empire stretched from northern Turkey into Iraq and Syria.[194] Fearless soldiers, they were famous for their lethal chariots and skill with horses. However, that was not all. Three thousand five hundred years ago, these people had already mastered the art of biological warfare.

Dr. Siro Trevisanato, a molecular biochemist who has been studying the Hittite empire for quite a long time, claims that their victories were down to the use of infected sheep, which they would slowly introduce inside those cities that they wanted to conquer. "There is no doubt that these were the

---

193 Eva Panagiotakopulu, "Pharaonic Egypt and the Origins of Plague," *Journal of Biogeography* 31, no. 2 (February 2004): 269–75.

194 Stefano de Martino, "Some Questions on the Political History and Chronology of the Early Hittite Empire," *Altorientalische Forschungen* 37, no. 2 (December 2010): 186–97.

first weapons of mass destruction," he said in an interview for *The Telegraph* in 2007. "They were waging bioterrorism."[195]

The sheep were infected with tularemia, also known as rabbit fever, a devastating disease caused by the bacterium *Francisella tularensis*. The bacterium can quickly jump from animals to humans, causing large skin ulcers and respiratory failure.

In 1325 BC, the Hittites entered the city of Symra, on the borders of Lebanon and Syria, and a mysterious plague was recorded. The disease was known as the Hittite Plague.[196] Political rivals of Egypt, the Hittites would often launch attacks against the Egyptian border.

After one of these encounters, the plague was described in letters reporting that donkeys were also infected and carried the disease. Right after, these animals were banned from the city in an attempt to stop the illness. At the same time, the London Medical papyrus was copied as the authorities thought it might be useful to disseminate the manual. This event might become one of the first movements in the handling of infectious diseases by society.[197]

---

195 Malcolm Moore, "Hittites 'used Germ Warfare 3,500 Years Ago' " *Telegraph*, December 8, 2007.

196 Siro Igino Trevisanato, "The 'Hittite Plague', an Epidemic of Tularemia and the First Record of Biological Warfare," *Medical Hypotheses* 69, no. 6 (January 2007): 1371–74.

197 Philip Norrie and Philip Norrie, "How Disease Affected the History of the Hittite Empire," in *A History of Disease in Ancient Times* (New York: Springer International Publishing, 2016), 37–59.

The Hittites' techniques were used for quite a long time. However, they were about to discover that there are forces in nature that cannot be contained or controlled. The Hittites paid a significant price for their tactics. An outbreak of the same disease that they were using was recorded among them. After a quick spread, it weakened their ranks a few years after the Symra attack. No more records of these practices were found after that time.

As happened with the Hittites, many other empires were vanishing from the records of history, while so many others were rising. Political and geographical stability was a distant memory for many in a time marked by wars and territorial expansions. The apogee of the Ancient World was about to erupt all over the Mediterranean, which would significantly affect the development of society in every aspect.

Still, humanity was living in the shadow of microorganisms that were starting to be noticed, but not understood. Humanity's last hope was to seek the knowledge of diseases to ultimately uncover the secrets that laid behind manuscripts of older civilizations. However, the path ahead was long and hard, with many ups and downs faced by a species that was destined to live and rise in an already fully developed bacterial world.

CHAPTER 8

GOD'S WRATH, HUMANITY'S AGONY

"But what does it mean, the plague? It's life, that's all."
—ALBERT CAMUS, THE PLAGUE

The last great pharaoh was long gone with the whispers of an empire whose greatness was lost to sandstorms. Days, months, and years gone, witnessing the rise and fall of new kings for almost a century. A new power ruled throughout the known world, one that was no man, but an ideal.

Humanity was at the edge of a new era in which rational thinking was about to burst at the same time that massive migrations of people from the countryside to the newly created city-states. Society became more organized and hierarchical, marked by the rise of new governmental powers and ways to rule.

The Mediterranean Sea became the nest of rationale movements triggering an expansion in both sciences and arts as the world had never seen before. Perfection became something worth seeking, and like that, humankind entered the Classical era, with Greeks and Romans becoming the protagonist of the masterpiece that was destined to be remembered for centuries to come.[198]

Perfection seeks knowledge, and with it comes questions. Undoubtedly, one of them was how to describe what no eyes could see. Buried deep down in the oblivion lay the answers destined to shed some light on the bacterial world and its inhabitants, invisibly crawling around and within us.

As such, we might be at the beginning of the birth of the germ theory, a nowadays-fundamental tenet of medicine, which states that microorganisms can invade the body and cause certain diseases.[199] By that time, mythology, gods, and the chaotic fate of men were always mixed with the medical and biological reality of maladies. Undoubtedly, among entropic conjectures, an absolute truth was waiting to be awakened by the constant wonder of alike minds.

Everything began with the *seeds*, spreading entities that were dispersible through the air and able to land in anyone's body. In his poem, *De Rerum Natura* (On the Nature of Things), written in 56 BC, the Roman poet Lucretius stated that the

---

198 Jonathan M. Hall, *A History of the Archaic Greek World, ca. 1200-479 BCE.* (Hoboken: Wiley-Blackwell, 2007).

199 K. Codell Carter, "The Germ Theory, Beriberi, and the Deficiency Theory of Disease," *Medical History* 21, no. 2 (April 1977): 119–36.

world contained various types of these seeds.[200] A few years later, the Roman statesman Marcus Terentius Varro wrote in his *Rerum Rusticarum Libri III* (Three Books on Agriculture) a statement that talks about *"certain minute creatures which cannot be seen by the eyes"* that live close to swamps and cause diseases.[201]

Undoubtedly, one of the most relevant contributions to this theory came by the handwriting of the Greek physician Galen, one of the fathers of anatomy and medicine whose practices were used for centuries.[202] He speculated in his *On Initial Causes*, written on 175 AD, that some patients might have "seeds of fever" while he also stated that diseases were spread by "certain seeds of plague."

Now, the Greek world did not just theorize and write about diseases and plagues for pure pleasure. They wanted to understand the reason behind them, a necessity that came from the suffering of its own people in what was the most lethal episode of illness in the Classical world.

Everything started in 430 BC, the second year of the Peloponnesian War. Athens and Sparta, the two most powerful city-states in ancient Greece at the time, were fighting for

---

200 Vivian Nutton, "The Seeds of Disease: An Explanation of Contagion and Infection from the Greeks to the Renaissance," *Medical History* 27, no. 1 (January 1983): 1–34.

201 J H Dirckx, "Pestilence Narratives in Classical Literature: A Study in Creative Imitation: I. Homer, Sophocles, Thucydides, and Lucretius.," *The American Journal of Dermatopathology* 22, no. 2 (April 2000): 197–202.

202 R. J. Littman and M. L. Littman, "Galen and the Antonine Plague.," *American Journal of Philology* 94 (1973): 243–55.

control of land and sea. In the fervor of the war, an outbreak of bubonic plague erupted in Athens.[203]

The original outbreak seemed to happen somewhere in sub-Saharan Africa, just south of Ethiopia. Trade routes allowed the pathogen to quickly sweep through Egypt and Libya across the Mediterranean Sea.[204] When the plague entered Athens through the city's port of Piraeus, it found a densely populated area in which to spread. By the end of the pandemic four years later, the disease killed around a third of the population, which numbered close to three hundred thousand in the fifth century BC.

Nowadays, all we know is thanks to the testimonies of the Greek historian and general Thucydides.[205] He was the first person to write about a pandemic in Ancient Greece, and probably in the whole Classical world.[206]

In his writings, Thucydides described patients whose fevers were so intense that they preferred to be naked than wear any clothes, while others preferred to be submerged in cold water. He wrote that the sick were "tormented by an unceasing thirst," which was never satiated. The sick could not sleep,

---

203 Robert J. Littman, "The Plague of Athens: Epidemiology and Paleopathology," *Mount Sinai Journal of Medicine: A Journal of Translational and Personalized Medicine* 76, no. 5 (October 2009): 456–67.

204 David M. Morens and Robert J. Littman, "Epidemiology of the Plague of Athens," *Transactions of the American Philological Association (1974-2014)* 122 (1992): 271-304.

205 D. L. Page, "Thucydides' Description of the Great Plague at Athens," *The Classical Quarterly* 3, no. 3–4 (July-October 1953): 97–119.

206 Arlene W. Saxonhouse, "Nature & Convention in Thucydides' History," *Polity* 10, no. 4 (June 1978): 461–87,.

and many displayed a constant restlessness, which made them zombies, wandering around the city with so much pain that they often collapsed and died in the streets.[207]

Furthermore, those who survived the plague had to live with serious disfigurements of their genitals, fingers, and toes. They also had permanent blindness and memory loss. Thucydides did also notice that in some instances, birds and other animals that often look to feed on human flesh were repulsed by the diseased bodies. He also observed that these animals died from consuming the rotting flesh.[208]

For nearly two thousand five hundred years, historians and scholars have attempted to identify precisely what exactly swept through Athens and resulted in so many deaths. In *The Plague of Athens: 430-428 B.C. Epidemic and Epizoötic*, J. A. H. Wylie and H. W. Stubbs discussed the possibility that the Athenian plague derived its origins from animals.[209]

The authors suggested that leptospirosis, a bacterial infection that is spread by dogs and cattle, existed in conditions that were prevalent in ancient Athens. Tularemia, also caused by pathogens shared by animals and humans, could be easily spread by rodents and infect humans through a flea or tick

---

207 Alexander D. Langmuir et al., "The Thucydides Syndrome: A New Hypothesis for the Cause of the Plague of Athens," *New England Journal of Medicine* 313, no. 16 (October 1985): 1027–30.

208 J McSherry and R Kilpatrick, "The Plague of Athens.," *Journal of the Royal Society of Medicine* 85, no. 11 (November 1992): 713.

209 H. W. Stubbs, "The Plague of Athens: 430–428 B.C. Epidemic and Epizoötic," *The Classical Quarterly* 33, no. 1 (January 1983): 6–11.

bite, or by contact with infected animals or contaminated water supplies.

In 1994, researchers found a mass grave containing over a hundred bodies deep beneath the Kerameikos cemetery in Athens. The arrangement of the bodies was chaotic, with the remains piled on top of one another, which was contrary to the Greek tradition. Manolis Papagrigorakis and her colleagues at the University of Athens were able to take some random teeth samples from the victims of this cemetery and extract the dental pulp. Once the materials were isolated, the team tested the pulp for many bacterial diseases before finding a match in *Salmonella enterica*, the bacterium responsible for typhoid fever.[210]

Typhoid fever, transmitted by contaminated food or water, causes fever, rash, and diarrhea, all closely matching Thucydides' account of the terrible plague. The only thing that did not match up is the quick onset of the disease, as the modern strains of the bacterium take longer to reproduce and show symptoms. "This inconsistency may be explained by a possible evolution of typhoid fever over time," the authors wrote in the report. "Considering the overcrowding and unsanitary conditions within the walls of the besieged Athens, a typhoid epidemic would have been likely to break out."[211]

---

210 Manolis J. Papagrigorakis, Christos Yapijakis, and Philippos N. Synodinos, "Typhoid Fever Epidemic in Ancient Athens," in *Paleomicrobiology: Past Human Infections*, ed. Didier Raoult and Michel Drancourt (Berlin: Springer Berlin Heidelberg, 2008), 161–73.

211 Manolis J. Papagrigorakis et al., "DNA Examination of Ancient Dental Pulp Incriminates Typhoid Fever as a Probable Cause of the Plague of Athens," *International Journal of Infectious Diseases* 10, no. 3 (May 2006): 206–214.

Whatever the exact cause was, the Plague of Athens was the first outbreak of an epidemic that humankind has ever cared to record with enough detail. However, the archives of such a plague and their content were quickly forgotten when, a few years later, the total control of Europe was shifted to a new king: the Roman Empire. A new dawn for the Classical world was beginning; Architecture, politics, economics, science, and so many other fields began to flourish or were re-shaped, leading to significant advancements, excellent pieces of art, strong laws, and magnificent monuments.

One of the reasons why the Roman Empire was famous was for their advanced sanitation and sewage systems, the employment of public baths, and extensive legislation and instructions for good sanitation practices.[212] Undoubtedly, these led to a healthier society. Nevertheless, Piers Mitchell, an expert on ancient diseases at Cambridge University's Department of Archaeology and Anthropology, might give you a totally different view.

He has studied archaeological pieces of evidence from sites all over the Roman Empire, and his conclusions are striking: The Romans may not have been any freer from diseases than the barbarians they often fought. Osseus material from Romans told us that they were prey to bedbugs, lice, and different species of fleas. Once they became vectors, they were able to spread bubonic plague and other bacterial infections

---

212 Stavros Yannopoulos et al., "History of Sanitation and Hygiene Technologies in the Hellenic World," *Journal of Water Sanitation and Hygiene for Development* 7, no. 2 (June 2017): 163–80.

across the empire to regions where the infestations were previously unknown.[213]

One of the main sources of such pathogenesis was the practice of regular bathing, the use of clean drinking water, and even the installation of public toilets with subsequent removal of human waste. Unlike what you might think, this brought more problems than solutions.

For instance, in public hot baths, while the biggest ones had daily water-recycling systems, in smaller and medium-sized baths, the water was changed only intermittently, entirely depending on slaves using buckets to empty them, leaving the bathers swimming in a warm soup of bacteria.

On the other hand, although they introduced systems of cleaning and removing human waste, it did not work as well as they may have expected. These wastes were spread on the fields surrounding the towns and cities, where it was used as an excellent soil fertilizer. However, the bacteria in the waste were also able to penetrate the soil and quickly reach water fountains and propagate across the air.

Consequently, these diseases were not contained in Rome. Samples of the same pathologies that originated in Rome have been found all over the old empire. The pathogens found an outstanding opportunity to spread with the conquest cravings of the Romans.

---

213 Piers D. Mitchell, "Human Parasites in the Roman World: Health Consequences of Conquering an Empire," *Parasitology* 144, no. 1 (January 2017): 48–58.

During the Imperial period, disease was a harsh reality of life all over five million square kilometers of Roman territory.[214] As the borders were continuously expanding and the population steadily growing, cities were exposed to a multitude of crowding people, lack of food, and poor sanitation conditions. What a wonderful world for pathogens.

The bacterial disease that most enjoyed such conditions was an old friend: TB. Research led by the University of Wisconsin-Madison revealed that the rise of the Roman Empire gave TB the chance to travel all around the known world.[215] This hypothesis, developed by the geneticist Caitlin Pepperell, has been formulated over the study of the bacterium's genome in a historical context.[216]

Seven dominant TB strains have been isolated to date with different origins, but all linked to a human disease that first appeared some tens of thousands of years ago in Africa. One of the most widespread strains went crazy around the first century AD. "The timing is consistent with the Romans causing an incredible amount of movement and exploration around the Mediterranean," Pepperell stated in an interview

---

214 Dennis C. Pirages, "Nature, Disease, and Globalization: An Evolutionary Perspective," *International Studies Review* 9, no. 4 (December 2007): 616–28.

215 Jared J. Eddy, "The Ancient City of Rome, Its Empire, and the Spread of Tuberculosis in Europe," *Tuberculosis* 95, no. S1 (June 2015): S23–28.

216 Mary B. O'Neill et al., "Lineage Specific Histories of *Mycobacterium Tuberculosis* Dispersal in Africa and Eurasia," *Molecular Ecology* 28, no. 13 (July 2019): mec.15120.

with *Daily Mail* in 2018.[217] "There was contact between human populations that had not had contact before."

With such widespread disease all over the empire, you might wonder if these illnesses had something to do with its fall. For hundreds of years, the Roman Empire occupied most of the Western world and land south of Asia, with an immense power and a vast array of resources. Therefore, what accounts for such a gigantic fall?

There is a wide range of answers, from class conflict or fiscal unsustainability to the technological development of barbarian tribes who were continually harassing the frontiers. All of them are plausible and perfectly fit with history. However, pathogen genomics providing new data shows that the fall of the Roman Empire may have been a biological phenomenon.[218] But how?

The beginning of the end took place in 285 AC when the Emperor Diocletian decided that the Roman Empire was too big to manage, so he broke it into two parts. The Western side officially ended on September 4, 476 AC, and the control of the empire was moved to the Eastern side and its capital Constantinople.[219]

---

217 Joe Pinkstone, "Ancient Romans to Blame for the Spread of Tuberculosis from Africa" *Daily Mail Online*, July 4, 2018.

218 Kyle Harper, *The Fate of Rome: Climate, Disease, and the End of an Empire.* (Princeton: Princeton University Press, 2017), 146.

219 Colin Michael Wells, *The Roman Empire* (Cambridge: Harvard University Press, 2004), 98.

Nevertheless, the most devastating enemy the Romans had ever faced was about to arrive. Regardless of what they might think, this enemy did not come from the barbaric lands, but from within their own walls. Its name was *Y. pestis.*

The first plague interrupted a remarkable renaissance of Roman power under the energetic leadership of the emperor Justinian, which is why it has been known to history as the Justinian plague.[220] The disease ravaged the capital. Those who recorded the outbreak believed they were witnessing the apocalyptic wrath of the gods in some extremely terrifying ways, such as the vision of enormous military towers filled with piles of purulent corpses.[221]

One of the best testimonies of the time comes from the Byzantine historian Procopius, who first reported the epidemic in July, 541 AD from the port of Pelusium, near Suez, in Egypt.[222] The origin of the disease was most likely linked to Asia and the westward migration of the Hun people.

DNA from a strain of the bacterium biologically related to the one involved in the Justinian pandemic was found in Hun individuals from Central Asia and North Ossetia in

---

220 Marcel Keller et al., "Ancient Yersinia Pestis Genomes from across Western Europe Reveal Early Diversification during the First Pandemic (541–750)," *Proceedings of the National Academy of Sciences of the United States of America* 116, no. 25 (June 2019): 12363–72.

221 William Rosen, *Justinian's Flea: The First Great Plague and the End of the Roman Empire.* (London: Penguin Books, 2007), 181.

222 J. A. S. Evans, "Procopius of Caesarea and the Emperor Justinian," *Historical Papers* 3, no. 1 (July 2012): 126.

Russia.[223] Researchers believe that the plague was brought through the Silk Road with intensified trade becoming the most likely factor for the outbreak.

Procopius wrote that at its peak, the plague was killing up to ten thousand people in Constantinople every day. He also wrote that it was not easy to see anyone out of their homes in the city. All craftsmen abandoned their work for months as a consequence of the disease, and the whole world was slowing down.

As Procopius wrote: "In some cases death came immediately, in others, after many days; and with some the body broke out with black pustules about as large as a lentil and these did not survive even one day, but all succumbed immediately." The whole society was struck by fear of a disease that was able to painfully kill you without hesitation and for which there was no cure.

Therefore, the Roman renaissance was stopped dead in its tracks Suddenly, state failure and economic stagnation came, from which the empire never recovered.[224] Some researchers and historians considered this plague as the biggest one in the old world, with deaths ranging from twenty-five to one hundred million people during two centuries of recurrence.[225]

---

223 Peter De Barros Damgaard et al., "137 Ancient Human Genomes from across the Eurasian Steppes," *Nature* 557, no. 7705 (May 2018): 369–74.

224 Ronald Findlay et al., "Demographic Shocks and the Factor Proportions Model: From the Plague of Justinian to the Black Death," in *The Economics of the Frontier.* (London: Palgrave Macmillan, 2016), 125–72.

225 Talha Burki, "Justinian's Flea: Plague, Empire and the Birth of Europe," *The Lancet Infectious Diseases* 7, no. 12 (December 2007): 774.

To help you with the numbers, we are talking about half of Europe's population at the time.

Recently, the actual DNA of the bacterium has been recovered from multiple victims of the pandemic, which has helped us understand how such a catastrophe could happen.[226] The bacterial strain of the plague was a relatively young species of *Y. pestis*, different from those which had existed before.[227] Therefore, when it hit the empire, it was an emerging infectious disease to which not many people had immunity.

The Justinian Plague might be the first time that humanity faced a real pandemic of catastrophic proportions. Subsequent waves continued to strike the continent throughout the sixth, seventh, and eighth centuries, with the disease becoming more localized and less virulent. Immunity started to build in the inhabitants of what now was just the shadow of an empire that had never knelt to human laws but had to do so to nature. Rome was the first advanced society shaken to its core by the explosive force of infectious diseases. However, it was not the last, as we are about to discover.

---

226 David M. Wagner et al., "Yersinia Pestis and the Plague of Justinian 541–543 AD: A Genomic Analysis," *The Lancet Infectious Diseases* 14, no. 4 (April 2014): 319–26.

227 Mark Achtman et al., "Microevolution and History of the Plague Bacillus, Yersinia Pestis," *Proceedings of the National Academy of Sciences of the United States of America* 101, no. 51 (December 2004): 17837–42.

CHAPTER 9

THE WHISPER THAT KILLED THE WORLD

—

"And so many died that all believed it was the end of the world."
—AGNOLO DI TURA

The fall of the Western Roman Empire marked the beginning of the Middle Ages. Around this time, the vast majority of people were living in the countryside, occupying their time with farming and livestock. Often, a local lord living in a fortified house or castle took control of everything, and then they wanted more. Life was owned as another mere possession, and the world was ruled by men who craved more while many others lived an unpleasant and poor life.[228] The Middle Ages were often witness to injustice, wars, and disease as no other time before.

---

228 Giovanna Belcastro et al., "Continuity or Discontinuity of the Life-Style in Central Italy during the Roman Imperial Age-Early Middle Ages Transition: Diet, Health, and Behavior," *American Journal of Physical Anthropology* 132, no. 3 (March 2007): 381–94.

The end of the Justinian plague marked a time where bacterial pathogens found their way to turn into nightmares of epic proportions. Names like leprosy, bubonic plague, TB, or anthrax, among many others, became endemic in many societies. Often represented as evil gods, their continuous waves destroyed entire communities, disrupted the economy, and left eternal stigmas all over the world. However, the worst was yet to arrive. The monster that came from the East had a name: *Yersinia pestis*. The Middle Ages were about to be the witness of the worst biological disaster in our history: the Black Death.

How did everything start? Or more accurately, where and why? Mark Achtman, a professor of Bacterial Population Genetics at Warwick Medical School in the UK, has concluded that all three of the great waves of the plague evolved in or near China.[229]

The Black Death came from a thirteenth-century China where the socioeconomical environment was perfect for the development of any bacterial disease.[230] The Mongols had recently captured part of the territory, disrupting farming and trading, and laying the foundation for an impending widespread famine. The population dramatically dropped

---

229 Stephanie Haensch et al., "Distinct Clones of Yersinia Pestis Caused the Black Death," ed. Nora J. Besansky, *PLoS Pathogens* 6, no. 10 (October 2010): e1001134.

230 John Norris, "East or West? The Geographic Origin of the Black Death," *Bulletin of the History of Medicine* 51, no. 0 (Spring 1977): 1–24.

from approximately one hundred twenty to sixty million.[231] Among the survivors, many developed vulnerabilities to diseases due to weakened immune systems.

In 1331, an outbreak erupted in the middle of the Yuan Empire. By 1356, the disease had killed over 90 percent of the Hebei Province's population, with deaths totaling over five million people, and ravaged other Chinese territories after several other outbreaks.[232]

With enough victims, *Y. pestis* had the longest ancient overland trade route to its entire use. From Xian, through Central Asia, and to Constantinople on the eastern edge of Europe, the Silk Road covered about 4000 miles of settlements full of people ready to be infected. The bacterium primarily used the Mongol armies and traders that were arriving in different lands via ship.[233]

By the end of 1346, news of a mysterious plague had reached the seaports of Europe. A chronicle wrote that "India was depopulated, Tartary, Mesopotamia, Syria, Armenia were covered with dead bodies." Others claimed that all of Asia was desolated. Using their testimonies, it is likely that each population center would have lost at least 40 percent of its

---

231 Ruth W. Dunnell, *China among Equals: The Middle Kingdom and Its Neighbors, 10th–14th Centuries* (Berkeley: University of California Press, 1983).

232 Johannes Nohl and C. H Clarke, *The Black Death. A Chronicle of the Plague.* (Yardley: Westholme Publishing, 1924).

233 Ole J. Benedictow, "Yersinia Pestis, the Bacterium of Plague, Arose in East Asia. Did It Spread Westwards via the Silk Roads, the Chinese Maritime Expeditions of Zheng He or over the Vast Eurasian Populations of Sylvatic (Wild) Rodents?," *Journal of Asian History* 47, no. 1 (2013): 1-31.

citizens, with some areas reaching death tolls as high as 70 percent.[234]

By 1335, the Black Death left a devastated Asia and moved closer to the Eastern border of Europe, a movement that was triggered by the Golden Horde. This army of Mongols, established by a grandson of Genghis Khan, was fighting and spreading their empire closer to Europe, bringing the deadly disease with them.[235] In 1344, they decided to recapture the Crimean port city of Kaffa from the Genoese, Italian traders. The Mongols set siege, which lasted three years. Exhausted by it, reinforcements were called. Instead of new men, they brought death.

The Italian lawyer Gabriele de Mussis recorded what happened: "The whole army was affected by a disease which overran the Mongols and killed thousands upon thousands every day." Consequently, the Mongols decided to end the siege, but not in a way that anyone could have ever expected.[236] Gabriele wrote that the Mongol leader "ordered corpses to be placed in catapults and lobbed into the city in hopes that the intolerable stench would kill everyone inside."

Regardless of how it played out, the Golden Horde's siege of Kaffa certainly did drive refugees to flee on ships bound for

---

234 Robert S. Gottfried, *The Black Death: Natural and Human Disaster in Medieval Europe* (New York: Free Press, 1985), 119-128.

235 Uli Schammoglu, "Preliminary Remarks on the Role of Disease in the History of the Golden Horde," *Central Asian Survey* 12, no. 4 (January 1993): 447–57.

236 Mark Wheelis, "Biological Warfare at the 1346 Siege of Caffa," *Emerging Infectious Diseases* 8, no. 9 (September 2002): 971–75.

Genoa, who became the primary source of the Black Death that went on to decimate Europe. All that was left was a dead city ready to host a few more ghosts.

In October 1347, a fleet of Genovese trading ships escaping from Kaffa reached the port of Messina in Sicily. By the time they arrived at the city, all the crew members were either infected or dead. However, no one stopped the rats from entering this new land.[237]

Consequently, many outbreaks started to erupt on shore, with the plague spreading to Genoa and Venice. From Italy, it moved northwest, striking France, Spain, Portugal, and England by June 1348.[238] Once it reached the North Sea, it then turned and spread east through Germany and Scandinavia. Finally, the plague reached northeastern Russia in 1351.

No one was safe from the disease. One of the most shocking testimonies came from the chronicler Agnolo di Tura, who was living in Siena (Italy) at the time of the epidemic.[239] He wrote, "They died by the hundreds, both day and night, and all were thrown in ditches and covered with earth. And as soon as those ditches were filled, more were dug. And I buried my five children with my own hands. And so many died that all believed it was the end of the world."

---

237 Jr. Samuel K. Cohn, *The Black Death Transformed: Disease and Culture in Early Renaissance Europe* (London: Bloomsbury Academic, 2003), 117–23.

238 Paul Slack, "The Black Death Past and Present. 2. Some Historical Problems," *Transactions of the Royal Society of Tropical Medicine and Hygiene* 83, no. 4 (July 1989): 461–63.

239 Daniel Lord Smail, "Accommodating Plague in Medieval Marseille," *Continuity and Change* 11, no. 1 (May 1996): 11–41.

On the other side of the world, the Moroccan historian Ibn Khaldun wrote about the outbreak in a shocking manner: "Civilization both in the East and the West was visited by a destructive plague which devastated nations and caused populations to vanish. It swallowed up many of the good things of civilization and wiped them out. Civilization fell with the decrease of humankind. Cities and buildings were laid waste, roads and way signs were obliterated, settlements and mansions became empty, dynasties and tribes grew weak. The entire inhabited world changed."[240]

Indeed, the world did change forever. The real impact of the Black Death is difficult to assess given the huge loss of life and subsequent inconsistent records. More importantly, the pandemic had a huge influence on the way people lived after.[241] Some of them took wild and immoral lives because there was nothing left for them, while others fell into deep despair and frustration.

The Black Death also brought down rich and poor alike. Having faced and survived the plague, people at the bottom of society were more prepared to question their position. Indeed, poor people began to hate their poverty and those above them, which helped destroy the feudal system.[242]

---

240 Robert Irwin, "Toynbee and Ibn Khaldun," *Middle Eastern Studies* 33, no. 3 (July 1997): 461–79.

241 Samuel Cohn, "After the Black Death: Labour Legislation and Attitudes towards Labour in Late-Medieval Western Europe," *The Economic History Review* 60, no. 3 (August 2007): 457–85.

242 Şevket Pamuk, "The Black Death and the Origins of the 'great Divergence' across Europe, 1300-1600," *European Review of Economic History* 11, no. 3 (December 2007): 289–317.

One of the greatest consequences of the pandemic came in the field of medicine. The management of the Black Death's crisis led to new advancements in subsequent physicians' generations with the aim to avoid the same mistakes committed in the past. Still, when the disease hit Europe, physicians wanted to help, but lacked essential resources.

However, bacteria were poorly understood at the time. The basis of medieval medicine was the theory of humor, based on Galen's work.[243] This theory explained that the four elements of earth, water, air, and fire are linked to bodily fluids, and each humor was associated with color, a particular taste, a kind of temperament, and a season of the year. If you take this as an accepted theory, and add the chaos of the time, what you get is poor and often useless care of patients.

As such, plenty of popular cures started to be used in the population. One of the most famous ones was known as the *Vicary Method*.[244] For this, a healthy chicken was taken, and its back and rear were plucked clean. Then, this bare part of the chicken, still alive, was applied to the swollen nodes of the sick person and the chicken strapped in place. When the poor chicken showed signs of illness, it was thought to be drawing the disease from the person. Then, the swollen nodes were removed, washed, and strapped back on. The process took place until the chicken or the patient died.

---

243 Elizabeth C. Evans, "Galen the Physician as Physiognomist," *Transactions and Proceedings of the American Philological Association* 76 (1945): 287.

244 J. F. Payne, "On an Unpublished English Anatomical Treatise of the Fourteenth Century; and Its Relation to the 'Anatomy' of Thomas Vicary," *British Medical Journal* 1, no. 1830 (January 1896): 200–203.

Eating or drinking a small number of crushed emeralds was another treatment offered to those who could pay.[245] On the other hand, the poor were able to use a freshly prepared solution of arsenic or mercury.[246] Of course, this method worked much quicker than others. At least, the patient did not die of the plague.

Y. pestis was easily spread through the air. Therefore, clearing the air was considered another effective remedy to get rid of the bacteria. The plague was considered part of the *bad air,* the reason why homes were fumigated with incense or simply smoke from burning thatch. People often carried bouquets of flowers, and when they were out in the streets, they held them to their faces.

After going home, people would often disinfect themselves by sitting close to a very hot fire. This would draw the disease out by heavy sweating. However, if they were out of wood to light, there was no problem. Anyone could easily go out and sit by an open sewer as the *bad air,* which was causing one's sickness, would gravitate to the *bad air* of the sewage of the pit. Unfortunately, these pits were used to dump human waste.[247] As you may imagine, most of the people who used this method never recovered.

---

245 Leah DeVun, *Prophecy, Alchemy, and the End of Time* (New York: Columbia University Press, 2009).

246 Zachary A. Matus, "Alchemy and Christianity in the Middle Ages," *History Compass* 10, no. 12 (December 2012): 934–45.

247 David Herlihy, *The Black Death and the Transformation of the West* (Cambridge: Harvard University Press, 1997), 122-24.

Undoubtedly, one of the most bizarre healing approaches involved the use of human waste. Carefully collected, it was made into a paste that was applied to the wounds. Despite the smart mind behind such a revolutionary treatment, its practice undoubtedly led to higher infection rates and more painful deaths. Besides, since it was believed that clean urine had medicinal properties, people would bathe in it or drink it.[248]

Pseudo-medicine aside, religious cures were the most common. These included public flagellation that were constantly moving from one town to another or was manifested by prayers carrying out any form of amulets and charms. The pope eventually put a stop to the public flagellations, as they were ineffective.[249] Sadly, by then, participants had spread the plague to every town or city they had visited.

Indeed, by this point, you might realize that the bacterium found most of the healing methods mentioned before pretty useful. Instead of stopping the spread, they would often make things worse. However, among all the chaotic treatments, a real effective measurement arose. Not one to cure, but to stop the spread.

The first time in history that the practice has been recorded was in the port city of Ragusa (modern-day Dubrovnik, in

---

248 Plinio Prioreschi, *A History of Medicine: Medieval Medicine* (Omaha: Horatius Press, 1996), 197.

249 Ole Jørgen Benedictow and Ole L. Benedictow, *The Black Death, 1346-1353: The Complete History* (Woodbridge: Boydell Press, 2004), 114-16.

Croatia).[250] The city imposed a thirty-day isolation period on arriving ships. The city's policy was active and soon adopted by other cities and extended to forty days under the law of *quarantino* (meaning "forty days"), which gives English the word "quarantine."[251]

Milan, on the other hand, imposed stricter measures and enforcement and had greater success in controlling the spread of the disease. The Milanese authorities tolerated no dissension among the citizenry in obeying the laws of quarantine. At one point, they took it too far, and completely sealed the infected occupants of three houses in their homes where, presumably, they all died. Still, it worked. In 1350, they built a structure outside the city walls, smartly named the *pesthouse*, where plague victims were housed, and caregivers could attend to them.

The casualties behind the plague were hugely influenced by the practices explained before, and despite the few initiatives of quarantine and some brilliant medical decisions, the death toll was over any conceivable limit. Historians have estimated that in just three years, an estimated thirty-five million people had died. This was two-thirds of the world's population at the time, being killed by a single bacterium.[252] Only in

---

250 Gian Franco Gensini, Magdi H. Yacoub, and Andrea A. Conti, "The Concept of Quarantine in History: From Plague to SARS," *Journal of Infection* 49, no. 5 (November 2004): 257-61.

251 Paul S. Sehdev, "The Origin of Quarantine," *Clinical Infectious Diseases* 35, no. 9 (November 2002): 1071–72.

252 Sharon N. DeWitte and James W. Wood, "Selectivity of Black Death Mortality with Respect to Preexisting Health," *Proceedings of the National Academy of Sciences of the United States of America* 105, no. 5 (February 2008): 1436–41.

Europe, it killed 30 percent to 60 percent of the population, and the continent became full of burned and abandoned ruins in which the smell of rotten wood and burned flesh was quickly spread out with the wind, along with the disease.

The whole word was dying, and every one of us was going down with it. However, a miraculous evolutionary event was about to show up. Regardless of not fully understanding how it worked, medieval people were developing an advanced counter-weapon to fight the disease: immunity. The physician Raimundo Chalmel de Vinario observed the decreasing mortality rate of successive outbreaks of plague in 1347, 1362, 1371, and 1382 in his treatise *On Epidemics*.[253]

In the first outbreak, two-thirds of the population contracted the illness, and most patients died. However, in the next wave, half the people became ill, but only some died. By the third, only one out of ten people was affected, and many survived. Lastly, in the fourth outbreak, only one in twenty people were sickened, and most of them survived. By the 1380s, the Black Death predominantly affected children and newborns.

By the beginning of the fifteenth century, most of the young and adult population were biologically blessed with a fighting chance toward the plague.[254] The light at the end of the tunnel was starting to be seen, and a feeling of peace was quickly spreading. Better times would come.

---

253 Iqbal Akhtar Khan, "Plague: The Dreadful Visitation Occupying the Human Mind for Centuries," *Transactions of the Royal Society of Tropical Medicine and Hygiene* 98, no. 5 (May 2004): 270–77.

254 Stephen R. Ell, "Immunity as a Factor in the Epidemiology of Medieval Plague," *Reviews of Infectious Diseases* 6, no. 6 (November 1984): 866–79.

But not in England. It was 1485, just at the beginning of the reign of Henry VII. Physicians started to notice and write about a new disease far different from the Black Death that had been destroying Europe. The first reports talk about an outbreak in September 19, 1485, at Milford Haven, just north of the islands. The outcome was several thousand people killed after a month.[255]

This alarming malady was soon named as The Sweat. It was regarded as being quite distinct from the Black Death because of the sweating. It reached Ireland in 1492, and recordings mentioned "an unusual plague of 24 hours duration." Surprisingly, it did not attack infants or little children.[256] "This disease is the easiest in the world to die of," reported the French ambassador, Cardinal du Bellay. "You have a slight pain in the head and at heart; all at once, you begin to sweat. There is no need for a physician; you are taken off without languishing."

Among all the potential causes for The Sweat, one origin is related to anthrax, according to microbiologist Edward McSweegan, which is caused by the bacterium *Bacillus anthracis*.[257] The symptoms of anthrax inhalation include

255 John L. Flood, "'Safer on the Battlefield than in the City': England, the 'Sweating Sickness', and the Continent," *Renaissance Studies* 17, no. 2 (June 2003): 147–76.

256 R. S. Gottfried, "Population, Plague, and the Sweating Sickness: Demographic Movements in Late Fifteenth-Century England," *Journal of British Studies* 17 (Autumn 1977): 12–37.

257 Edward McSweegan, "Anthrax and the Etiology of the English Sweating Sickness," *Medical Hypotheses* 62, no. 1 (January 2004): 155–57.

copious sweating, exhaustion, and sudden onset, which mostly match the descriptions of that time.

Luckily for a devastated continental Europe, the outbreaks were mostly contained within England, where they occurred over the summers between 1485 and 1551.[258] Just in London, it killed fifteen thousand people in six weeks.[259] Then, it suddenly vanished without a trace, leaving behind more questions than answers.

Undoubtedly, death could be used as the best-suited term of the Middle Ages, a period that witnessed an almost constant wartime and injustice where suffering became the life of many. As such, the divergence between the medieval world and a new way of modernity was cut open in a society whose time of intellectual, economical and societal transformation was arriving. A time of discoveries, ideological ascension, and geographical expansion was about to arrive, one in which our bacterial companions will have plenty to say.

---

258 Alan Dyer, "The English Sweating Sickness of 1551: An Epidenmic Anatomized," *Medical History* 41, no. 3 (July 1997): 362–84.

259 Paul R. Hunter, "The English Sweating Sickness, with Particular Reference to the 1551 Outbreak in Chester," *Reviews of Infectious Diseases* 13, no. 2 (March 1991): 303–6.

CHAPTER 10

SUNKEN HOPES IN THE SHORES OF DESPAIR

"This is a world of corpses strewn in streets and pits, yet in the deadcart itself a drunken piper wakes up to cry, 'But I am not dead though, am I?'"

—DANIEL DEFOE, A JOURNAL OF THE PLAGUE YEAR

On the evening of August 3, 1492, Cristopher Columbus departed from Palos de la Frontera, Spain, with three ships: the Niña, Pinta, and Santa Maria. He was determined to find a direct water route west from Europe to Asia, but never did. It was around 2 a.m. on October 12 when a lookout on the Pinta spotted land. Thirty-six days after their departure, Columbus and his crew landed on the Bahamian Island of Guanahani. He baptized the land as San Salvador.[260]

---

260 Wendy R. Childs, "1492–1494: Columbus and the Discovery of America," *The Economic History Review* 48, no. 4 (November 1995): 754.

Soon after their arrival, a small group of natives appeared and gathered around them: the Taíno people. He described them in letters as naked as the day they were born. The Taíno had little idea of who these people were, but they laid down their weapons willingly and brought the foreign sailors tokens of friendship.[261] Christopher later wrote that the Taíno "remained so much our friends that it was a marvel." The first cultural exchange between continents in a long time had begun.

However, despite the celebration and the discovery of a new world, that day, something else landed on that shore. A peaceful handshake, a close breath in the air, or the droplets hitting the floor from the hands of a thirsty explorer. That was all that it took. What was that strange passenger that the Spanish ships brought? Death, as no other the new continent had ever seen.

The first victims were the Taíno people. A year after his arrival, Columbus built the first town on the nearby island of Hispaniola, where the Taíno numbered as many as eight million people, according to some estimates. Fifty years later, only five hundred of them remained alive.[262] How do you bring an entire civilization to the brink of extinction in such a short time?

---

261 Kathleen A. Deagan and José María Cruxent, *Columbus's Outpost Among the Taínos: Spain and America at La Isabela, 1493–1498* (London: Yale University Press, 2002), 177.

262 Kathleen Deagan, "Reconsidering Taíno Social Dynamics after Spanish Conquest: Gender and Class in Culture Contact Studies," *American Antiquity* 69, no. 4 (October 2004): 597–626.

When Columbus bridged the old world (Europe, Africa, and Asia) with the new one in the Americas, he brought a massive wave of settlers, hopes for exploration, and the intention of expansion. But not just that—a devastating suite of diseases, with bacteria on the frontline, was unleashed on the shores of America.

Geographically isolated millennia ago, entire civilizations and cultures that did not have any contact with the bacterial pathogens of the old world were now exposed to them.[263] A gigantic biological collision that resulted in one of the quickest extinctions that the planet has ever seen. "It was a culture clash, obviously," said Stephen Prescott, Oklahoma Medical Research Foundation (OMRF) president in an article in 2013.[264] "But it also launched a clash of infectious diseases."

For quite a long time, more native North Americans died each year from infectious diseases brought by European settlers than were born. OMRF reports that the impact of these diseases was far more catastrophic than the Black Death in medieval Europe. By 1517, only twenty-five years after the arrival of the first explorers, nearly 95 percent of the native population had perished due to these new pathogens, while many regions in the continent lost 100 percent of their indigenous people.[265]

---

263 Nathan Nunn and Nancy Qian, "The Columbian Exchange: A History of Disease, Food, and Ideas," *Journal of Economic Perspectives* 24, no. 2 (March 2010): 163–88.

264 Greg Elwell, "Oklahoma Scientists Still Study Explorers' Impact on Disease," *The Oklahoman*, October 12, 2013.

265 Noble David Cook, *Born to Die: Disease and New World Conquest, 1492 –1650* (Cambridge: Cambridge University Press, 1998), 109–22.

Medical records were sparse or did not exist back then, so
it is challenging to say precisely where and when certain
diseases emerged. However, there is a list of thirty diseases
that were believed to have either been introduced to the new
world or worsened in the post-Columbian era, most of them
carried by bacteria.[266]

One important aspect to mention is that some bacterial diseases are experts at hiding behind the effects of viral pandemics, and the Americas were witness of this in April of
1520. The Spanish forces landed in what is now Veracruz,
Mexico. Two months after their arrival, the troops entered
the capital of the Aztec empire, Tenochtitlán.[267]

By October, a strange disease was sweeping through the city,
killing nearly half of the population, leaving the Spanish
troops unharmed. Scholars today estimate that between fifty
thousand and three hundred thousand people died within a
few months. By the time that the conqueror Hernán Cortés
and his troops began their final assault on Tenochtitlán, bodies lay scattered over the city, allowing the small Spanish
force to overwhelm the shocked defenders. This time, the
silent enemy was not a bacterium, but a virus: smallpox,

---

266 Alfred W. Crosby, *The Columbian Exchange: Biological and Cultural
Consequences of 1492* (Westport: Praeger, 2003).

267 Robert McCaa, "Spanish and Nahuatl Views on Smallpox and Demographic Catastrophe in Mexico," *Journal of Interdisciplinary History* 25,
no. 3 (Winter 1995): 397.

which killed between five and eight million people in a few weeks.[268]

Now, what matters here is that you understand that a catastrophe like this is prompt to leave a decimated and weakened population, famine, and instability. If you put all these together, you have a hotbed for the development of new diseases, and bacteria are undoubtedly the most opportunistic microorganisms in the whole world to trigger such a disaster. Basically, because they are everywhere.

Then, what had to happen, happened. In 1545, a new outbreak appeared. However, it was not smallpox. A new illness quickly spread throughout what is now Mexico and part of Guatemala.[269] The symptoms were unlike anything the doctors have seen back in Europe. Victims were slowly turning yellowish, and blood ran from their ears and noses. Hallucinations and agonizing convulsions that were prolonged for a few days led to a terrible generalized pain. Then, death.

Aztecs called it the *cocoliztli*, a word that meant pestilence in the native language. "The cocoliztli appeared from almost nowhere. Nobody knew what it was," said Rodolfo Acuña-Soto, a historical epidemiologist at the National Autonomous

---

268 Kristine B. Patterson and Thomas Runge, "Smallpox and the Native American," *American Journal of the Medical Sciences* 323, no. 4 (April 2002): 216–22.

269 Rodolfo Acuna-Soto et al., "Megadrought and Megadeath in 16th Century Mexico," *Emerging Infectious Diseases* 8, no. 4 (April 2002): 360–62.

University of Mexico in Mexico City.[270] Historical records suggest that the disease was some type of hemorrhagic fever, like Ebola, that killed an estimated 45 percent of the entire native population.[271]

However, recently discovered DNA evidence suggests that the culprit might have been caused by a pathogen well-known to humans from our very own origins: *Salmonella*, and a particular strain that was brought by European colonizers, hence not known in the Americas.[272]

The evidence was extracted from the teeth of twenty-nine skeletons. Kirsten Bos, a molecular paleobiologist at the Max Planck Institute for the Science of Human History, and her colleagues found that the genetic material in the skeletons matched fragments of *Salmonella enterica*, the pathogen linked to enteric fever.[273]

Bos knows that in order to detect the pathogen, these people must have had massive amounts of the bacteria in their blood. "When you get a very advanced bacterial infection,

270 Åshild J. Vågene et al., "Salmonella Enterica Genomes from Victims of a Major Sixteenth-Century Epidemic in Mexico," *Nature Ecology and Evolution* 2, no. 3 (March 2018): 520–28.

271 Rodolfo Acuna-Soto et al., "Drought, Epidemic Disease, and the Fall of Classic Period Cultures in Mesoamerica (AD 750–950). Hemorrhagic Fevers as a Cause of Massive Population Loss," *Medical Hypotheses* 65, no. 2 (January 2005): 405–9.

272 José Luis Puente and Edmundo Calva, "The One Health Concept-the Aztec Empire and Beyond," *Pathogens and Disease* 75, no. 6 (August 2017): ftx062.

273 Vågene et al., "Salmonella Enterica Genomes from Victims of a Major Sixteenth-Century Epidemic in Mexico." *Nature Ecology & Evolution* 2 (January 2018): 520–28.

you can get bleeding from orifices and symptoms very similar to hemorrhagic fever," she mentioned in an interview for *Science*.[274] "The historical records match a hemorrhagic fever, but we shouldn't be too dismissive on what biologic agent it really was."

The natives lacked a strong natural immune response to the disease, which made them extremely susceptible. At the time, the Spanish historian Fray Juan de Torquemada wrote, "In the year 1576, great mortality and pestilence that lasted for more than a year overcame the Indians. . . . the place we know as New Spain (Mexico) was left almost empty."[275]

Hundreds of new and similar outbreaks were recorded in the following years, and the spread of new diseases became a regular event. Noble David Cook, professor at the Florida International University, is the voice of a community of scholars who have dedicated their lives to understanding the epidemiologic consequences of the arrival of Columbus to the New World.[276] Their conclusions are clear: the rampant spread of epidemic diseases, to which the natives had no prior exposure or resistance, was the primary cause of the massive population decline of the Native Americans.

274 Angus Chen, "One of History's Worst Epidemics May Have Been Caused by a Common Food Poisoning Microbe," *Science*, January 16, 2018.

275 Angela Herren Rajagopalan, *Portraying the Aztec Past: The Codices Boturini, Azcatitlan, and Aubin* (Texas: University of Texas Press, 2018), 88.

276 Noble David Cook, *Demographic Collapse: Indian Peru, 1520-1620* (Cambridge: Cambridge University Press, 1982), 104–9.

A commonly accepted and demonstrated explanation for the population reduction of the American natives included the European immigrants' accounts of the brutal practices of the European conquerors, as often recorded by themselves. However, a large percentage of such dramatic contribution might be entirely explained from the epidemic's point of view.

After reading this, you might wonder why all of this happened so quickly. We know that the lack of immunity was an important factor, which can be explained in terms of the Virgin Soil Effect (VSE).[277] This concept refers to epidemics "in which the populations at risk have had no previous contact with the diseases that strike them and are therefore immunologically almost defenseless," as was defined by William McNeill in his work *Plagues and Peoples*.[278]

This theory plays around the idea that contact and exchange among civilizations are what drives human history forward. Then, it is possible to connect the development of agriculture and more sedentary life with the emergence of new diseases. Therefore, virgin soil epidemics can be traced back to European colonization that took place in the Americas, Australia, and the Pacific Islands.

In simple words, when a population has not had contact with a particular pathogen, individuals in that community have not built up an immunity to that organism. Therefore, new generations have not received immunity passed from mother

277 A. W. Crosby, "Virgin Soil Epidemics as a Factor in the Aboriginal Depopulation in America.," *The William and Mary Quarterly* 33 (April 1976): 289–99.

278 William McNeill, *Plagues and Peoples* (New York: Anchor, 1976), 123.

to child. Epidemiologist Francis Black has suggested that some isolated populations within the Americas may not have mixed enough to become as genetically heterogeneous as the European colonizers.[279] Consequently, this had a huge impact to their natural immunity as well.

Another important fact to keep in mind is that when a disease is introduced in a new environment, there is an increase in the morbidity and mortality rates. Historically, this increase has often been devastating and always noticeable. However, no one could have expected the impact behind the Columbus exchange, a planetary-sized clash. The European colonization of the Americas killed so many people that it contributed to climatic change and temporary global cooling, according to scientists from University College London.[280]

This human tragedy meant that there were simply not enough workers left to manage the fields and forests. Without this intervention, previously managed landscapes returned to their natural states, thereby absorbing carbon from the atmosphere. The extent of this regrowth of the natural habitat was so vast that it removed enough carbon dioxide to cool the planet.

The lower temperatures prompted feedbacks in the carbon cycle, which eliminated even more carbon dioxide from the

---

279 Francis L Black, "An Explanation of High Death Rates among New World Peoples When in Contact with Old World Diseases," *Perspectives in Biology and Medicine* 37, no. 2 (Winter 1994): 292–307.

280 Alexander Koch et al., "Earth System Impacts of the European Arrival and Great Dying in the Americas after 1492," *Quaternary Science Reviews* 207 (March 2019): 13–36.

atmosphere. This rapid cooling phenomenon led to a significant drop in carbon dioxide at the beginning of the seventeen centuries that we can notice nowadays in the Antarctic ice cores. It was the full reverse of today's climate change crisis—human action removing greenhouse gases from the atmosphere rather than adding them.

The cooling of the planet caused severe winters and cold summers all over the world, which triggered famines and rebellions, especially across Europe and Japan. Death is cold and always carries consequences, but would you imagine something like this?

Now, if I told you that there is a version of karma in the epidemic's world, would you believe me? Everything goes back one way or another. Those who once arrived, also returned, and when they reached home, they brought something else with them.

Skeletal evidence suggested that Columbus and his crew brought back a bacterial strain from the Americas that was far more lethal than the ones found in Europe.[281] We are talking about *Treponema pallidum*, the bacterium behind syphilis, a disease that is transmitted upon sexual contact, which can cause damage to the brain, nerves, eyes, or heart.[282]

This illness was prevalent in the Native American population back before Columbus arrived. Exactly five hundred

281 M. H. Grieco, "The Voyage of Columbus Led to the Spread of Syphilis to Europe," *Allergy Proceedings* 13, no. 5 (September-October 1992): 233–35.

282 William L. Fleming, "Syphilis Through the Ages," *Medical Clinics of North America* 48, no. 3 (May 1964): 587–612.

thirty-eight skeletal remains in the Dominican Republic have shown evidence characteristic of syphilis in up to 14 percent of the afflicted population.[283] This makes the bacterium a common endemic pathology, the reason why it might have been so easy for the explorers to bring it back home.

Indeed, soon after Columbus went back to Europe, the first outbreak of the new syphilis was recorded there. By the summer of 1495, early symptoms were found among French troops besieging Naples, in Italy. It is believed that the bacteria might have been transmitted to the French via Spanish mercenaries serving King Charles of France in the siege.[284] Many of the crew members who served on the Columbus voyage later joined the army of the king seeking more gold.

From this epicenter, the disease swept across a Europe that was still slowly recovering from the consequences of the Black Death. The tropical strain of the bacteria might have mutated at its arrival to the continent. Then, it became extremely deadly for Europeans with no immunity, leading to as many as five million deaths.[285]

This particular strain was especially virulent, and its symptoms were far worse than the ones already recorded. As the

---

283 Bruce M. Rothschild et al., "First European Exposure to Syphilis: The Dominican Republic at the Time of Columbian Contact," *Clinical Infectious Diseases* 31, no. 4 (October 2000): 936–41.

284 Robert J. Knell, "Syphilis in Renaissance Europe: Rapid Evolution of an Introduced Sexually Transmitted Disease?," *Proceedings of the Royal Society of London. Series B: Biological Sciences* 271, no. suppl 4 (May 2004): S174–S176.

285 B. M. Rothschild, "History of Syphilis," *Clinical Infectious Diseases* 40, no. 10 (May 2005): 1454–63.

American geographer, historian, and anthropologist Jared Diamond described, "When syphilis was first definitely recorded in Europe in 1495, its pustules often covered the body from the head to the knees, caused flesh to fall from people's faces, and led to death within a few months."[286] Records have shown that the disease was much more lethal than it is today, but it took its time to kill the hosts, who wandered around the streets or lay in beds in extreme pain.

The same George Armelagos that we met before in this book has been studying syphilis for quite a long time. He initially doubted the so-called Columbian theory for syphilis when he first heard about it some decades ago. "I laughed at the idea that a small group of sailors brought back this disease that caused a major European epidemic," he recalled. Critics of the Columbian theory have proposed that syphilis had always bedeviled the Old World but simply had not been set apart from other rotting bacterial diseases such as leprosy.[287]

However, upon further investigation, Armelagos and his colleagues got a shock. All of the available evidence they found supported the Columbian theory. Emory researchers were studying twenty-six geographically scattered strains of the Treponemes family, as well as related nonvenereal infections such as yaws. They found that the venereal syphilis-causing strains arose relatively recently in humans and are closely

---

286 Lester Bivens, *Basic Health Care Series: Sexually Transmitted Diseases (STD)* (New Delhi: Alpha Editions, 2017), 112.

287 George J. Armelagos, Molly K. Zuckerman, and Kristin N. Harper, "The Science Behind Pre-Columbian Evidence of Syphilis in Europe: Research by Documentary," *Evolutionary Anthropology: Issues, News, and Reviews* 21, no. 2 (March 2012): 50–57.

associated with an ancient infection isolated in South America that gives rise to yaws.[288] The findings clearly support the hypothesis that syphilis came from the New World.

In an interview in 2011, Armelagos said, "What it really shows to me is that globalization of disease is not a modern condition. The lesson we can learn for today from history is that these epidemics are the result of the unrest," and added, "With syphilis, wars were going on in Europe at the time, and all the turmoil set the stage for the disease. Nowadays, a lot of diseases jump the species barrier due to environmental unrest."[289]

If something was common in this new world, it was the environmental unrest. Entire societies, cultures and ideas were changing, bringing down substantial modifications of the geography, with the exhaustion of entire ecosystems or reorganization of territories.[290] European people began to enjoy luxuries, nicer clothes, finer foods, and the arts. The whole society was changing, allowing a growing scientific and medical revolution. Scientists learned more about how the human body works, and new discoveries, such as vaccination, came into being.

---

288 B. J. Baker and G. J. Armelagos, "The Origin and Antiquity of Syphilis: Paleopathological Diagnosis and Interpretation.," *Current Anthropology* 29, no. 5 (October 1988): 703–38.

289 Charles Q. Choi, "Case Closed? Columbus Introduced Syphilis to Europe," *Scientific American*, December 27, 2011.

290 Kevin H. O'Rourke and Jeffrey G. Williamson, "After Columbus: Explaining Europe's Overseas Trade Boom, 1500-1800," *Journal of Economic History* 62, no. 2 (June 2002): 417–56.

However, if there is a lesson that should be taken after this chapter it is that any cultural exchange carries out an unavoidable bacterial trade that can affect both sides with dramatic consequences. No action is taken without a tradeoff when written in words of bacteria. The modern world began with a catastrophe of near-unimaginable proportions, which marked the beginning of a new era that was ready to tell some secrets about the hidden world around us.

CHAPTER 11

SAND TO THE NAKED EYE

———

"I am being narrowed down to the field of the microscope. I see details, not wholes nor the shadow of the whole. I count some parts, and say, 'I know.'"

—HENRY DAVID THOREAU

Many of those who embarked on long overseas journeys looking for the resources and cultural opportunities of the New World never returned. However, those who came back witnessed a homeland that was far from being fully recovered from the stigma of the Black Death. In a time where *Yersinia pestis* had turned into a natural, mostly endemic, bacterial nightmare, humanity's only hopes were put in scientific breakthroughs that were taking too long to arrive.[291]

---

291 Richard Palmer, "The Church, Leprosy and Plague in Medieval and Early Modern Europe," *Studies in Church History* 19 (1982): 79–99.

While Western Europe was taking steps to counteract the pandemics that were inherited from the past, the scientific community was trying to understand the truth that lies beyond them. The work of a few was moved by the desperation of many, uncovering pathogens that were moving from invisible enemies to something which had a shape and a physical existence. A live form that, as with everything material, could be ended.

As such, humanity was about to enter into a time where disastrous outbreaks led to brilliant scientific breakthroughs. Consequently, we will see the rise and fall of both calamitous epidemics and great men who stood up and decided to fight them. While the former brought us death, the latter offered a hope whose light was about to burst through the end of the dark era of bacterial pathogens.

So, where do we begin? Our first stop takes place in a warm and humid April in 1665 in London.[292] The capital of England was the perfect example of a modern European city that was growing at an exponential rate. The arms of the city were able to embrace every piece of land for miles around. A monster of machinery, steel, and fire, whose veins were crowded with people and animals constantly feeding resources to a heart made of oil and coal.[293] Besides, a heavily polluted Thames was not reflecting the choking black smoke that was continuously belching forth from the factories, breweries, and iron

---

292 Valerie Pearl, "Change and Stability in Seventeenth-Century London," *The London Journal* 5, no. 1 (July 2013): 3–34.

293 Jeremy Boulton, "Wage Labour in Seventeenth-Century London," *The Economic History Review* 49, no. 2 (May 1996): 268–90.

smelters and from approximately fifteen thousand houses that were burning coal day and night.[294]

Outside the city walls, suburbs had sprung up, now providing shelter for the craftsmen and tradespeople who flocked to the already overcrowded city. Towns full of houses made of wood were piling up at both sides of streets swelling blood and sweat, crawling with rats, and made filthy by a lack of sanitation. The government had tried to control the development of these suburbs but had failed. Now, over a quarter of a million people lived here.

As you may already be aware, London had become a paradise for bacterial pathogens. Then, the unavoidable happened when a Dutch trading ship coming from a plagued Amsterdam arrived at the docks.[295] A few suspicious deaths were recorded soon after the arrival of the ship in the outskirt of the city, but no one said a word.

Soon after, a quarantine was established in the suburbs. Working was forbidden, and the poor, with no income, started to worry about famine. A riot broke out in the suburb of St. Giles when the first house was sealed up. The crowd fought the police and broke down the door, releasing the captive. They were warmly welcomed and took care of by

---

294 P. E. Jones and A. V. Judges, "London Population in the Late Seventeenth Century," *The Economic History Review* 6, no. 1 (October 1935): 45–63.

295 R. S. Roberts, "Tercentenary of the Plague of London 1665: The Place of Plague in English History," *Journal of the Royal Society of Medicine* 59, no. 2 (February 1966): 101–5.

their saviors. Sadly, all of them were already sick, and that was all it took.[296]

The Black Death's last major outbreak in Great Britain had already begun, quickly spreading through the hot summer months. In June, the Plague was rampant in the city. The rich ran away, including King Charles II. Businesses were closed when merchants and professionals fled away. In a few days, much of the population was all gone. Only a small number of clergymen and physicians remained to cope with an increasingly large number of victims, trying to save as many as possible in a rush that often took their lives.

Undoubtedly, the worst side of the disease was chasing the poor. They could not afford to leave the city. Whether they stayed or left, death followed. When things got worse, everyone was required to possess a certificate of good health signed by government officers. As most people at the administration were already gone, this paperwork became increasingly difficult to obtain. They were trapped in a city that had already dug their tombs.

Within time, people living in the villages around London began to resent the city's exodus and were no longer prepared to accept more people. Refugees were turned back, often violently, and not allowed to pass through towns. Those who

---

296 W. G. Bell. *The Great Plague in London in 1665* (London: Random House UK Ltd, 1995), 155.

decided not to come back were forced to wander across the country, surviving with what they had.[297]

By August, the epidemic peaked. Death tolls increased from two thousand people to over seven thousand per week in September.[298] These figures are likely to be a considerable underestimate as those taking the numbers refused to cooperate, and many of the poor were just dumped into mass graves unrecorded.

Luckily, by late fall, the number of victims in London and the suburbs began to decrease. In February of 1666, it was considered safe enough for the king to come back to the city. His return was followed by a mass exodus, and life returned to the city. The desolation that they found was evidenced by the odor coming from the pyres that were lit from the guts of a decimated city.

Just when everything was supposed to go back to normal, it didn't. That same year, on midnight of September 2, a fire broke out at a bakery close to the center of the city. The flames quickly spread and did not stop burning for five entire days. What was then known as the Great Fire of London destroyed

---

297 Stephen Greenberg, "Plague, the Printing Press, and Public Health in Seventeenth-Century London," *Huntington Library Quarterly* 67, no. 4 (December 2004): 508–27.

298 Mary F. Hollingsworth and T. H. Hollingsworth, "Plague Mortality Rates by Age and Sex in the Parish of St. Botolph's without Bishopsgate, London, 1603," *Population Studies* 25, no. 1 (March 1971): 131–46.

everything that it encountered, alive or not. Hundreds of people were killed, and thousands were left homeless.[299]

When everything was extinguished, some people started to believe that the flames healed the city. Whatever the truth was, the later cases of *Y. pestis* were found in the suburbs that were not consumed by the fire.[300]

Those who survived both the fire and the Plague were afraid of having to live through the same again. An imperative need to rebuild the city from the ashes was found in the hands of the Londoners, and the government pushed toward important sanitation improvements. Not only was the capital rejuvenated, but it became a healthier environment in which to live. People in the city had a greater sense of community after that. The Plague made them better. It brought them together.

That same year that the Plague started killing in London, the English Royal Society published its first popular science book, *Micrographia*.[301] The manuscript, written by Robert Hooke, a thirty-year-old English scientist and an original fellow of the society, was a wonder. Its pages contained a collection of dozens of beautiful engravings based on meticulous illustrations made by Hooke himself. He provided a clear description of the architecture of the small world that was surrounding us: fleas, seeds of thyme, the eyes of ants,

---

299 S. Atallah, "Some Observations on the Great Fire of London, 1666," *Nature* 211 (July 1996): 105–06.

300 Alan Rosen, "Plague, Fire, and Typology in Defoe's A Journal of the Plague Year" *Connotations* 1, no. 3 (July 1991): 258–82.

301 Robert Hooke, *Micrographia* (Scotts Valley, CreateSpace Independent Publishing Platform, 2014), 108–9.

the internal structures of sponges, fungi, and the building blocks of a wide variety of plants.[302]

The book also contained a detailed description of Hooke's microscope, a simple machine with two lenses well-made under the standards of the time.[303] The optics system of the instrument was poor, limited by its own design. The microscope suffered from large optical aberration, which happens when light spreads out over some region of space instead of focusing to a point. By that time, no lens-makers were able to avoid such problem.[304] Therefore, images were fuzzy, and often a bit of imagination was required to reconstruct the structure of the object in view.

However, Hooke was able to outstandingly transmit this imagination on paper. His book sparked interest in the construction of better lenses all over Europe, a task that became extremely difficult for everyone, except for a young Dutch fabric merchant in Delft. A copy of *Micrografia* ended up in his hands, and an already established passion for lenses and microscopes became then an obsession. His name was Anton van Leeuwenhoek.

---

302 Michael Aaron Dennis, "Graphic Understanding: Instruments and Interpretation in Robert Hooke's Micrographia," *Science in Context* 3, no. 2 (Autumn 1989): 309–64.

303 C. Ash, "Hooke's Microscope," *Trends in Microbiology* 6, no. 10 (October 1998): 391.

304 Ian Lawson, "Crafting The Microworld: How Robert Hooke Constructed Knowledge about Small Things," *Notes and Records* 70, no. 1 (March 2016): 23–44.

In 1671, Anton developed a novel type of microscope.[305] It was smaller, simpler, and had better optics, a system like no other before, and allowed a much higher magnification without the distortion of the more complicated, expensive instruments. He used the best Venetian glass that was polished in a way that we will never understand, as he decided to keep his technique a secret.[306]

Another quality of Anton was that he loved to write letters. He handwrote a considerable amount of them over his life, most of which were recording his findings and fascination. This passion drove him to what could be named the most important discovery in microbiology.[307] In October of 1674, he took a piece of paper and wrote: "Last winter, while being very sickly and nearly unable to taste, I examined the appearance of my tongue, which was very furred, in a mirror and judged that my loss of taste was caused by the thick skin on the tongue."[308]

Anton found an ox's tongue and took a sample. He then put it under the microscope, where he observed "very fine pointed projections" containing small globules in quantity. Unknowingly, he was describing the taste buds, also known

305 M Karamanou et al., "Anton van Leeuwenhoek (1632-1723): Father of Micromorphology and Discoverer of Spermatozoa," *Rev Argent Microbiol* 42, no. 4 (October-December 2010): 311–14.

306 J. Zuylen, "The Microscopes of Antoni van Leeuwenhoek," *Journal of Microscopy* 121, no. 3 (March 1981): 309–28.

307 J. R. Porter, "Antony Van Leeuwenhoek. Tercentenary of His Discovery of Bacteria," *Bacteriological Reviews* 40, no. 2 (June 1976): 260–69.

308 Joseph G. O'Mara, "On Leeuwenhoek's Magnifications," *Antonie van Leeuwenhoek* 45, no. 2 (June 1979): 161–64.

as receptor or gustatory cells. It was then that Anton became curious about how we sense taste.

Trying to find answers, Anton started making infusions of various spices, such as black pepper mixed with water. Within time, he did manage to prepare a vast collection of infusions.[309] After intense days of work, many of them were pulled out or left forgotten in his studio.

In 1676, Anton found a flask of black pepper in water that had been sitting on a shelf for three or more weeks. The liquid had turned strangely cloudy, almost nasty. He took a few drops and put them under his microscope.[310] And just like that, for the first time in human history, one of us was able to see them.

But what exactly did Anton see? He found microscopic organisms, one to two micrometers in diameter, swimming around. They were moving with random trajectories all over the liquid.[311] Anton quickly sketched them and wrote, "I saw a great multitude of living creatures in one drop of water, amounting to no less than 8,000 or 10,000. They appear to my eye through the microscope as common as sand does to the naked eye."

---

309 H. Gest, "The Discovery of Microorganisms by Robert Hooke and Antoni van Leeuwenhoek, Fellows of The Royal Society," *Notes and Records of the Royal Society of London* 58, no. 2 (May 2004): 187–201.

310 D Bardell, "The Roles of the Sense of Taste and Clean Teeth in the Discovery of Bacteria by Antoni van Leeuwenhoek.," *Microbiological Reviews* 47, no. 1 (March 1983): 121–26.

311 John O. Corliss, "Three Centuries of Protozoology: A Brief Tribute to Its Founding Father, A. van Leeuwenhoek of Delft," *The Journal of Protozoology* 22, no. 1 (February 1975): 3–7.

He called them *animalcules*, a Latin word meaning little animals. The discovery of these animalcules was itself unforeseen as Anton had no idea what the organisms really were. He imagined that those things were literally tiny animals.[312]

Then, Anton wondered where these animalcules might be and where they came from. Soon after, he examined scrapings from his own mouth and was astonished to see, for the first time, the presence of animalcules on his teeth and gums. Here, Anton really stood out among the other scientists of his time, and revealed, for the first time, that we are not alone in our bodies. We are carriers of animalcules. He theorized that humans and other animals harbor huge numbers of animalcules in their body.[313]

Obsessed with this idea, he started to take samples everywhere all the time. For instance, he noted that when he drank hot coffee in the morning, the animalcules in our mouth died. It was the first observation that heat killed microbes. Furthermore, he described the various shapes and relative sizes of these microorganisms from his own saliva and in other secretions.

Right after, as he would do with any other of his discoveries, he sketched what was seen. Hundreds of these drawings were collected in dozens of letters and notebooks that would

---

312 Nick Lane, "The Unseen World: Reflections on Leeuwenhoek (1677) 'Concerning Little Animals,'" *Philosophical Transactions of the Royal Society B: Biological Sciences* 370, no. 1666 (April 2015): 20140344.

313 B. J. Ford, "Bacteria and Cells of Human Origin on van Leeuwenhoek's Sections of 16741,2.," *Transactions of the American Microscopical Society* 101, no. 1 (January 1982): 1–9.

later become the basis for microbial taxonomy. However, he realized that the letters were useless in his possession. It was time to tell the world. Anton sent a famous seventeen-and-a-half-page letter to the Royal Society describing his discovery of animalcules for publication in the new, and first, scientific journal, *Philosophical Transactions*.[314]

When they got the letter, the feeling that the other scientists at the society felt was unanimous: skepticism. Even Hooke, one of the fathers of the society, thought it was a delusion. The man had to be just crazy. It was then when the Society sent a vicar and some other reputable observers to Delft to verify Anton's reports. They were hoping to find lies and fraud, ready to destroy the reputation of the young Anton. However, nothing other than fascination was collected after the visit.

Anton's now-verified observations were published by the society in English. This task would not have been possible without the help of Hooke, who, astonished by the findings, quickly learned Dutch so that he could read Leeuwenhoek's papers and translate them. The world had to know, and it did.

Years after the publications, he is known and often viewed as the father of microbiology. However, he did not achieve that title alone, as Anton had the incredible help of Hooke, who led him to fame. Both remarkable men were critical catalysts for the impending discovery of the invisible world.

---

314 Rachel K. Zwick and Barbara A. Schmidt, "When Anton van Leeuwenhoek Looked through His Early Microscopes in the 1600s, He Realized That the World Was Teeming with Microbial Organisms. Introduction," *The Yale Journal of Biology and Medicine* 87, no. 1 (March 2014): 1.

By the end of his life, Anton had written approximately 560 letters to the society and other scientific institutions concerning his observations and discoveries, as well as built over five hundred microscopes, most of them lost to date. Even during the last weeks of his life, Anton continued to send letters full of comments to London.

The last few letters contained an accurate description of his own illness, in which he recorded how close he was to his own death. He suffered from a rare disease and uncontrolled movement of the midriff (a region of the front of the body between the chest and the waist), which now is named van Leeuwenhoek's disease.[315]

On August 26, 1723, Anton died at the age of ninety. That day, humanity lost "the first even to think of looking—certainly, the first with the power to see," as the British biochemist Nick Lane wrote. However, his legacy did not die with him, as many others were now using his vision to develop new methods to unravel the mysteries of the bacterial world.

---

315 Andrew J. Larner, "Antony van Leeuwenhoek and the Description of Diaphragmatic Flutter (Respiratory Myoclonus)," *Movement Disorders* 20, no. 8 (August 2005): 917–18.

CHAPTER 12

CONTROL AND CONTAINMENT

—

"When I look back upon the past, I can only dispel the sadness which falls upon me by gazing into that happy future when the infection will be banished. But if it is not vouchsafed for me to look upon that happy time with my own eyes the conviction that such a time must inevitably sooner or later arrive will cheer my dying hour."

—IGNAZ SEMMELWEIS

The beginning of the eighteenth century brought a new way of thinking to humanity with the Age of Enlightenment, where a vast array of ideas was shared in newly created scientific academies, Masonic lodges and numerous books and journals. Reason and the evidence of the senses become the primary sources of knowledge, where many renowned figures sought the empiricism behind theories of the past.

Nonetheless, infectious diseases did not need a renaissance in their ideas, as their dogma was still present in many parts of Europe. The worst side of these epidemics was about to be deployed over southeastern France. This time, the threat was already known, which was the reason why a quite effective health surveillance was instituted, along with quarantine. However, the accumulation of small negligent acts led to one of the worst epidemics that the country had ever seen: the Great Plague of Marseille, also known as the last major outbreak of bubonic plague in Western Europe.[316]

In 1720, the Grand-Saint-Antoine, a merchant ship, arrived in the city with an extra and unwanted bacterial charge. The crew was all sick and it was promptly placed under quarantine by the port authorities. However, some powerful city merchants who wanted the silk and cotton cargo from the ship for a local fair pressured authorities to lift the quarantine.[317]

A few days later, the epidemics broke out in the city. Hospitals were quickly overwhelmed, and residents panicked, driving the sick from their homes and out of the city. Mass graves were dug but quickly filled. Eventually, the number of dead overcame city public health efforts, until thousands of corpses lay scattered and in piles around the streets.

---

316 M. Signoli, "La Rechute Epidemique de La Grande Peste de Marseille [Mai-Juillet 1722] : Le Charnier de l'observance," *Medecine Tropicale* 58, no. 2 SUPPL. 1 (January 1998): 7–13.

317 Christian A. Devaux, "Small Oversights That Led to the Great Plague of Marseille (1720–1723): Lessons from the Past," *Infection, Genetics and Evolution* 14, no. 1 (March 2013): 169–85.

It was then that Marseille established a novel quarantine system never before seen. Members of an emergency sanitation board inspected all incoming ships and gave them one of three "bills of health," which then determined the level of access to the city by the ship and its cargo. Furthermore, a governmental act was instituted, allowing the death penalty for any communication between the city and the rest of Provence.

In order to centralize control of the outbreak, a Council of Health was created in Paris that regularly met to oversee all aspects of crisis management.[318] Representatives were sent to the city and took care that food and relief were distributed, that dogs and cats were slaughtered, and that merchandise and other properties suspected of infection were burned.

In addition, pin implantation was instituted during the plague. Physicians and other health representatives would implant bronze pins into the toes of the victims. The aim was to successfully identify those who died of the disease and separate them from others.[319]

Streets, homes, and merchandise likewise underwent regular disinfection and perfuming with vinegar or herbs. Social events of all kinds were forbidden, and markets were either

---

318 Alexandre Wenger, "[Regulations in the Struggle against the Plague. Geneva Facing the Great Plague of Marseille (1720-1723)].," *Gesnerus* 60, no. 1–2 (January 2003): 62–82.

319 Georges Leonetti et al., "Evidence of Pin Implantation as a Means of Verifying Death During the Great Plague of Marseilles (1722)," *Journal of Forensic Sciences* 42, no. 4 (July 1997): 1419J.

closed or regulated, along with taverns and houses of ill. Martial law was established.

To enforce the separation between the city and the rest of the country, a twenty-seven-kilometer long plague wall, or *mur de la peste* was erected around the city. The wall, built of dry stone, was two meters high and seventy centimeters thick. Heavily armed guards were posted and ordered to kill anyone who wanted to cross it without permission.

Faced with the impossibility of leaving the city, during a two-year period, 60 percent of Marseille's total population perished. At its peak, the disease was taking one thousand lives per day, and all together, between seventy-six thousand and one hundred twenty-six thousand lives were lost in southeastern France.[320] Ultimately, the Marseille Plague represented one of the last chapters in the book of medieval plagues and the introductory section in the records of modern disease outbreaks and disasters.

Simultaneously, more and more people in the scientific community, now armed with microscopes, started theorizing about the origins of diseases with the aim to stop them. However, most of these scientists were also convinced of the classical miasma theory, which limited their search for a truth beyond.

This medical premise had its origin in the first century BC, when the Roman writer Vitruvius described the effects of

---

320 Barbara Bramanti et al., "Plague: A Disease Which Changed the Path of Human Civilization," in *Advances in Experimental Medicine and Biology*, ed. John D. Lambris (New York: Springer New York LLC, 2016): 1–26.

miasma from fetid swamps. The theory explained that diseases were caused by a kind of bad air, known as miasma, that emanated from rotting organic matter.[321] The miasma theory, employed all along the Middle Ages, was anchoring the scientific community far from the truth.

However, new ideas started to spark. One of the early fruits of this race against contagious diseases was accomplished in 1720, when the English botanist Richard Bradley wrote that the plague and other similar pathologies were caused by poisonous insects, living creatures that could only be observed with the help of microscopes. These organisms lived and reproduced under the appropriate conditions and were present in both plants and animals, including humans.[322]

This theory went unchallenged until 1762, when the Austrian physician Marcus Antonius von Plenciz published his *Opera medico-physica*. In this manuscript, Marcus extended the previous theory and explained that specific animalcules in the soil and the air were responsible for causing diseases.[323] He wrote that a disease could be epidemic and contagious, like dysentery—or contagious but not an epidemic, like leprosy.

---

321 Marianna Karamanou et al., "From Miasmas to Germs: A Historical Approach to Theories of Infectious Disease Transmission," *Le Infezioni in Medicina* 20, no. 1 (March 2012): 58–62.

322 Richard Bradley et al., "The Germ Theory of Disease. Neglected Precursors of Louis Pasteur," *Annals of Science* 11, no. 1 (June 2006): 44–57.

323 Gaylord W. Anderson, "The Conquest of Epidemic Disease: A Chapter in the History of Ideas," *The American Historical Review* 49, no. 2 (January 1944): 272–73.

Along new theories and the skepticism of the experts, a new horror was propagating in the East. Russia was facing a chaotic time. War was becoming a real concern in the southern border of its territory, a situation that made diseases totally unpredictable and almost impossible to handle. Sadly, Russians were to find out about that the hard way.

In January of 1770, the Russian troops in Moldova discovered the first signs of *Y. pestis*, where the bacterium was indigenous and contracted by prisoners of war. The infected soldiers just wanted to return home, unaware that escaping death on the frontline did not mean they did not have to face it at home.[324]

By 1770, the plague had reached Moscow, where it peaked in fall of the following year, killing an estimated thousand Muscovites a day, leaving a third of the population in graves. However, many more deaths happened, as they often escaped the statistics; residents, fearing that the infested properties would be destroyed by authorities, routinely concealed the casualties, burying the dead at night, or simply throwing them on the streets.[325] Authorities set up chain gangs of prisoners to collect and bury the bodies, but their forces were insufficient, and their deaths were not even counted.

Soon after, a state of emergency was declared on the city. Businesses, taverns, factories, and even churches were shut down and people were asked (often, not politely) to stay in

---

324 John T. Alexander, *Bubonic Plague in Early Modern Russia: Public Health and Urban Disaster* (Oxford: Oxford University Press, 2002), 81.

325 N. K. Borodi, "The History of the Plague Epidemic in the Ukraine in 1770–74.," *Soviet Studies in History* 25, no. 4 (1987): 33–43.

their homes. The city was placed under a total lockdown. Then, the pressure started to rise within it.[326]

On September 15, 1771, Moscow residents revolted against the authorities. The mob perceived any emergency measures of the state as a conspiracy to spread the disease. The riot was prolonged for a few days. Angry citizens captured a few crowded places and destroyed quarantine zones.[327]

In the following days, thousands of people gathered again calling for the elimination of quarantines. Indeed, this was probably not the smartest movement, as cases continued to rise. Luckily for the population, with the onset of cold weather, the outbreak began to subside. In the end, around two hundred thousand people died in Moscow, and many more citizens also perished in its outskirts.[328]

That same winter, two thousand miles south of Moscow, an outbreak took place in the city of Baghdad, in Iraq. However, unlike any other, the disease spread to other parts of the Persian Empire with a speed never seen before. The epidemic, known as the Persian Plague, ravaged the whole empire for only one year, claiming more than two million lives, with a mortality rate and a quick effect that have denoted it as

326 J. T. Alexander, "Plague in Russia and Danilo Samoilovich: An Historiographical Comment and Research Note.," *Canadian-American Slavic Studies. Revue Canadienne-Americaine d"etudes Slaves* VIII, no. 4 (December 1974): 525–31.

327 M. F. Prokhorov, "The Moscow Uprising of September 1771.," *Soviet Studies in History* 25, no. 4 (1987): 44–78.

328 Charles de Mertens, *An Account of the Plague Which Raged at Moscow in 1771* (Scotts Valley, CreateSpace Independent Publishing Platform, 2015), 148–52.

the most devastating bubonic plague epidemic in human history.[329]

By its end, only a few other outbreaks were recorded, while in Western Europe, people started to breathe and felt some kind of peace.[330] Quarantine and improvements in the sanitation systems all over the main cities were leading to a safer environment and healthier inhabitants, who now did not fear the ghosts of the past. Entire communities were now flourishing and growing, unchained from the shadow of contagious diseases.

On the other hand, hospitals and the medical sector became more professionalized, with a reorganization at the management level along more bureaucratic and administrative lines. Funding was increased, with an exponentially growing number of research projects oriented to the prevention and treatment of infectious diseases.[331]

Still, mortality rates were high, but surprisingly, only in hospitals. But why? To find the answer, we have to travel to mid-nineteenth-century Austria, a place famous for its notable physicians who became pioneers of a significant expansion of the basic medical sciences and specialties.

---

329 Abdolrazagh Hashemi Shahraki, Elizabeth Carniel, and Ehsan Mostafavi, "Plague in Iran: Its History and Current Status," *Epidemiology and Health* 38 (July 2016): e2016033.

330 Boris V. Schmid et al., "Climate-Driven Introduction of the Black Death and Successive Plague Reintroductions into Europe," *Proceedings of the National Academy of Sciences of the United States of America* 112, no. 10 (March 2015): 3020–25.

331 W. F. Bynum, *Science and the Practice of Medicine in the Nineteenth Century* (Cambridge: Cambridge University Press, 1990), 104.

One of them was Ignaz Semmelweis. Ignaz was born in Budapest, Hungary, in 1818 and started working at Vienna General Hospital's maternity clinic in 1846. Soon after, he became deeply unsettled by the extraordinarily high maternal mortality rate in one of the wards.[332]

In this particular ward, staffed by physicians and medical students, 18 percent of new mothers were dying of a mysterious illness known as the childbed fever, a bacterial infection of the upper genital tract, in which the most common cause is the bacteria beta *Haemolytic streptococcus.* By comparison, in the ward staffed by midwives, about 2 percent of women died of the fever. At the time, no one knew the cause behind the extreme discrepancy.[333]

Ignaz scrutinized everything, from the climate to the crowds at each maternity clinic, trying to discover factors that might cause a spike in fever cases at one. After a few months of study, there was only a single difference: the midwives. What were the doctors doing to the women that midwives were doing differently? "Everything was in question; everything seemed inexplicable; everything was doubtful," he wrote in his book *The Etiology, Concept, and Prophylaxis of Childbed Fever* in 1861.[334] "Only the large number of deaths was an unquestionable reality."

---

332 M. Best and D. Neuhauser, "Ignaz Semmelweis and the Birth of Infection Control," *Quality and Safety in Health Care* 13, no. 3 (June 2004): 233–34.

333 K. Codell Carter, "Ignaz Semmelweis, Carl Mayrhofer, and the Rise of Germ Theory," *Medical History* 29, no. 1 (January 1985): 33–53.

334 Ignaz Semmelweis, *The Etiology, Concept, and Prophylaxis of Childbed Fever,* trans. K. Codell Carter (Madison: University of Wisconsin Press, 1983), 40.

In 1847, Ignaz's good friend Jakob Kolletschka died after being accidentally poked with a student's scalpel while performing a *post-mortem* examination. Kolletschka's own autopsy showed a pathology similar to that of the women who were dying from puerperal fever.

Ignaz discovered that the physicians had been dissecting infected cadavers with their bare hands, with no sanitation after. Then, with those same contaminated hands, they were delivering babies and helping those women.[335] The science of bacteria was not yet understood, a reason why Ignaz theorized that the physicians were carrying around invisible particles of decaying animal-organic matter on their fingers. Then, after not washing their hands, they were putting those particles on the bodies of their patients.

Ignaz required anyone examining a woman in the labor room to wash their hands in a chlorinated lime solution before entering the operating room, especially those who had just touched dead bodies. Within months, the maternal mortality rate dropped to 1 percent, matching that of the women in the midwives' ward.[336]

Could a task like washing hands be responsible for the elimination of bacteria and for saving all those lives? Nowadays,

---

335 Joshua Manor, Nava Blum, and Yoav Lurie, "'No Good Deed Goes Unpunished': Ignaz Semmelweis and the Story of Puerperal Fever," *Infection Control and Hospital Epidemiology* 37, no. 8 (August 2016): 881–87.

336 Pierre La Rochelle and Anne-Sophie Julien, "How Dramatic Were the Effects of Handwashing on Maternal Mortality Observed by Ignaz Semmelweis?," *Journal of the Royal Society of Medicine* 106, no. 11 (November 2013): 459–60.

the answer is clear. However, to some of Ignaz's colleagues in the medical community, it sounded crazy and extremely foolish. As we know, the miasma theory was widely accepted, and everyone believed that miasmas were responsible for spreading diseases. If people cared about washing their hands in earlier decades, it was because they were trying to get rid of the smell, not the particles.

Now Ignaz was claiming that those invisible particles on doctors' hands were to blame. "Nobody was pleased to think that doctors were responsible for killing all these women," Dana Tulodziecki, a professor at Purdue University, said in an interview with *The Washington Post*.[337] "Nobody liked that. Especially because the ward with the midwives had a lower mortality rate, but of course, the doctors were supposed to know much more than them."

Many doctors were deeply offended at the suggestion that they should wash their hands, feeling that their social status as gentlemen was inconsistent with the idea that their hands could be dirty. Unfortunately, Ignaz could not seem to communicate why handwashing solved the problem. And people around started to get extremely annoyed at him.[338]

After a few political changes within Europe's hospitals, Ignaz lost his job. Soon after, he started to work in a small clinic as a relatively insignificant, unpaid, honorary head physician.

---

337 Meagan Flynn, "The Man Who Discovered That Unwashed Hands Could Kill — and Was Ridiculed for It," *The Washington Post*, March 23, 2020.

338 Daniel B. Raemer, "Ignaz Semmelweis Redux?," *Simulation in Healthcare: The Journal of the Society for Simulation in Healthcare* 9, no. 3 (June 2014): 153–55.

When he arrived, childbed fever was rampant. After taking over in 1851, he virtually eliminated the disease by instituting his handwashing policy. In the four years that he worked there, only eight patients died from childbed fever out of 933 births (0.85 percent).[339]

His method was working, and it had the potential to save thousands of lives all over the world. But nobody was listening. Frustrated by that, everything started to fall apart. At the beginning in 1861, Ignaz had various nervous breakdowns. He suffered from severe depression and became absentminded. It was common to find him wandering around meetings turning every conversation to the topic of childbed fever.

After a number of unfavorable foreign reviews of his book, Ignaz decided to complain in a series of open letters. They were addressed to various prominent European obstetricians and full of bitterness, desperation, and fury, with content that was pretty offensive. He called critics of his work irresponsible murderers. In 1865, his public behavior became exasperating and embarrassing to everyone around him.

Soon after, Ignaz was sent to a mental institution. When he tried to escape, he was severely beaten by guards, secured in a straitjacket, and confined to a darkened cell for days. Two weeks later, on August 13, 1865, at the age of forty-seven, he died from a gangrenous wound, due to an infection on

---

339 Nicholas Kadar, Roberto Romero, and Zoltán Papp, "Ignaz Semmelweis: The 'Savior of Mothers': On the 200th Anniversary of His Birth," *American Journal of Obstetrics and Gynecology* 219, no. 6 (December 2018): 519–22.

his right hand, which might have been caused by the struggle.[340] The autopsy gave the cause of death as sepsis, caused by bacteria. We will never know if those who treated him washed their hands before touching the wound, but most likely, they did not.

Ignaz was buried in Vienna on August 15, 1865. Only a few people attended the service. Although the rules of the Hungarian Association of Physicians and Natural Scientists specified that a commemorative address was to be delivered in honor of members who had died, there was no address for him. His death was never even mentioned.

Years later, Western Europe and North America witnessed a new bacterial enemy, which pushed them to institute new sanitation practices that set the beginning of a new era in infectious disease control. The subsequent development of the germ theory of infectious diseases allowed Ignaz's work and theories to be accepted. However, his legacy was forever tarnished, an important loss in a war that was about to turn in humanity's favor.

---

340 K. Codell Carter and Barbara R. Carter, *Childbed Fever: A Scientific Biography of Ignaz Semmelweis* (Abingdon: Routledge, 2005), 107–9.

CHAPTER 13

DEATH IN THE TIME OF CHOLERA

———

"Messieurs, c'est les microbes qui auront le dernier mot." (Gentlemen, it is the microbes who will have the last word.)

—LOUIS PASTEUR

By the late nineteenth century, the world had already changed dramatically. Europe and North America became the two most significant powers with favorable economic development and a bright industrial future ahead. People were enjoying better and longer lives in societies of rapidly increasing size. Widespread industrialization and urbanization had allowed the introduction of substantial commodities to the cities, as well as improved resources in terms of sanitation and hygiene.[341]

———

341 Paul Bairoch and Gary Goertz, "Factors of Urbanisation in the Nineteenth Century Developed Countries," *Urban Studies* 23, no. 4 (August 1986): 285–305.

Now, don't get me wrong; bacteria did not stop hurting us. From the ashes of the absence of the great plagues, emerging chronic diseases were now taking their chances. The bacterial world still had one "last" word, which was about to be translated in three important events: the birth of a new emerging threat; the prevalence and rise of an long-known pathology; and the death of the most devastating weapon of the microscopic world.

Let us start with the birth of that emerging threat that today is commonly known as the Forgotten Pandemic. We are talking about *Vibrio cholerae* and its disease, cholera, the world's longest-running pandemic.[342] It may also be known as the nightmare from which we might never wake up.

One of the first detailed accounts of cholera comes from Gaspar Correa, a Portuguese historian who described a mysterious outbreak in the spring of 1543 in the Ganges Delta, located in Bangladesh and the Indian state of West Bengal.[343] The disease, locally known as *moryxy*, was able to kill people within eight hours of the first sign of symptoms. Soon after, numerous reports of *moryxy* were recorded on the west coast of India.[344]

---

342 Edward T. Ryan, "The Cholera Pandemic, Still with Us after Half a Century: Time to Rethink," *PLoS Neglected Tropical Diseases* 5, no. 1 (January 2011): e1003.

343 Norman Howard-Jones, "Rminolog Cholera Nomenclature and Nosology: A Historical Note," *Bulletin of the World Health Organization* 51, no. 3 (1974): 317.

344 R Pollitzer and George Williams Hooper Foundation, "Cholera Studies," *Bull. Org. Mond. Sante* 10, no. 3 (1954): 421–61.

The first cholera pandemic emerged from the Ganges Delta with an outbreak in the city of Jessore, Bangladesh, in 1817, as a result of contaminated rice.[345] Over the next few weeks, thousands of people collapsed and died, including hundreds of British soldiers.

Cholera quickly spread throughout most of India, modern-day Myanmar, and Sri Lanka by traveling along trade routes established by Europeans.[346] From there, the bacterium made its way to China. Eventually, it also spread beyond Asia, as in 1821, British troops traveling from India brought it to the Persian Gulf. At that moment, the rest of the world realized the problem. It seemed inevitable and highly expected that cholera was going to make its way to Europe.[347]

However, it did not. The pandemic died out six years after it began. One of the most accepted causes is related to the severe winter in 1823–1824. The unusually cold temperatures may have killed the bacterium living in water supplies and reservoirs. In the end, the first of the seven waves left an unknown death toll, with numbers that scattered from different countries, and was estimated to be as high as two to eight million deceased in British India.

---

345 A. K. Siddique and Richard Cash, "Cholera Outbreaks in the Classical Biotype Era," *Current Topics in Microbiology and Immunology*, no. 379 (2014): 1–16.

346 R. E. McGrew, "The First Cholera Epidemic and Social History," *Bulletin of the History of Medicine* 34, no. 1 (1960): 61–73.

347 Dhiman Barua, "History of Cholera," in *Cholera*, ed. Dhiman Barua William and B. Greenough III (New York: Springer US, 1992), 1–36.

Six years after, the second wave found its source at the Ganges River. After an outbreak in 1829, the bacteria rapidly spread along with trade and military routes throughout Asia and the Middle East. By autumn of 1830, with unprecedented speed, it had made it to Moscow. The spread temporarily slowed during the winter but picked up again in the spring of 1831, reaching Finland and Poland before passing into Hungary and Germany.[348]

For the first time, cholera cases moved to Great Britain. Quarantines were implemented and people became gripped. The tension led to a general feeling of distrust of authority figures and doctors, with people, led by an untruthful press, starting to think that more victims died in the hospital than their homes.[349] People also believed that victims were taken to hospitals and killed by doctors for anatomical dissection and study of the new disease.[350]

In 1832, the bacterium had also made it to the Americas with thousands of deaths in Quebec, New York, and Philadelphia.[351] The pandemic would eventually die around 1851. It

348 Mh Azizi and F Azizi, "History of Cholera Outbreaks in Iran during the 19(Th) and 20(Th) Centuries.," *Middle East Journal of Digestive Diseases* 2, no. 1 (January 2010): 51–55.

349 Samuel Cohn, "Fear and the Corpse: Cholera and Plague Riots Compared," in *Histories of Post-Mortem Contagion*, ed. Christos Lynteris and Nicholas H. A. Evans (New York: Springer International Publishing, 2018), 55–81.

350 Geoffrey Gill, Sean Burrell, and Jody Brown, "Fear and Frustration — The Liverpool Cholera Riots of 1832," *Lancet* 358, no. 9277 (July 2001): 233–37.

351 Alison M. Devault et al., "Second-Pandemic Strain of *Vibrio Cholerae* from the Philadelphia Cholera Outbreak of 1849," *New England Journal of Medicine* 370, no. 4 (January 2014): 334–40.

was the first wave to affect the planet, a world that had yet not seen the worst.

A few years before the end of the second episode, a third wave exploded again in India. It prolonged the suffering of people for nearly twenty years. Historians and scientists agreed that the third one was the deadliest pandemic that had ever affected the whole world, with the bacteria already accustomed to the cold winters.[352]

Around this time, when the third wave was ravaging Great Britain, John Snow, an English physician who is nowadays known as a leader in the development of anesthesia and medical hygiene, and one of the fathers of modern epidemiology, stood up to the rest of his community. In 1849, he published an essay that contained his theory of contagion diseases. In his writing, John showed a skeptic vision of the dominant miasma theory and suggested that cholera's bacterium was transmitted between humans via the fecal-oral route.[353]

John's view quickly gained more critics than supporters. However, proof of it was about to come, and the moment of truth happened in 1854, the single worst year of cholera pandemics in the story of humanity. The disease had already killed twenty-three thousand people in Great Britain alone in just a few weeks.

---

352 Anne Hardy, "Cholera, Quarantine and the English Preventive System, 1850–1895," *Medical History* 37, no. 3 (July 1993): 250–69.

353 John Snow, *On the Mode of Communication of Cholera* (London: Wilson and Ogilvy for John Churchill, 1849).

While the city was submerged in chaos, John took the time to carefully map the cholera cases in the Soho area of London. By merely talking to residents, he identified the source of the outbreak as the public water pump on Broad Street.[354] He persuaded the local council to disable the pump by removing its handle. The result was significant. Cholera cases dramatically dropped in the area, which demonstrated how the disease was spreading according to his work.

He also recommended that water should be filtered and boiled before use, which became one of the first practical applications of germ theory in the area of public health. John also used statistics to illustrate the connection between the quality of the water source and cholera cases. Unknowingly, John was behind what is nowadays considered the founding event of the science of epidemiology.[355]

Also, in 1854, across the English Channel, the University of Lille appointed an experienced scientist as a professor of chemistry and dean of the science faculty. His name was Louis Pasteur. He quickly used the influence and resources of his position to further work on a germ theory that was slowly taking its final shape. Indeed, Louis' findings eventually convinced most of Europe that bacteria were responsible for some of the most useful wonders that society could enjoy, such as souring wine, beer, and even milk. However, he also

---

354 Sandra Hempel, *The Strange Case of the Broad Street Pump: John Snow and the Mystery of Cholera* (Berkeley: University of California Press, 2007), 16.

355 Tom Koch and Kenneth Denike, "Crediting His Critics' Concerns: Remaking John Snow's Map of Broad Street Cholera, 1854," *Social Science and Medicine* 69, no. 8 (October 2009): 1246–51.

knew that these resources were a source of disease if not properly handled.

By that time, Emperor Napoleon III enlisted Pasteur to save France's wine industry from what was known as the "diseases of wine." On April 20, 1862, he completed the first test by boiling and then cooling the liquid. The outcome allowed wine makers to significantly extend the shelf-life of the treated substance and remove pathogens. He patented the process and called it pasteurization.

Pasteurization turned out to be a significant strike to the pathogen-side of the bacterial world and helped society's consumption of food become safer and healthier. Pleased at the success of his new technique, Louis turned his attention into a different field: vaccines. After the development of a vaccine to cure chicken cholera, a bacterial disease caused by *Pasteurella multocida*, he focused on anthrax, a disease that was killing a large number of sheep in Europe.[356] Louis provided experimental evidence that the anthrax bacillus was indeed responsible for the infection.[357]

Studying the origins of the disease, he unraveled the concept of virulence, He theorized that virulence is a variable property that can be lost and later recovered. Indeed, it could be both decreased and increased. Louis believed that increased virulence was what gave rise to epidemics.

---

356 M. Pasteur, "An Address on Vaccination in Relation to Chicken Cholera and Splenic Fever," *British Medical Journal* 2, no. 1076 (August 1881): 283–84.

357 A. Scorpio et al., "Anthrax Vaccines: Pasteur to the Present," *Cellular and Molecular Life Sciences* 63, no. 19–20 (January 2006): 2237–48.

His theory was matched by the behavior of cholera. The fourth and fifth pandemics almost happened at the same time, between 1863–1875 and 1881–1896, respectively.[358] However, they were overall less severe than previous outbreaks but had their fair share of deadly waves.

The time between these two epidemics supposed a period full of changes in our understanding of the bacterial world. A single man, the German physician and microbiologist Heinrich Hermann Robert Koch, considered one of the fathers of modern bacteriology, led most of these breakthroughs. Over his lifetime, Robert identified the specific causative agents of TB, cholera, and anthrax. Also, he gave experimental support for the concept of infectious disease, which included experiments on humans and animals.[359]

He began investigating anthrax, a disease that, like what had happened in France with Pasteur, was ravaging his country.[360] Robert designed inoculation studies using mice and other animals and soon discovered that inoculating a mouse with blood from a sheep that had died of anthrax caused the mouse to die the following day. At the autopsy, rod-shaped structures were present in the dead animal.[361]

---

358 J. Sepulveda, H. Gomez-Dantes, and M. Bronfman, "Cholera in the Americas: An Overview," *Infection* 20, no. 5 (September 1992): 243–48.

359 Steve M. Blevins and Michael S. Bronze, "Robert Koch and the 'golden Age' of Bacteriology," *International Journal of Infectious Diseases* 14, no. 9 (September 2010): e744–51.

360 Ragnhild Münch, "Robert Koch," *Microbes and Infection* 5, no. 1 (January 2003): 69–74.

361 A. M. Friedlander, "Microbiology: Tackling Anthrax," *Nature* 414, no. 6860 (November 2001): 160–61.

Attempting to isolate the bacterium, he developed artificial culture techniques that could allow one to observe changes in bacteria over time. He placed a piece of infected splenic tissue in a drop of aqueous humor. Then, he would seal it on a concave slide, creating a living environment that allowed the observation of bacterial growth over days.[362] Using a petroleum lamp, a humid chamber, an incubator, and variable amounts of vegetable oil for a seal, Robert could control the temperature, humidity and aeration of his specimens.

Using this technique, he found that the anthrax could form spores, resilient structures that appear in harsh environments. He demonstrated that these spores, in the absence of bacteria, could cause anthrax. Because of this, he recommended that diseased animals be burned or buried in soil cold enough to preclude spore formation.[363] The fields were then full of fumes and the odor of burned meat, a bad storm just before the peace of an area free of anthrax.

In a makeshift laboratory in the back room of his house, Robert had elucidated the life cycle of a single bacterium, *Anthrax bacillus*. So now, what? In 1883, Robert moved to Egypt and Calcutta to study the origins of cholera. He developed a

---

362 Maxime Schwartz, "Dr. Jekyll and Mr. Hyde: A Short History of Anthrax," *Molecular Aspects of Medicine* 30, no. 6 (December 2009): 347–55.

363 Joseph A. Witkowski and Lawrence Charles Parish, "The Story of Anthrax from Antiquity to the Present: A Biological Weapon of Nature and Humans," *Clinics in Dermatology* 20, no. 4 (July 2002): 336–42.

technique allowing him to grow and describe the bacterium and its presence in the intestines.[364]

By the time of this discovery, the fifth cholera pandemic was also beginning. This wave was the last one to rampage through Western Europe. Important sanitation and health-care improvements were pushing the spread of cholera back. Partially because of this, the sixth cholera pandemic, which started in 1899, primarily did not affect the developing world. By its end in 1923, cholera cases had dissipated throughout much of the world, except India, where it killed more than half a million people in both 1918 and 1919.

The seventh cholera pandemic began in Indonesia with a new strain named El Tor in the 1960s. In the late 1970s, there were small outbreaks, but most of them were known to have a pretty self-limited life, meaning they come to an end after peaking without human intervention.[365] Nowadays, almost four million cases of cholera, resulting in close to one hundred fifty thousand deaths, occur worldwide per year.

However, cholera was not the only bacterial disease causing problems, as it was sharing its human playground with of a long-known bacterial friend: *Mycobacterium tuberculosis*. Indeed, TB was still the leading cause of death in the world despite the emergence of cholera. The disease, now

---

364 N. Howard-Jones, "Robert Koch and the Cholera Vibrio: A Centenary.," *British Medical Journal (Clinical Research Ed.)* 288, no. 6414 (February 1984): 379–81.

365 Carlos Seas and Eduarde Gotuzzo, "Cholera: Overview of Epidemiologic, Therapeutic, and Preventive Issues Learned from Recent Epidemics," *International Journal of Infectious Diseases* 1, no. 1 (July 1996): 37–46.

known as the White Death, became endemic in Europe and caused millions of deaths, particularly in the poorer classes of society.[366]

The nature of the disease was elucidated when Koch discovered the bacterium behind the epidemics. As he wrote: "If the importance of a disease for humanity is measured from the number of fatalities which are due to it, then tuberculosis must be considered much more important than those most feared infectious diseases."[367] In 1882, he published his findings in a report that explained that the causative agent of the disease was slow-growing *Mycobacterium tuberculosis*.[368]

The advancement of scientific understanding of TB and its contagious nature created the need for institutions for the sick. These places were separate from the rest of civilization and housed in environments with pure and fresh air, which supposed the birth of sanatoriums.[369] One of the first and most famous examples of this practice was found in the United States in 1842, when Dr. John Croghan, the owner of Mammoth Cave, brought fifteen patients into the cave.[370]

366 René Jules Dubos and Jean Dubos, *The White Plague: Tuberculosis, Man, and Society* (New Brunswick: Rutgers University Press, 1987), 45–7.

367 Richard K. Riegelman, *Public Health 101: Healthy People-Healthy Populations* (Burlington: Jones & Bartlett Learning, 2010), 112.

368 Helen D. Donoghue et al., "Tuberculosis: From Prehistory to Robert Koch, as Revealed by Ancient DNA," *Lancet Infectious Diseases* 4, no. 9 (September 2004): 584–92.

369 Barbara Bates, *Bargaining for Life: A Social History of Tuberculosis, 1876–1938* (Philadelphia: University of Pennsylvania Press, 1992), 67.

370 Thaddaeus Zajaczkowski, "Genitourinary Tuberculosis: Historical and Basic Science Review: Past and Present," *Central European Journal of Urology* 65, no. 4 (December 2012): 182–87.

By late January, two patients were dead, and the rest had left and were found dead after, with John Croghan dying himself from TB later on.

On the other side of the Atlantic, the German physician Hermann Brehmer proposed that regions well above sea level, where the atmospheric pressure was less, would help the sick.[371] He created the first TB sanatorium in 1854 in Görbersdorf, Germany, which quickly became famous all over Europe. Back in the US, an American physician from New York, Dr. Edward Livingston Trudeau, was diagnosed with TB. To cope with the disease, Trudeau moved his family to Saranac Lake and founded the Adirondack Cottage Sanatorium.[372] One of his early patients was author Robert Louis Stevenson. Sadly, Trudeau died of the disease within a room of the sanatorium that he founded.

Partially because of these sanatoriums and because of the advancements in medicine and infection prevention, at the beginning of the twentieth century, TB was becoming a smaller problem all over the world. Still, regardless of social status, 50 percent of those who entered a sanatorium were dead within five years, which helped to encourage fear of the disease.[373]

---

371 F. Kobarfard, "Tuberculosis and Traditional Medicine: Fighting the Oldest Infectious Disease Using the Oldest Source of Medicines," *Iranian Journal of Pharmaceutical Research*, vol. 0 (November 2004): 182–87.

372 John F. Murray, Dean E. Schraufnagel, and Philip C. Hopewell, "Treatment of Tuberculosis: A Historical Perspective," *Annals of the American Thoracic Society* 12, no. 12 (December 2015): 1749–59.

373 Thomas M. Daniel, "The History of Tuberculosis," *Respiratory Medicine* 100, no. 11 (November 2006): 1862–70.

The end of the nineteenth century also witnessed the decline of the most efficient bacterial killer that humans had ever seen, *Y. pestis*. What does the death of a pandemic look like? Painful and horrible, just like any other outbreak.

By the time that America and the Western World were utterly free of the plague, a mysterious outbreak happened in the Chinese city of Yunnan in 1855. The Third Plague was the last known pandemic of the disease that the world had seen, but it had also been one of the worst ones.[374]

A natural reservoir for plague was growing in western Yunnan, which is nowadays still an ongoing health risk. By 1850, the population had exploded to over seven million people. Increasing transportation throughout the region brought people in contact with plague-infected fleas, the primary vector between the yellow-breasted rat and humans.[375] People brought the fleas and rats back into growing urban areas, where small outbreaks often reached epidemic proportions. Soon after, these were happening everywhere.[376]

In 1894, during an outbreak in Hong Kong, the organism behind the plague was isolated independently by two bacteriologists. On one side, we had the French Alexandre Yersin,

---

374 Myron Echenberg, "Pestis Redux: The Initial Years of the Third Bubonic Plague Pandemic, 1894–1901," *Journal of World History* 13, no. 2 (Fall 2002): 429–449.

375 Lei Xu et al., "Nonlinear Effect of Climate on Plague during the Third Pandemic in China," *Proceedings of the National Academy of Sciences of the United States of America* 108, no. 25 (June 2011): 10214–19.

376 Maria A. Spyrou et al., "Historical Y. Pestis Genomes Reveal the European Black Death as the Source of Ancient and Modern Plague Pandemics," *Cell Host and Microbe* 19, no. 6 (June 2016): 874–81.

working for the Pasteur Institute, while on the other we had the Japanese bacteriologist Kitasato Shibasaburo, who was a former associate of Koch.[377]

Both men found bacteria in fluid samples taken from plague victims, then injected them into animals and observed that the animals died quickly of plague. Yersin named the new bacillus *Pasteurella pestis*, after his mentor. In 1970, the bacterium was renamed *Yersinia pestis* in honor of Yersin himself.[378]

With no cure, the plague, which was brought from Hong Kong to British India, killed around 12.5 million people over the next thirty years. According to the World Health Organization, the pandemic was considered active until 1960, when worldwide casualties dropped to two hundred per year.

What are the chances of humanity beating its worst bacterial nightmare? Almost none, but it only took one discovery to completely transform the field. As Louis Pasteur said, chances only favor the prepared minds, and our collective conciseness was craving, after centuries of suffering, for a chance. However, nobody was expecting it to come in the way of an accident caused by an odd mixture of distraction and luck that took place in a small laboratory at the end of the 1920s.

---

377 Thomas Butler, "Yersinia Infections: Centennial of the Discovery of the Plague Bacillus," *Clinical Infectious Diseases* 19, no. 4 (October 1994): 655–6.

378 Robert D. Perry and Jacqueline D. Fetherston, "Yersinia Pestis — Etiologic Agent of Plague," *Clinical Microbiology Reviews* 10, no. 1 (January 1997): 35–66.

CHAPTER 14

THE GOLDEN BULLET

———

"One sometimes finds what one is not looking for."
—ALEXANDER FLEMING

Alexander Fleming was born on August 6, 1881, on a small farm in Scotland. After he inherited some money, he moved to London.[379] In 1903, he enrolled at St Mary's Hospital Medical School in Paddington, where he earned a Bachelor of Medicine with distinction in 1906.

Soon after, he joined the research department at St Mary's, where he became an assistant to Sir Almroth Wright, a pioneer in vaccine therapy and immunology. Everything was set around him to allow for a suitable research environment.

---

379 B. Lee Ligon, "Sir Alexander Fleming: Scottish Researcher Who Discovered Penicillin.," *Seminars in Pediatric Infectious Diseases* 15, no. 1 (January 2004): 58–64.

However, Alexander had to serve his country throughout World War I in the Royal Army Medical Corps.[380]

At that time, bacterial infections were killing more people than the bullets of the enemies. As a consequence, by late 1914, the British Army asked Sir Almroth Wright to set up a research laboratory in the field to explore how to improve the treatment of war wounds. Alexander accompanied him to a makeshift lab based on the top floor of a casino in Boulogne.[381]

The only way possible to save these soldiers was to use antiseptics. These drugs had been used since the 1860s to combat the risk of infection. After months of work, Alexander wrote an article where he reported a detailed explanation of why antiseptics were killing more soldiers than the infections themselves.[382] Simply, these drugs were suppressing the body's natural defenses and encouraging the growth of bacteria.

He was able to demonstrate that then commonly used chemical antiseptics, like carbolic acid, did not sterilize the wounds

---

380 Joan W. Bennett and King Thom Chung, "Alexander Fleming and the Discovery of Penicillin," *Advances in Applied Microbiology* 49 (January 2001): 163–84.

381 Siang Yong Tan and Yvonne Tatsumura, "Alexander Fleming (1881–1955): Discoverer of Penicillin," *Singapore Medical Journal* 56, no. 7 (July 2015): 366–67.

382 Alexander Fleming, "A Comparison of the Activities Antiseptics on Bacteria and on Leucocytes," *Proceedings of the Royal Society of London. Series B, Containing Papers of a Biological Character* 96, no. 674 (April 1924): 171–80.

at all.[383] Indeed, the body was able to sterilize itself by producing pus, a thick yellowish liquid produced in infected tissue, which consists of dead white blood cells and bacteria. Antiseptics were damaging those cells, making the body more vulnerable to infections.

The article caused controversy, and over the course of the war, physicians continued to use antiseptics even in cases where this worsened the condition of the patients. In 1918, when the war was over, Alexander returned to St Mary's Hospital. Far from the frontlines, he could concentrate more on his investigations into antibacterial substances as a way to eradicate bacterial infections.

Results came pretty soon. In 1921, he demonstrated that his own nasal mucus had the ability to inhibit the growth of a certain strain of bacteria in culture. The mechanism of action was related to a protein within the mucus that caused the bacterial cells to lyse. Hence, Alexander named the protein lysozyme.[384] Despite its antimicrobial activity toward harmless airborne bacteria, lysozyme proved to be ineffective against pathogenic bacteria. Alexander, realizing that there were no broad medical applications for his discovery, moved on to other studies with the hope of yielding better results elsewhere, but his findings were more groundbreaking than he or anyone else could have expected.

---

383 S. S. Brennan, M. E. Foster, and D. J. Leaper, "Antiseptic Toxicity in Wounds Healing by Secondary Intention," *Journal of Hospital Infection* 8, no. 3 (November 1986): 263–67.

384 Pierre Jollès and Jacqueline Jollès, "What's New in Lysozyme Research? — Always a Model System, Today as Yesterday," *Molecular and Cellular Biochemistry* 63, no. 2 (September 1984): 165–89.

Returning from holiday on September 3, 1928, Alexander found the chaos left behind in his laboratory before the vacation. He began to sort through Petri dishes containing colonies of *Staphylococcus aureus*, a common bacterium that we carry in the skin. He was cultivating them as part of his routine work.[385] When he started looking at the plates before throwing them, a specific one caught his attention from among the rest.

This particular plate was dotted with colonies of the bacteria (the usual form in which they grow in agar plates), perfectly shaped. Everything looked normal except for a specific area. In there, a blob of what seemed to be a mold was growing, utterly free of the presence of bacteria. The zone immediately around this organism was clear, as if it had secreted something that inhibited bacterial growth.[386]

Alexander was then able to isolate and grow a pure culture of the mold. Soon after, he discovered that it was a *Penicillium* mold and was able to isolate a filtrate which was later named penicillin. The growing mold was later identified as a rare specific strain of *Penicillium notatum*.

This organism, along with the substance that was able to produce, was about to change our perception of the bacterial world forever. Such an experience could not be better described than by Fleming himself: "When I woke up just after dawn on September 28, 1928, I certainly didn't plan to

---

385 B. Lee Ligon, "Penicillin: Its Discovery and Early Development," *Seminars in Pediatric Infectious Diseases* 15, no. 1 (January 2004): 52–57.

386 Alexander Fleming, "Penicillin," *British Medical Journal* 2, no. 4210 (September 1941): 386.

revolutionize all medicine by discovering the world's first antibiotic, or bacteria killer. But I suppose that was exactly what I did." [387]

Alexander kept the plate and started to experiment with the mold growing out of it. He found that his *mold juice* (as he used to called it) was capable of killing a wide range of harmful bacteria, such as streptococcus, meningococcus, and the diphtheria bacterium.[388] Fascinated by this ability, he called his students, Stuart Craddock and Frederick Ridley, and gave them a difficult task: isolating pure penicillin from the mold juice, which soon proved to be a hell of an experience.

For starters, penicillin proved to be very unstable, which created many challenges in rendering useful yields. In spite of that, Alexander published his findings in the *British Journal of Experimental Pathology* in June 1929. In the article, there was only a passing reference to penicillin's potential therapeutic benefits.[389] No detailed analysis, characterization, or applicability of the drug in the future was reported.

The task of transforming penicillin into a lifesaving drug was not for Alexander, but for two men whose interest on the compound stood up among the rest: the Australian pharmacologist Howard Florey and the British biochemist Ernst

---

387 Mark Jackson, *The History of Medicine: A Beginner's Guide* (London: Oneworld Publications, 2014).

388 A. B. Weisse, "The Long Pause: The Discovery and Rediscovery of Penicillin," *Hospital Practice* 26, no. 8 (August 1991): 93–118.

389 Alexander Fleming, "On the Antibacterial Action of Cultures of a Penicillium, with Special Reference to Their Use in the Isolation of B. Influenzæ," *British Journal of Experimental Pathology* 10, no. 3 (June 1929): 226–36.

Chain, who both worked at Oxford University.[390] With plenty of hope and a compelling vision, Howard and Ernst started to work in 1939.

However, World War II erupted and much of the funds were dedicated to helping those on the frontline, so doing research far from the battlefield became almost impossible. Still, they were able to set up a laboratory with a simple objective: to understand the chemistry and purification process of penicillin. Their final task was to design and set animal and clinical trials as soon as possible to demonstrate the therapeutic efficacy of the drug.[391]

The lab was entirely dedicated to growing the mold and slowly turned into a giant incubator where the organism was grown in a wide variety of culture vessels: from baths, bedpans, milk churns, or even food tins. Soon after, they designed a customized fermentation vessel for an easier removal of the filtrate. By that time, a team of "penicillin girls" (as they were known) were employed, who were paid £2 a week, to inoculate and generally look after the mold. In effect, the Oxford laboratory was being turned into a penicillin factory.[392]

In the meantime, the English biologist and biochemist Norman Heatley ideated a system to extract penicillin from huge

---

390 R. Sykes, "Penicillin: From Discovery to Product," Bulletin of the World Health Organization 79, no. 8 (2001): 778–79.

391 Ernst Chain, "The Early Years of the Penicillin Discovery," *Trends in Pharmacological Sciences* 1, no. 1 (January 1979): 6–11.

392 Hans T. Clarke, *Chemistry of Penicillin* (Princeton: Princeton University Press, 1949), 34-8.

volumes of the filtrate.[393] Thanks to this and other modifications, the team was able to produce enough of the antibiotic to run a set of experiments with mice. Despite the difficulties and an unsuccessful array of experiments, the team did not lose hope and decided to jump into human studies.

The first patient to be treated with penicillin was Albert Alexander, a policeman from the county of Oxford. He had developed sepsis after puncturing himself while trimming roses in the garden of the police house in the early autumn of 1940.[394] Now in the Radcliffe Infirmary in Oxford, he was covered in abscesses and had already lost an eye.

Alexander received a single dose of 200 mg of penicillin on February 12, 1941, followed by another 300 mg doses every three hours over five days. Over the course of the treatment, his recovery was remarkable. His urine was collected and rushed to the penicillin production unit, where the scientists desperately tried to purify the excreted drug for reuse. It was too precious to be wasted.

However, they could not recover enough. The bad news was accompanied by worse reports from the infirmary, where Alexander relapsed and eventually died. His temporary recovery, however, helped convince the penicillin team that

393 Carol L. Moberg, "Penicillin's Forgotten Man: Norman Heatley; Although He's Been Overlooked, His Skills in Growing Penicillin Were a Key to Florey and Chain's Clinical Trials," *Science* 253, no. 5021 (August 1991): 734–36.

394 Kavita Raja, "Editorial on Penicillin-Sensitive Bacteria," *Journal of The Academy of Clinical Microbiologists* 16, no. 1 (2014): 17–19.

curing him would have been possible if only enough of the drug could have been made.

Florey then turned his attention to children, who would need fewer amounts of penicillin to be treated. For this task, a four-year-old was cured of an infection but sadly died of an unrelated brain hemorrhage.[395] Florey realized that they needed more material in order to test more patients. More results would allow for a better analysis of penicillin's efficacy.

Unfortunately, the only way to scale up required asking the big pharmaceutical companies in Europe for help. However, their efforts were already immersed in the ongoing war.[396] Therefore, with the support of the Rockefeller Foundation, Florey and Heatley traveled to the United States in the summer of 1941 to see if they could get the interest of the American pharmaceutical industry.[397]

Once in the US, they were first referred to Robert Thom, a foremost mycologist and authority on the penicillium mold who eventually joined the department's Northern Regional Research Laboratory (NRRL) in Peoria, Illinois.[398] This laboratory was about the become one of the most important key players in the development of penicillin.

---

395 Charles M. Grossman, "The First Use of Penicillin in the United States," *Annals of Internal Medicine* 149, no. 2 (July 2008): 135–6.

396 H. Harris, "Howard Florey and the Development of Penicillin," *Notes and Records of the Royal Society of London* 53, no. 2 (May 1999): 243–52.

397 John Warren Henderson, "The Yellow Brick Road to Penicillin: A Story of Serendipity," *Mayo Clinic Proceedings* 72, no. 7 (July 1997): 683–87.

398 Robert Bud, *Penicillin: Triumph and Tragedy* (Oxford: Oxford University Press, 2007), 99.

The director of the NRRL agreed to have the Peoria laboratory be used to produce higher quantities of penicillin. Within a few weeks, the team discovered that it was possible to significantly increase the yield by substituting lactose for sucrose as the carbon source for the mold.

Still, there was something missing. The Oxford group had been growing the mold on the surface of a nutrient medium from the beginning. After deliberation, the Peoria lab decided that growing it on a submerged culture would be a superior process.[399] The process seemed feasible, and the yield improvement significant.

Unfortunately, the strain of the mold that Florey brought from the UK was able only to produce traces of penicillin when grown in a submerged culture. They had to find a different strain, one that would be able to facilitate the scale-up of the process.

Soon after, the Army Air Corps pilots were instructed to scoop up a sample of dirt from anywhere they landed, and then, send it to Peoria.[400] Different samples coming from all over the planet were screened day after day. Ironically, after a few intensive months, the most productive strain came from a moldy cantaloupe (or sweet melon) from Peoria's fruit market.

---

399 W H Schmidt and A J Moyer, "Penicillin: I. Methods of Assay.," *Journal of Bacteriology* 47, no. 2 (February 1944): 199–209.

400 Nelson Kardos and Arnold L. Demain, "Penicillin: The Medicine with the Greatest Impact on Therapeutic Outcomes," *Applied Microbiology and Biotechnology* 92, no. 4 (November 2011): 677–87.

Things were moving fast when Florey visited his old friend and pharmacologist Alfred Newton Richards, the chair of the Committee on Medical Research of the Office of Scientific Research and Development (OSRD). The OSRD, created in June of 1941, had the goal of assuring that adequate attention was given to research on scientific and medical problems relating to national defense, and bacterial bugs were one of them.

Richards set a meeting between Florey and representatives of Merck, Squibb, Lilly, and Pfizer, and informed them that they would be serving the national interest if they undertook penicillin production. Richards mentioned that there might be a significant contribution from the federal government. That meeting became an essential factor that changed the course of medical history, as these pharmaceutical companies started to collaborate together toward the same goal.

By March 1942, enough penicillin had been produced to treat Anne Miller, who made medical history as the first patient ever saved by the antibiotic.[401] Mrs. Miller was near death at New Haven Hospital, suffering from a streptococcal infection. As she slipped in and out of consciousness, the doctors obtained a tiny amount of penicillin and injected her with it.

Her hospital chart, now at the Smithsonian Institution as a famous item of the history of medicine, registered a sharp overnight drop in temperature, and by the next day, she was no longer delirious and soon was eating full meals. Mrs.

---

401 R. D.G. Cooper, "The Enzymes Involved in Biosynthesis of Penicillin and Cephalosporin; Their Structure and Function," *Bioorganic and Medicinal Chemistry* 1, no. 1 (July 1993): 1–17.

Miller became the first of many more patients who came after her.[402]

Soon after, and with the help of the pharma industry, the scale of production increased. Still, assuring enough purity of the final product was something challenging that brought some engineering problems. John L. Smith, executive of Pfizer at the time, captured the complexity and uncertainty that the pharma companies faced trying to achieve a suitable scale-up process: "The mold is as temperamental as an opera singer, the yields are low, the isolation is difficult, the extraction is murder, the purification invites disaster, and the assay is unsatisfactory."[403]

On March 1, 1944, Pfizer opened the first commercial plant for large-scale production of penicillin, using a submerged culture method, in the heart of Brooklyn, in New York. The plant contained fourteen 7,500-gallon tanks, and soon, the company was producing massive amounts of the drug.

The increasingly apparent value of penicillin quickly caught the attention of the military. As such, the War Production Board (WPB) was created in 1943 to take responsibility for the increased production of the antibiotic and make sure that

---

402 John Oxford et al., "Factors Influencing Inappropriate Antibiotic Prescription in Europe," *Education for Primary Care* 24, no. 4 (July 2013): 291–93.

403 "Penicillin Production through Deep-Tank Fermentation—National Historic Chemical Landmark," American Chemical Society, accessed July 7, 2020.

industry generated enough dosages for the D-Day invasion of Europe.[404]

The general public heard the echoes of the wonder drug, and the pressure made it so that exceptionally small quantities of penicillin were given to civilians through doctors, who had to administer them in low dosages and often make tough decisions.

As such, the first mass civilian use of penicillin happened in Boston after a dramatic fire accident at the Cocoanut Grove, a restaurant and night club near Park Square, in downtown. It was a cold Saturday of Thanksgiving weekend in 1942. About a thousand people packed the club that night, nearly double the building's rated capacity.[405] Suddenly, a fire started and within minutes the whole building went up in flames. Four hundred ninety-two people died as a result and more than a hundred survivors were sent to the hospital.

At the Massachusetts General Hospital, the thirty-nine survivors who lived long enough to be treated underwent an experimental protocol with penicillin. In early December, under police escort, the pharmaceutical firm Merck & Co. rushed 32 liters of a medication containing penicillin from

---

404 Peter Neushul, "Science, Government, and the Mass Production of Penicillin," *Journal of the History of Medicine and Allied Sciences* 48, no. 3 (October 1993): 371–95.

405 Stuart B. Levy and Stuart B. Levy, "From Tragedy the Antibiotic Age Is Born," in *The Antibiotic Paradox: How the Misuse of Antibiotics Destroys Their Curative Powers* (Cambridge: Da Capo Press, 2002), 1–12.

New Jersey to Boston.[406] The deployment of the drug was a complete success.

Amid the successful deployments of the drugs, the production of the drug began to increase dramatically by early 1944, jumping from twenty-one billion units in 1943 to 1,660 billion units in just a year after, to almost seven trillion units in 1945. The US government removed restrictions on the drug, prices dramatically dropped, and penicillin then became widely distributed and available to the consumer in their closest pharmacy. This, as we will see soon, marked the beginning of the end of the antibiotic era, which had started seventeen years ago.[407]

The world became a safer place for the first time. The cooperative efforts of chemists, chemical engineers, microbiologists, mycologists, government agencies, and chemical and pharmaceutical manufacturers all over the planet had produced a real medical miracle.

The long night was over; the pre-antibiotic era became a symbol of the past. Humanity had an effective treatment for infections such as pneumonia, gonorrhea, or rheumatic fever, which were affecting thousands. Those who ended up in hospitals with pathologies such as blood poisoning or sepsis were given the hope that they had never been granted before.

---

406 N. W. Faxon and E. D. Churchill, "The Cocoanut Grove Disaster in Boston: A Preliminary Account," *Journal of the American Medical Association* 120, no. 17 (December 1942): 1385–88.

407 Judith Walzer Leavitt and Ronald L., *Sickness and Health in America: Readings in the History of Medicine and Public Health* (Madison: University of Wisconsin Press, 1997), 33.

Penicillin heralded the dawn of the antibiotic age, becoming the first weapon of its kind that was able to effectively fight bacterial infections. However, in the summit of such euphoria, nobody could have expected what the bacterial world was preparing for us.

CHAPTER 15

WHAT DOES NOT KILL YOU MAKES THEM STRONGER

"Bacteria are not going to be destroyed. They have been here and they have seen dinosaurs come and go . . . so any attempt to sterilize our home is fraught with failure."

—STUART LEVY

The end of World War II marked the beginning of the antibiotic era, a real revolution in our history. Hospitals, clinics, and healthcare centers became the frontline of a battle that both physicians and patients could face with hope. Not just hospital personnel, but the general public was now stocking up on antibiotics and using them to treat bacterial infections as they pleased.

The consequence was significant. Infectious diseases that previously killed or severely disabled people were now regarded as easily treatable. One of the most widely known examples comes with the survival rate of bacterial pneumonia, which increased from 20 percent to 85 percent between 1937 and 1964.[408]

Most of the advancements in healthcare that we all enjoy today exist because of the successful implementation of antibiotics.[409] For instance, they allowed organ transplants to be performed and made chemotherapy treatments possible, along with intensive care and other surgical procedures, in a safe and bacterial-controlled setting.[410] People did not have to fear going to the hospital. We entered into a bubble, characterized for a state of euphoria that was spreading quicker than any disease on the planet.[411]

The Nobel Prize in Physiology or Medicine was awarded jointly to Fleming, Chain, and Florey on December 10, 1945, for "the discovery of penicillin and its curative effect in various infectious diseases." That night, everyone was prepared for Alexander's speech at the Nobel Banquet. He seemed extraordinarily calm and full of serenity. While someone

408 Rustam Aminov, "History of Antimicrobial Drug Discovery: Major Classes and Health Impact," *Biochemical Pharmacology* 133 (June 2017): 4–19.

409 David M. Simon and Stuart Levin, "Infectious Complications of Solid Organ Transplantations," *Infectious Disease Clinics of North America* 15, no. 2 (June 2001): 521–49.

410 Christine Herbst et al., "Prophylactic Antibiotics or G-CSF for the Prevention of Infections and Improvement of Survival in Cancer Patients Undergoing Chemotherapy," *Cochrane Database of Systematic Reviews* 21, no. 1 (January 2009): CD007107.

411 Daniel M. Laskin et al., "The Influence of Preoperative Antibiotics on Success of Endosseous Implants at 36 Months," *Annals of Periodontology* 5, no. 1 (December 2000): 166–74.

could have expected some degree of shaking from the man who had been called the savior of humanity, it did not happen.

Amid a wave of optimism among the attendees, Alexander gave a different version of the speech than the whole crowd was expecting. "It is not difficult to make microbes resistant to penicillin in the laboratory by exposing them to concentrations not sufficient to kill them, and the same thing has occasionally happened in the body," he started while the audience remained in silence. "The time may come when penicillin can be bought by anyone in the shops. Then, there is the danger that the ignorant man may easily underdose himself, and by exposing his microbes to non-lethal quantities of the drug make them resistant."[412]

Resistance. What was that about? How could bacteria, an enemy that we had just learn to defeat, become resistant to our most brilliant weapon? Alexander just gave a glimpse of a future that was not alive in anyone's mind. However, drug resistance was real. For instance, the existence of sulfa drug resistance in World War II had placed clinicians on high alert for subsequent resistance to other drugs.[413] However, everything was just a theory that not many people subscribed to.

Indeed, nobody seemed to care about something that might not even ever happen. Antibiotics were a new wonder and a significant need, and where there is a necessity, there is

---

412 I. Patrick Guilfoile and Edward Alcamo, *Antibiotic-Resistant Bacteria* (New York: Chelsea House Publications, 2006), 66.

413 George A. Jacoby, "History of Drug-Resistant Microbes," in *Antimicrobial Drug Resistance*, ed. Douglas L. Mayers (New York: Springer International Publishing, 2017), 3–8.

both profit and opportunity. The race for the discovery of new antibiotics had just begun, from broad-spectrum antibiotics to those that were prescribed to treat specific conditions. During the period between 1950 and 1960, one-half of the antibiotics commonly used today were discovered and released to the market. This time was known as the golden age of antibiotic discovery.[414]

By 1947, the pipeline of production was growing at an exponential rhythm. That same year, the first case of resistance to penicillin was observed, just two years after Alexander's speech and four years after the release of the antibiotic to the market.[415]

Would you imagine which bacterium was the first one to be reported to show resistance to human-made antibiotics? *Staphylococcus aureus*, ironically, the same bacterium that was growing on the famous plate from which the drug was isolated. It was then that Alexander's warnings came to life. Somehow, it seemed like humanity was full of those "ignorant men" that he was talking about after all.

The penicillin-resistance of *Staphylococcus aureus* was reported by the British pathologist and bacteriologist Mary Barber. She found out that this resistance was a source of hospital outbreaks and deaths worldwide. Between 1948 and 1958, Mary's focus shifted to cross-infection by *Staphylococcus*

---

414 Dane Lyddiard, Graham L. Jones, and Ben W. Greatrex, "Keeping It Simple: Lessons from the Golden Era of Antibiotic Discovery," *FEMS Microbiology Letters* 363, no. 8 (March 2016): fnw084.

415 Mary Barber, "Staphylococcal Infection Due to Penicillin-Resistant Strains," *British Medical Journal* 2, no. 4534 (November 1947): 863–65.

in hospitals.[416] She discovered that the penicillin-resistant strain was becoming endemic in the noses of the nurses after working in the wards.

It was then that she proposed a solution that indeed was pretty straightforward: to limit the use of the antibiotic and combine it with other drugs for maximum effect. This policy was adopted at St. Thomas' Hospital in London, leading to a significant decrease in cases.[417]

Her work did more than save lives—it awakened a growing concern that was roaming the ears of many by the beginning of the 1950s. As the British general practitioner Lindsay Batten stated before the Royal Society of Medicine in 1954: "Those deadly staphylococci are not pirates or privateers accidentally encountered, they are detachments of an army. They are also portents. We should study the balance of nature in the field and hedgerow, nose and throat, and gut before we seriously disturb it. Again, we may come to the end of antibiotics. We may run clean out of effective ammunition and then how the bacteria and molds will lord it."[418]

The echoes of testimonies like that one reached the World Health Organization (WHO), which convened a small

---

416 Mary Barber et al., "Reversal of Antibiotic Resistance in Hospital Staphylococcal Infection," *British Medical Journal* 1, no. 5165 (January 1960): 11–17.

417 Mark Ridley et al., "Antibiotic-Resistant Staphylococcus Aureus and Hospital Antibiotic Policies," *The Lancet* 295, no. 7640 (January 1970): 230–33.

418 Scott H. Podolsky, *The Antibiotic Era: Reform, Resistance, and the Pursuit of a Rational Therapeutics* (Baltimore: Johns Hopkins University Press, 2015), 55–7.

meeting of experts from the US and the UK in 1959 to discuss antibiotics and antibiotic resistance.[419] Despite being the first meeting of its kind, it did not have the impact that it was envisioned to, and no further actions were taken.

Resistance was, at its last, a mere laboratory definition, not a worldwide concern. Society continued to be shielded from it, and there was a general optimism regarding the pharmaceutical industry's ability to keep up in the microbial arms race. There was no bacterial disease for which we could not find a cure. If they became resistant, we would just use different antibiotics.

By the early 1960s, a new class of chemically modified antibiotics was developed, with methicillin on the frontline.[420] This particular drug would go down to history as the trigger of one of the most worrisome forms of resistance.

Methicillin was released to the public as a definitive and highly effective weapon. Such was the confidence that the drug was often sprayed into ward air to reduce the presence of *Staphylococcus aureus* and carriage of its infections among the newborn in hospital nurseries.[421] Less than a year after

---

419 National Academies of Sciences, Engineering, and Medicine. "Combating Antimicrobial Resistance: A One Health Approach to a Global Threat, " Proceedings of a Workshop (Washington, DC: The National Academies Press, 2017).

420 L. L. Silver and K. A. Bostian, "Discovery and Development of New Antibiotics: The Problem of Antibiotic Resistance," *Antimicrobial Agents and Chemotherapy* 37, no. 3 (March 1993): 377–83.

421 Michio Kurosu, Shajila Siricilla, and Katsuhiko Mitachi, "Advances in MRSA Drug Discovery: Where Are We and Where Do We Need to Be?," *Expert Opinion on Drug Discovery* 8, no. 9 (September 2013): 1095–1116.

its commercial release, MRSA (methicillin-resistant *Staph-ylococcus aureus*) was first detected in Britain as common pathogens in hospitals, which also became prevalent in the community.

Despite the concerns behind MRSA, the term antibiotic resistance only justified the need for the antibiotic market to constantly introduce new and improved drugs. Nevertheless, in the 1960s, a team of scientists in Japan demonstrated resistance could be spread not only vertically to descendant bacteria, but also horizontally across strains and even species.[422]

Such behavior was explained through mobile genetic elements that would eventually come to be known as plasmids. These independent strands of DNA were first found in bacterial cells in the late 1940s by researchers investigating how bacteria developed resistance, and their final name was given by the American molecular biologist Joshua Lederberg in 1952.[423]

A year later, the double-helix structure of DNA was presented, which then proved that DNA was made up of genetic material. This fact helped scientists determine that plasmids were composed of small sequences of genetic material, meaning that they could carry genes, and among them, those involved in resistance.[424]

---

422 Christian J.H. Von Wintersdorff et al., "Dissemination of Antimicrobial Resistance in Microbial Ecosystems through Horizontal Gene Transfer," *Frontiers in Microbiology* 7 (February 2016): 173.

423 Joshua Lederberg, "Cell Genetics and Hereditary Symbiosis," *Physiological Reviews* 32, no. 4 (October 1952): 403–30.

424 N. Patrick Higgins and Alexander V. Vologodskii, "Topological Behavior of Plasmid DNA," *Microbiology Spectrum* 3, no. 2 (April 2015).

Simultaneously, some researchers became worried about the use of antibiotics for growth promotion in farm animals, reporting on the putative spread of resistant bugs from animals to humans at a rhythm that has not been seen before.[425] By the end of the decade, more and more articles with titles like "Infectious Drug Resistance" were all warning society with statements such as, "Unless drastic measures are taken very soon, physicians may find themselves back in the pre-antibiotic Middle Ages in the treatment of infectious diseases."[426]

Despite that, the situation remained the same until 1969 when the Swann report was released in Great Britain. This collaborative effort concluded with the ban of therapeutically relevant antibiotics for agricultural growth promotion.[427] The Swann recommendations were partially adopted in some other European countries with policies that rarely worked. While non-therapeutic antibiotic usage could be banned, veterinarians could simply switch to therapeutic overprescribing, which made the problem far worse.

In the meantime, the scientific community continued to describe plasmid-mediated resistant infections at the same time that more and more cases of antibiotic-resistant

---

425 Geoff Watts, "Ephraim Saul Anderson," *The Lancet* 367, no. 9520 (April 2006): 1392.

426 Claas Kirchhelle, *Picking One's Poisons* (New Brunswick: Rutgers University Press, 2020), 78–9.

427 Frederick R. Falkiner, "Antibiotics in Plant Tissue Culture and Micropropagation—What Are We Aiming At?" in *Pathogen and Microbial Contamination Management in Micropropagation*, ed. A. C. Cassells (New York, Springer, 1997), 155–60.

infections were reported every day. Outbreaks were happening in every corner of the world. However, since most of them were quickly controlled and treated, for example, by switching to another antibiotic to which those bugs did not have reported resistance, the public remained silent.

The world had to wait a bit more until a pivotal moment in the fight toward antimicrobial resistance to antibiotics, or AMR, would come from the mind of the American researcher and physician Stuart Levy, an already well-known expert on antibiotic resistance.[428] Stuart, who was working at Tufts University (Boston), convened a conference in Santo Domingo, Dominican Republic, that was held in January of 1981, around the "Molecular Biology, Pathogenicity, and Ecology of Bacterial Plasmids." At an evening session of the meeting, 147 scientists from twenty-seven countries signed a joint "Statement Regarding Worldwide Antibiotic Misuse."

The collaborative statement pointed out that antibiotic resistance was a "worldwide public health problem" and that there was a need for an increased awareness of the dangerous consequences of antibiotic misuse at all levels of usage, from consumers, prescribers, dispensers, and manufacturers to even the governmental regulatory agencies.[429]

Stuart used the statement as a launching point from which to form the Alliance for the Prudent Use of Antibiotics (APUA). This organization aimed to educate the medical profession

---

428 Stuart B. Levy, "Antibiotic Resistance: Consequences of Inaction," *Clinical Infectious Diseases* 33, no. s3 (September 2001): S124–29.

429 Stuart B. Levy, "Antibiotic Resistance — The Problem Intensifies," *Advanced Drug Delivery Reviews* 57, no. 10 (July 2005): 1446–50.

and society alike about appropriate antibiotic use.[430] This effort became an enormous step in the race to fight antibiotic resistance. However, in the US and Great Britain, little attention was paid to it at the federal level. Somehow, it was not just the right time yet.

Nevertheless, by the late 1980s, Levy's efforts would receive a significant boost thanks to the help and call to attention coming from Joshua Lederberg. In 1988, right in the middle of the AIDS epidemic in the US, Lederberg described the linked pragmatic and moral necessity of confronting infectious diseases as a shared global concern.[431]

Across the Atlantic, the echoes of the Western world were heard, and Scandinavia came to serve as a global model for antibiotic stewardship. The country turned as a leader in the crusade to prove that antibiotics are precious resources that should not be wasted or misused. Sweden became the first country to eliminate the usage of antibiotics for growth promotion in food-producing animals in 1986.[432]

430 Kathleen T. Young and Thomas F. O'Brien, "Alliance for the Prudent Use of Antibiotics: Scientific Vision and Public Health Mission," in *Frontiers in Antimicrobial Resistance: A Tribute to Stuart B. Levy*, ed. David G. White, Michael N. Alekshun and Patrick F. McDermott (Washington, D.C.:American Society of Microbiology, 2014), 519–27.

431 Thomas M. Hooton and Stuart B. Levy, "Antimicrobial Resistence: A Plan of Action for Community Practice," *American Family Physician* 63, no. 6 (March 2001): 1087.

432 Ulf R. Dahle, Charlotte Ulstad, and Sophie Berg, "Norwegian Public Health Investigation Shows That Antibiotic Resistance Concerns Us All," *BMJ (Online)* 351 (July 2015): h4055.

However, it was already too late. Over the decade, Europe witness the horrors of resistance. Do you remember how MRSA was first reported in the UK less than a year after its release? By that time, MRSA was responsible for 37 percent of fatal cases of blood poisoning in the country. With penicillin and methicillin out of the equation, vancomycin was the only antibiotic left to be used.[433] However, reports of VISA (vancomycin-intermediate *Staphylococcus aureus*) began appearing in the late 1990s.[434]

Due to this and other cases, the WHO fully re-engaged with the issue and stated that antibiotic resistance was a "major public health problem in both developed and developing countries."[435] In the US, the Infectious Diseases Society of America (IDSA) took the lead in drawing attention to the apparent inability of the pharmaceutical industry to respond appropriately.[436]

Despite these efforts, the first documented strain with complete resistance to vancomycin, termed VRSA (Vancomycin-resistant *Staphylococcus aureus*), appeared in the US in

---

433 Paul Crawford et al., "The 'Moral Careers' of Microbes and the Rise of the Matrons: An Analysis of UK National Press Coverage of Methicillin-Resistant *Staphylococcus Aureus* (MRSA) 1995–2006," *Health, Risk & Society* 10, no. 4 (August 2008): 331–47.

434 Keiichi Hiramatsu, "The Emergence of Staphylococcus Aureus with Reduced Susceptibility to Vancomycin in Japan," *American Journal of Medicine* 104, no. 5 A (May 1998): 7S-10S.

435 "Antimicrobial Resistance," World Health Organization, accessed July 8, 2020.

436 B. Spellberg et al., "The Epidemic of Antibiotic-Resistant Infections: A Call to Action for the Medical Community from the Infectious Diseases Society of America," *Clinical Infectious Diseases* 46, no. 2 (January 2008): 155–64.

2002.[437] Now, there was nothing much left to use. A class of antibiotics that became available in the 1990s, known as oxazolidinones, was employed instead of vancomycin. The first commercially available of these drugs was linezolid, with an effect comparable to vancomycin in effectiveness against MRSA. As it was probably expected by many, linezolid-resistance in *Staphylococcus aureus* was reported in 2003.[438]

When these strains left hospitals and entered the community, they became emerging epidemics. Nowadays, all these bacterial populations are responsible for rapidly progressive and fatal diseases, including necrotizing pneumonia and severe sepsis, among others. Indeed, MRSA is the most frequently identified antimicrobial drug-resistant pathogen in US hospitals.[439]

Unfortunately, the epidemiology of the bacterium changes so quickly that research is struggling to keep up. In the past ten years, thousands of outbreaks of MRSA infections in the community have been reported in correctional facilities, among athletic teams and military recruits, as well as in newborn nurseries. These infections, some of them resistant

437 D. M. Sievert et al., "Vancomycin-Resistant Staphylococcus Aureus in the United States, 2002-2006," *Clinical Infectious Diseases* 46, no. 5 (March 2008): 668–74.

438 Michael J. Peeters and Juan C. Sarria, "Clinical Characteristics of Linezolid-Resistant Staphylococcus Aureus Infections," *American Journal of the Medical Sciences* 330, no. 2 (August 2005): 102–4.

439 François Vandenesch et al., "Community-Acquired Methicillin-Resistant Staphylococcus Aureus Carrying Panton-Valentine Leukocidin Genes: Worldwide Emergence," *Emerging Infectious Diseases* 9, no. 8 (August 2003): 978–84.

to many of the antibiotics in use, now appear to be endemic in many urban regions.[440]

Almost half a century after Alexander Fleming's warning, the world finally found that antibiotic resistance is not only a shared, global problem but also one mandating collaborative, multi-sectoral intervention that would need the support of every aspect of society.

And yet, despite such a seemingly dire need and such multi-sectoral enthusiasm, reformers still considered existing funding and measures as insufficient to forestall the end of antibiotics. In a way, the chance that *the cure might be the problem* behind antibiotic resistance is a crude, almost irrational reality for many. We have not learned from our past mistakes while we are fighting an opportunistic enemy that knows how to use them against us. Time will tell, and unfortunately, it is counting down for us.

---

440 Helen W. Boucher and G. Ralph Corey, "Epidemiology of Methicillin-Resistant *Staphylococcus Aureus*," *Clinical Infectious Diseases* 46, no. S5 (June 2008): S344–49..

CHAPTER 16

INVISIBLE VOICES

"Maybe there is a beast . . . maybe it's only us."
—WILLIAM GOLDING, LORD OF THE FLIES

Undoubtedly, two-thirds of the twentieth century demonstrated that bacteria were developing the ability to defeat the drugs that we had designed to kill them. There was not much room left for improvement after such a failure. We have to realize that we might be closer than we think to a dystopian future. Humanity may be heading toward a reflection of its own self, surrounded by the ruins of a time that was not supposed to arrive. A time in which the only thing left to do would be to wonder why we allowed this to happen in the first place.

However, as dystopic as it might seem, a future is a future. There is still time; there is hope. We are in a plateau of realization, a time for asking questions, whose many answers we can now seek, instead of regret. Nowadays, information is power, and we better carry the best version of it with us.

Despite years of experiments, studies, and reports throughout the entire worldwide scientific community, the most
important question does not have a final answer yet. How
does it happen? How can a simple organism like bacteria
go from being a harmless life form to a resistant superbug?

Let us find an answer. Starting simply, antibiotics are weapons to fight bacteria, and they do what they do through a
variety of mechanisms. For instance, the well-known miracle drug, penicillin, kills bacteria by damaging or inhibiting
the synthesis of the bacterial cell walls.[441] In contrast, other
antibiotics act by altering or destroying genetic material or
proteins, or by changing the metabolism of the bacterial cells
that they encounter.[442]

Such a wide array of complex interactions relies on a paradigm of understanding that is characterized by a void in
knowledge. Regardless of how antibiotics operate, resistance
eventually appears, sooner or later. Still, how does it happen?

The best person to explain this is a fictional patient that we
are about to create. Just close your eyes and imagine a regular
human being doing whatever anyone would do with their
normal life. The patient has been recently infected with a
bacterial pathogen through a scratch in their leg. After a few
days of not feeling well, they go to the hospital, and the doctor
prescribes antibiotics. They come back home and swallow the

---

441 P. E. Reynolds, "Structure, Biochemistry and Mechanism of Action of
     Glycopeptide Antibiotics," *European Journal of Clinical Microbiology &
     Infectious Diseases* 8, no. 11 (November 1989): 943–50.

442 J. William Lown, "The Mechanism of Action of Quinone Antibiotics,"
     Molecular and Cellular Biochemistry 55, no. 1 (March 1983): 17–40.

pill along with some water. A few hours after, the prescription indicates that it is safe to take the next dosage.

The active components of the pill—the antibiotic itself—get to the problem soon after by reaching those bacterial cells that are happily growing and causing problems. Once a single bacterial cell enters into contact with an antibiotic, two things can happen: either it dies, or does not.

Now, we care about the "*it does not.*" The bacterial cell survives through the development of resistance. The antibiotic will kill other bacteria that are not resistant as well. Sadly, the ones dying are often those native species around the patient's microbiota, those who had been living there all this time.[443] They do not know how to fight the drug. When the antibiotic reaches them, they die. End of the story.

What do we have after? Imbalance. The harmful bacteria have plenty of free space and a vast amount of nutrients, so they grow even quicker than before. Then, it does not matter that the patient, still feeling ill, takes two or more dosages of the same antibiotic time after time. The treatment is not going to kill the bug nor work in any manner. Instead, it is going to continue to devastate the natural microbiota.

However, the critical question now arises: how did this bad bacterium acquire resistance in the first place? Let us start with a clear statement: Bacteria are either "born" or "made"

---

443 Carles Ubeda and Eric G. Pamer, "Antibiotics, Microbiota, and Immune Defense," *Trends in Immunology* 33, no. 9 (September 2012): 459–66.

resistant, thanks to either evolution or the action of other bacteria, respectively.[444]

Antibiotic resistance can be acquired through two main mechanisms, leading to what is known as intrinsic or acquired resistance.[445] To make things easier, let us consider two bacteria that can survive in the presence of the antibiotic: bacterium A and B. While the first one was born resistant, the second one acquired this power from another bacteria.

Getting to know them better, let's start with bacterium A, a Gram-negative bacterium that has a cell wall. This physical barrier is composed of a thin layer of peptidoglycan, a polymer consisting of sugars, and amino acids.[446] The bacterium was born resistant, so it survived in the presence of the drug because of the named intrinsic resistance.

How does this intrinsic resistance work? Bacterium A has natural features that render immunity to the killing mechanisms of the drug.[447] It is like if you were born without an allergy to pollen; while everyone else is struggling to breathe in spring, you would be able to happily go and grab

---

444 Dan I. Andersson, "Persistence of Antibiotic Resistant Bacteria," *Current Opinion in Microbiology* 6, no. 5 (October 2003): 452–56.

445 Abiola O. Olaitan, Serge Morand, and Jean Marc Rolain, "Mechanisms of Polymyxin Resistance: Acquired and Intrinsic Resistance in Bacteria," *Frontiers in Microbiology* 5 (November 2014): 643.

446 J. W. Costerton, J. M. Ingram, and K. J. Cheng, "Structure and Function of the Cell Envelope of Gram Negative Bacteria," *Bacteriological Reviews* 38, no. 1 (March 1974): 87–110.

447 Georgina Cox and Gerard D. Wright, "Intrinsic Antibiotic Resistance: Mechanisms, Origins, Challenges and Solutions," *International Journal of Medical Microbiology* 303, no. 6–7 (August 2013): 287–92.

an ice cream in the middle of a windy Sunday without any problems.

However, in the microscopic bacterial world, this immunity to antibiotics is reflected in the outer membrane of our bacterium A, which is a major intrinsic resistance determinant. Why? This biological wall is thick enough that it does not allow large molecules to pass through, like antibiotics.

Another remarkable example of inherent resistance occurs with vancomycin, one of the most critical last-resort antibiotics. This drug interferes with the cell wall structure in bacteria. Still, it is only active against Gram-positive bacterial cells (we will get to them in just a second) because vancomycin cannot cross the outer membrane of the Gram-negative species.

Alternatively, a smart way of intrinsic resistance is found in some bacteria that can temporarily express or suppress different genes to enable survival in the presence of antibiotics.[448] Those genes allow for the generation of some expression patterns, which return to normal once the threat posed by those particular drugs has passed.[449]

In summary, bacterium A has intrinsic resistance, a direct consequence of the natural evolution of the organism.

---

448 D. P. Josey et al., "Strain Identification in Rhizobium Using Intrinsic Antibiotic Resistance," *Journal of Applied Bacteriology* 46, no. 2 (April 1979): 343–50.

449 Hany S. Girgis, Alison K. Hottes, and Saeed Tavazoie, "Genetic Architecture of Intrinsic Antibiotic Susceptibility," ed. Christophe Herman, *PLoS ONE* 4, no. 5 (May 2009): e5629.

Because of that, it is not affected by the misuse of antibiotics. It has been like that since the very beginning, and most likely, will be. Forever. No matter how many times we throw that antibiotic at it, there is no way it is going to kill it.

On the other hand, we have our bacterial friend B, a Gram-positive bacterium. Its cell wall is composed of a thick layer of peptidoglycan, and unlike bacterium A, it does not have a second physical barrier.[450] Still, it can withstand the attack of antibiotics. Bacterium B has acquired resistance, a feature that it did not have before. But how?

The bacteria got the ability to resist antibiotics through either a sudden gene mutation (for instance, caused by stress, as we will explain later) or through the transfer of genetic material from other bacteria that were already resistant, for instance, bacterium A.[451]

Let us go back to the example of vancomycin mentioned before. Naturally, bacterium B would die after exposure to the drug. However, it can get the ability to resist the drug from bacterium A. Once it gets that, the bacterium can show changes in its membrane, preventing vancomycin from entering the cell, or they can secrete enzymes to break down

---

450 Carol L. Friedrich et al., "Antibacterial Action of Structurally Diverse Cationic Peptides on Gram-Positive Bacteria," *Antimicrobial Agents and Chemotherapy* 44, no. 8 (August 2000): 2086–92.

451 Michael Teuber, Leo Meile, and Franziska Schwarz, "Acquired Antibiotic Resistance in Lactic Acid Bacteria from Food," *Antonie van Leeuwenhoek, International Journal of General and Molecular Microbiology* 76, no. 1–4 (November 1999): 115–37.

the antibiotic even before it gets close.[452] Another possible way, and quite often seen in bacteria, would be the use of a structure called the efflux pump that quickly removes the drug entirely within the bacterial environment or reduces its concentration below adequate levels.

Now, the key in all of this is how does bacterium B get resistance from A? It is not like a lecture or reading a memo, and it does not happen by a teaching process as we might think. Instead, there is something known as promiscuous gene transfer systems, which allow the sharing of genetic material between bacteria.[453] Among these transfer systems, conjugative plasmids are the ones we need to know more about.

Plasmids, as we know from before, are circular DNA molecules that contain genes that have the resistance superpower in them. These circles of genetic materials are to bacteria as antibiotics are to humanity, something that is protective. Plasmids can replicate independently and move between bacteria carrying antibiotic resistance genes with free will, eventually reaching other bacteria that are in need of this ability to survive.[454] Then, they multiply and spread antibi-

---

452 Susan S. Huang, Rupak Datta, and Richard Platt, "Risk of Acquiring Antibiotic-Resistant Bacteria from Prior Room Occupants," *Archives of Internal Medicine* 166, no. 18 (October 2006): 1945–51.

453 P. M. Bennett, "Plasmid Encoded Antibiotic Resistance: Acquisition and Transfer of Antibiotic Resistance Genes in Bacteria," *British Journal of Pharmacology* 153, no. SUPPL. 1 (March 2008): S347–57.

454 Stuart B. Levy, George B. Fitzgerald, and Ann B. Macone, "Spread of Antibiotic-Resistant Plasmids from Chicken to Chicken and from Chicken to Man," *Nature* 260, no. 5546 (March 1976): 40–42.

otic resistance among successive generations.[455] Now, this wonder of a process takes place at a rate that no other living organisms on the face of the Earth can achieve. And this makes them extremely dangerous.

However, other than plasmids, there is another mechanism of resistance communication far worse: integrons. They are something like mobile DNA elements that can capture and carry genes.[456] Why should we be worried about them? These communication channels are becoming prevalent in many bacterial species, indeed, in more than we expected. For instance, integrons now appear in up to 70 percent of Gram-negative pathogens in clinical and agricultural samples.[457] This means that they acquired resistance through these channels.

Over the years, bacteria have become more and more fluent in the art of communicating resistance. Long before humans were able to throw a word to each other, they dominated the art of generating and releasing plasmids, integrons, and other similar structures of which we might not even have noticed yet. That void in knowledge is what makes them dangerous and unpredictable, and what make us an easy prey.

455 R. K. Sizemore and R. R. Colwell, "Plasmids Carried by Antibiotic Resistant Marine Bacteria," *Antimicrobial Agents and Chemotherapy* 12, no. 3 (September 1977): 373–82.

456 Alexandra Moura et al., "Novel Gene Cassettes and Integrons in Antibiotic-Resistant Bacteria Isolated from Urban Wastewaters," *Research in Microbiology* 163, no. 2 (February 2012): 92–100.

457 Thibault Stalder et al., "Integron Involvement in Environmental Spread of Antibiotic Resistance," *Frontiers in Microbiology* 3 (April 2012): 119.

As you may imagine, the resistances of bacterium A and B, either inherited or acquired, are not exclusive. A bacterium is also able to perform more than one of these functions simultaneously, hence becoming resistant to more than one type of antibiotic. This super-superpower results in probably the most worrisome kind of resistance: multidrug resistance (MDR), in which a single bacterium can become immune to more than two antibiotics.[458]

The problem here is that this MDR is often seen as too many antibiotics are considered last-resort drugs, and that is a huge problem. Besides, outcomes in patients infected with multidrug resistant (MDR) bacteria tend to be worse as compared to patients infected with more susceptible organisms.

Undoubtedly, this leads to a tremendous added cost associated with these infections, not only for the patient, but for the hospitals and clinics. In the US, associated annual additional costs of infections caused by MDR organisms as compared to susceptible organisms are estimated to cost up to $34 billion. Now, that is a lot of money, but bacteria are not the ones to blame here. The prevalence of specific MDR bacteria is closely linked to the use of broad-spectrum antibiotics.[459] This increased use in turn leads to even higher rates of MDR bacteria, thus creating a vicious cycle whose outcome is going to blow up in our face one way or another.

---

458 Laura Freire-Moran et al., "Critical Shortage of New Antibiotics in Development against Multidrug-Resistant Bacteria — Time to React Is Now," *Drug Resistance Updates* 14, no. 2 (April 2011): 118–24.

459 David van Duin and David L. Paterson, "Multidrug-Resistant Bacteria in the Community: Trends and Lessons Learned," *Infectious Disease Clinics of North America* 30, no. 2 (June 2016): 377–90.

Now, MDR might sound like the tip of the iceberg, but it is not. In recent years, a new term has been used to define a novel class of extremely hazardous bacteria: pan-drug resistant strains.[460] For instance, an isolate of *Pseudomonas aeruginosa* becomes pan-drug-resistant if it is resistant to all seven available anti-pseudomonal classes of antimicrobial agents.[461]

One of the most shocking cases of these extremely worrisome infections was reported in 2016 in an American woman who had recently arrived from India. When she was admitted to a Nevada hospital, her blood was carrying pan-drug resistant *Klebsiella pneumoniae*.[462] When the bacterium was isolated from her hip abscess, it was shown to be resistant to all twenty-six antimicrobials tested, including b-lactams, colistin, and aminoglycosides, some last-resort antibiotics. Unfortunately, the patient died from septic shock within one month. No antibiotics were left to treat her. There was no miracle weapon; there was no way, nothing. That was it.

Now we know how resistance happens, and how easily and quickly it is spread among bacterial species and strains. In war, communication is key. Better communication allows

---

460 M. Souli, I. Galani, and H. Giamarellou, "Emergence of Extensively Drug-Resistant and Pandrug-Resistant Gram-Negative Bacilli in Europe.," *Euro Surveillance : Bulletin Européen Sur Les Maladies Transmissibles = European Communicable Disease Bulletin* 13, no. 47 (November 2008): 19045.

461 C. Y. Wang et al., "Pandrug-Resistant Pseudomonas Aeruginosa among Hospitalised Patients: Clinical Features, Risk-Factors and Outcomes," *Clinical Microbiology and Infection* 12, no. 1 (January 2006): 63–68.

462 David P. Calfee, "Recent Advances in the Understanding and Management of Klebsiella Pneumoniae," *F1000Research* 6 (September 2017): 1760.

for a suitable response and a much faster way to adapt to different situations. Therefore, well-transmitted information and instructions, delivered in the right moment in the precise way, separates the winners from the losers

However, there is no possible way to fight this enemy. This war is like no other. Bacteria transmit information at a rate that no one can predict, using a wide array of channels and vehicles that not even a supercomputer could decipher in a million years. They are among the simplest organisms on the planet, and yet their complexity is light years beyond the limits of our own knowledge. All that we have left is what we learn from the battle. Nothing else will stand or remain. How we use that information, how we share that knowledge, is all that matters.

CHAPTER 17

THE STONE THAT WE THROW OVER THE SKY

———

"But you can't make people listen. They have to come around in their own time, wondering what happened and why the world blew up around them"

—RAY BRADBURY, FAHRENHEIT 451

Resistance is a reality. Whatever you call it: single, multi- or pan-resistance, it is already here. It grows among us, spreads quicker than anything we can imagine, and silently kills while remaining unnoticed. In the previous chapter, we learned *how* this all happens, but now, we may seek a different truth in a new scenario: the post-antibiotic world, a place and time where we might wonder if all this is happening that fast simply because of antibiotics.

Most cases of resistance arise when the antibiotic kills susceptible bacteria. Then, among the ashes of the weak, those microorganisms that are resistant prevail and spread.

However, there is a difference between killing the guards and freeing the beast.

In other words, antibiotics are not directly causing resistance. Instead, they are selecting for resistant bacteria and increasing their proportional prevalence.[463] By annihilating the natural microbiota and disrupting balance, drug-resistant pathogens are making their way out. Maybe, in our search to find weapons to fight bacteria, we have revealed those superbugs that now are immune to everything we throw at them.

Resistance was always there; we already know that. Although bacteria would indeed be able to spontaneously acquire this resistance through mutation, we would most likely not have to worry about them in ours and our close future generations' lifetime. Bacteria would not need to develop resistance if we were not continuously throwing drugs at them, am I right?

However, there is more. Resistance grows faster than before, but antibiotics are not the only factor speeding up the wheels. Human-derived antibiotic aside, what else can be contributing to the problem?

As we already know, and as early as 1945, Alexander Fleming raised the alarm regarding antibiotic overuse. His words were warning the public, telling them that they were not wrong to demand so much of the drug. The era of abuses

---

463 Johan Bengtsson-Palme and D. G.Joakim Larsson, "Concentrations of Antibiotics Predicted to Select for Resistant Bacteria: Proposed Limits for Environmental Regulation," *Environment International* 86 (January 2016): 140–49.

is already here, with overuse as one of the most concerning driving points of the evolution of resistance.[464]

The Centers for Disease Control and Prevention (CDC) estimates that more than 70 percent of the bacteria responsible for the two million infections acquired in hospitals annually in just the US are resistant to at least one commonly used antibiotic.[465] Why? Mostly because between 20 percent to 50 percent of antibiotics prescribed in the country's hospitals are unnecessary or inappropriate.[466]

If we study antibiotic consumption based on volume sold in retail and hospital pharmacies. we realize that around twenty-two standard units of antibiotics are prescribed per person in the US.[467] In some states, the number of prescribed courses of treatment with antibiotics per year exceeds the population, amounting to more than one treatment per person per year.[468]

Now, this happens in the US where the government regulates antibiotic use and consumption with a pretty solid

---

464 Martin J. Blaser, *Missing Microbes: How the Overuse of Antibiotics Is Fueling Our Modern Plagues* (New York: Henry Holt and Co, 2014), 187.

465 "Antibiotic Use in Outpatient Settings" Centers for Disease Control and Prevention, accessed July 9, 2020.

466 Laura J. Shallcross, "Editorials: Antibiotic Overuse: A Key Driver of Antimicrobial Resistance," *British Journal of General Practice* 64, no. 629 (December 2014): 604–5.

467 Thomas P. Van Boeckel et al., "Global Antibiotic Consumption 2000 to 2010: An Analysis of National Pharmaceutical Sales Data," *The Lancet Infectious Diseases* 14, no. 8 (August 2014): 742–50.

468 C Lee Ventola, "The Antibiotic Resistance Crisis: Causes and Threats.," *P & T Journal* 40, no. 4 (April 2015): 277–83.

foundation. However, what does happen in those countries where antibiotics are unregulated and available over the counter without a prescription? Chaos.

Globalization and the extensive use of the internet have helped spread resistant bacteria in the same way that the born of society helped their ancestors in the dawn of humankind. Nowadays, it is possible to purchase antibiotics online, making them accessible in countries where they are not regulated—one of the most shocking examples being in Mongolia, a country that has by far the highest level of antibiotic consumption in the entire planet, with almost sixty-five defined daily doses per one thousand people.

Then we have the giants of the west: China and India, two countries that are quickly catching up with the thresholds.[469] As such, daily dosage per person has risen by 70 percent in China and 65 percent in India since the beginning of the century[470] If you consider that they are the first and second most populated countries in the world, with a raising antibiotic consumption and with weak regulations, what you end up with is an atomic-scale ticking time bomb.

We also have to realize that incorrectly prescribed antibiotics have questionable therapeutic benefits and expose patients to potential complications related to antibiotic therapy.

469 Jin Wang et al., "Use and Prescription of Antibiotics in Primary Health Care Settings in China," *JAMA Internal Medicine* 174, no. 12 (December 2014): 1914–20.

470 Anita Kotwani and Kathleen Holloway, "Trends in Antibiotic Use among Outpatients in New Delhi, India," *BMC Infectious Diseases* 11, no. 1 (April 2011): 1–9.

Subinhibitory and subtherapeutic antibiotic concentrations can promote the development of antibiotic resistance, allowing strain diversification in organisms such as *Pseudomonas aeruginosa*, leading to new strains whose effect we are far from fully understanding.[471]

Misdiagnosis of bacterial pathologies also helps to make the problem worse. One US study reported that an infectious pathogen was defined in only 7.6 percent of almost eighteen thousand patients hospitalized with community-acquired pneumonia.[472] Furthermore, 30 percent to 60 percent of the antibiotics prescribed in intensive care units, one of the settings most affected by bacterial infections, are unnecessary, inappropriate, or suboptimal.[473] We can do things to lower these numbers, but not doing them is always easier.

The antimicrobial resistance to antibiotics (AMR) crisis is also fueled by the use of antibiotics in livestock and agriculture.[474] For instance, an estimated 80 to 90 percent of all antibiotics sold in the US are employed in animals.[475]

471 Elli A. Wright et al., "Sub-Inhibitory Concentrations of Some Antibiotics Can Drive Diversification of Pseudomonas Aeruginosa Populations in Artificial Sputum Medium," *BMC Microbiology* 13, no. 1 (July 2013): 1–12.

472 John G Bartlett, David N Gilbert, and Brad Spellberg, "Seven Ways to Preserve the Miracle of Antibiotics," *Clinical Infectious Diseases* 56, no. 10 (May 2013): 1445–50.

473 S. M. Walther et al., "Antibiotic Prescription Practices, Consumption and Bacterial Resistance in a Cross Section of Swedish Intensive Care Units," *Acta Anaesthesiologica Scandinavica* 46, no. 9 (October 2002): 1075–81.

474 Anthony E. Van Den Bogaard and Ellen E. Stobberingh, "Antibiotic Usage in Animals. Impact on Bacterial Resistance and Public Health," *Drugs* 58, no. 4 (November 1999): 589–607.

475 Stanley Falkow and Donald Kennedy, "Antibiotics, Animals, and People—Again!," *Science* 291, no. 5503 (January 19, 2001): 397–397.

Why? These drugs promote growth and prevent infection.[476] Besides, they improve the overall health of the animals, producing larger yields and a higher-quality product that we all can enjoy in our supermarkets and then in our dishes.

But at what cost? Despite the different grades of meat and those who claim to be antibiotic-free, the crude reality is different: Most people do not consume them, either because of choice or because of the lack of stock. When someone purchases standard meat produced on a livestock farm that employs antibiotics for growth promotion, they will likely ingest residues of the drugs when consuming the food and foodborne pathogens carrying resistance.[477]

The use of antibiotics in livestock is leading to a diversification of microbial contamination routes. For example, up to 90 percent of the antibiotics given to animals are excreted in urine and stool and then dispersed through fertilizer, groundwater, and surface runoff.[478] Consequently, resistant strains of bacteria can reach fruits and vegetables, which can get contaminated through contact with the soil, water, or

476 Jay P. Graham, John J. Boland, and Ellen Silbergeld, "Growth Promoting Antibiotics in Food Animal Production: An Economic Analysis," *Public Health Reports* 122, no. 1 (January 2007): 79–87.

477 Lieve Okerman and Jan Van Hoof, "Evaluation of the European Four-Plate Test as a Tool for Screening Antibiotic Residues in Meat Samples from Retail Outlets," *Journal of AOAC INTERNATIONAL* 81, no. 1 (January 1998): 51–56.

478 Wolfgang Witte, "Selective Pressure by Antibiotic Use in Livestock," *International Journal of Antimicrobial Agents* 16, no. SUPPL. 1 (November 2000): 19–24.

fertilizer that contains such animal waste.[479] And then back to the grocery store again.

A recent international study gathered nearly a thousand publications and unpublished veterinary reports from around the world.[480] Between 2000 and 2018, the proportion of antibiotic resistance rates in those species was way above 50 percent in developing countries. The authors found that antibiotics that could be used for treatment failed more than half the time they were used in chickens and pigs raised for human consumption.

Our traditional use of antibiotics in these settings is starting to fail. Still, we use them as if nothing was happening. Regardless of that, everything gets worse in the developing world. Since the beginning of the century, meat production has accelerated way over 60 percent in Africa and Asia, and by 40 percent in South America. Due to the mediocre regulation in antibiotic use for meat production and a low production price, they can export high-quality meat with low fees.

In addition to animals, plant food production is affected. Tetracyclines and streptomycin, two common types of antibiotics, are sprayed on fruit trees to act as pesticides in the

---

479 Alan G. Mathew, Robin Cissell, and S. Liamthong, "Antibiotic Resistance in Bacteria Associated with Food Animals: A United States Perspective of Livestock Production," *Foodborne Pathogens and Disease* 4, no. 2 (June 2007): 115–33.

480 Thomas P. Van Boeckel et al., "Global Trends in Antimicrobial Resistance in Animals in Low- And Middle-Income Countries," *Science* 365, no. 6459 (September 2019): eaaw1944.

western and southern US.[481] While their use accounts for a much smaller proportion of the overall antibiotic use, the resultant geographical spread is far more extensive than in livestock settings.[482]

Human, livestock, and agricultural use of antibiotics are all critical factors in the spread of AMR, continually feeding new nightmares a vicious cycle that has not known an end. However, there is another pivotal factor increasing the burden of resistance: how the drugs are produced.

Nowadays, most of the world's antibiotic drugs are manufactured in China and India due to cheap labor and capital costs, and of course, a lighter regulatory burden.[483] For these reasons, China has become the world's largest producer and exporter of active pharmaceutical ingredients (API), the part of any drug that produces the intended effects.

Currently, the country exports up to 90 percent of all raw materials for antibiotics, increasing AMR pressure in the area. Recent reports indicated that Indian and Chinese drug makers routinely release untreated waste fluid containing active ingredients into surrounding soil and waterways.[484]

---

481 Patricia S. McManus et al., "Antibiotic Use in Plant Agriculture," *Annual Review of Phytopathology* 40, no. 1 (September 28, 2002): 443–65.

482 Patricia S. McManus and Virginia O. Stockwell, "Antibiotic Use for Plant Disease Management in the United States," *Plant Health Progress* 2, no. 1 (January 2001): 14.

483 Carl Nathan and Otto Cars, "Antibiotic Resistance — Problems, Progress, and Prospects," *New England Journal of Medicine* 371, no. 19 (November 2014): 1761–63.

484 Xiaohui Liu et al., "Antibiotics in the Aquatic Environments: A Review of Lakes, China," *Science of the Total Environment* 627 (June 2018): 1195–1208.

These residues will eventually end up in the food of livestock and within the roots of plants that will reach the tables of many people worldwide.

One recent study showed that antibiotic concentrations downstream of drug manufacturing plants in these countries exceed those expected in someone being treated for the infection.[485] Moreover, researchers from some Chinese universities concluded that for every bacterium that entered a waste treatment plant in northern China, four or five antibiotic-resistant bacteria were released into the water system.[486]

Lastly, one of the most forgotten factors contributing to AMR's rise is related to an activity that most of us do almost every day as part of our routines: cleaning. A clean surface is synonymous to order and self-care. However, too much of a good thing becomes a bad one, and if this involved bacteria, it becomes more accessible than you might believe.

Antibiotics aside, antimicrobial products sold for hygienic or cleaning purposes are an essential resistance trigger.[487] Traditionally, people washed bacteria from their bodies and homes using soap and hot water, alcohol, chlorine bleach, or hydrogen peroxide, among some mixtures of the previous.

---

485 D. G. Joakim Larsson, "Pollution from Drug Manufacturing: Review and Perspectives," *Philosophical Transactions of the Royal Society B: Biological Sciences* 369, no. 1656 (November 2014): 20130571.

486 Wilfried Sanchez et al., "Adverse Effects in Wild Fish Living Downstream from Pharmaceutical Manufacture Discharges," *Environment International* 37, no. 8 (November 2011): 1342–48.

487 Allison E. Aiello et al., "Antibacterial Cleaning Products and Drug Resistance," *Emerging Infectious Diseases* 11, no. 10 (October 2005): 1565–70.

These products act nonspecifically. What does that mean? They wipe out almost every type of microbe in sight, from fungi and bacteria to even some viruses, rather than selecting a particular one. For instance, soap works by loosening and lifting dirt, oil, and microbes from surfaces to be easily rinsed away with water.

When technological innovation reached these cleaning products, generic cleaners and brands we all know nowadays became widely available. They were cheap, and most importantly, they worked pretty well. Unlike traditional cleaners, this new generation of products contained variable amounts of antibacterial substances. Moreover, as it would happen with alcohol-based cleaners or traditional approaches, these products leave surface residues, creating conditions that may foster the development of resistant bacteria.

Therefore, something similar to what happens inside our body after an antibiotic course might be happening in our home's surfaces. How? For instance, when wiping the kitchen counter, active chemicals are left behind. These can chemically attack bacteria, not just at the application moment, but also after. This interaction supposes stress for the bacteria. When one subpopulation is placed under such a stressor, resistance may arise.[488]

These lineages will survive and reproduce as their weaker relatives perish, as we know, leaving plenty of space and

488 Jean-Yves Maillard et al., "Does Microbicide Use in Consumer Products Promote Antimicrobial Resistance? A Critical Review and Recommendations for a Cohesive Approach to Risk Assessment," *Microbial Drug Resistance* 19, no. 5 (October 2013): 344–54.

nutrients in the environment. We can now quickly identify a case of "what doesn't kill you makes you stronger." Most antibacterial chemicals select bacteria that endure their presence, and then we have to deal with them.[489] And just like that, a new source of resistance is well-integrated in the core of your house.

However, things can always get worse. When these bacteria develop a tolerance for the antibacterial compounds, there is also a chance of developing resistance for certain antibiotics. This phenomenon, called cross-resistance, has been demonstrated in several laboratory studies. For instance, triclosan, one of the most common chemicals found in antibacterial hand cleaners, dishwashing liquids, and other wash products, is an essential trigger of cross-resistance.[490]

When bacteria are exposed to triclosan for long periods, genetic mutations arise. Some of these mutations endow the bacteria with resistance to isoniazid, a common antibiotic used for treating TB. Now, take that both triclosan and its close chemical relative triclocarban (also widely used as an antibacterial), are present in 60 percent of America's streams and rivers.[491] Although both chemicals are efficiently removed from wastewater in treatment plants, they still end

---

489 Bonnie M. Marshall et al., "The Frequency of Antibiotic-Resistant Bacteria in Homes Differing in Their Use of Surface Antibacterial Agents," *Current Microbiology* 65, no. 4 (October 2012): 407–15.

490 Daniel E. Carey and Patrick J. McNamara, "The Impact of Triclosan on the Spread of Antibiotic Resistance in the Environment," *Frontiers in Microbiology* 5, (January 2014): 780.

491 Lucia Birošová and Mária Mikulášová, "Development of Triclosan and Antibiotic Resistance in Salmonella Enterica Serovar Typhimurium," *Journal of Medical Microbiology* 58, no. 4 (April 2009): 436–41.

up getting trapped in the produced sludge, which is used as fertilizer for crops, thereby opening a potential pathway for contamination of the food we eat.

Besides, we do clean surfaces and products not only in our household but also when treating the food we eat. Ironically, one of the settings where the stress of bacteria related to cleaning happens more often is in the food preservation chain.[492] In this industrial setting, the use of sublethal bacteriostatic methods may contribute to antibiotic resistance among food-related pathogens making their way to our tables if not careful.[493]

Despite such a wide variety of sources, AMR is not fully considered a crisis, rather than an emerging one. Many public health organizations have described its rapid emergence as a nightmare scenario that could end having catastrophic consequences. As such, MDR bacteria have been declared a substantial threat to US public health and national security, leading to more than 2.8 million antibiotic-resistant infections each year, and more than thirty-five thousand deaths.[494]

Nowadays, MRSA kills more Americans each year than HIV/AIDS, Parkinson's disease, emphysema, and homicide

---

492 Ana Alonso et al., "Environmental Selection of Antibiotic Resistance Genes," *Environmental Microbiology* 3, no. 1 (2001): 1–9.

493 Rosa Capita and Carlos Alonso-Calleja, "Antibiotic-Resistant Bacteria: A Challenge for the Food Industry," *Critical Reviews in Food Science and Nutrition* 53, no. 1 (January 2013): 11–48.

494 "Biggest Threats and Data | Antibiotic/Antimicrobial Resistance," Centers for Disease Control and Prevention, accessed July 10, 2020.

combined.[495] On the other hand, vancomycin-resistant enterococci (VRE) and a growing number of additional pathogens are developing resistance to many common antibiotics, most of them used as last resorts. Besides, the global spread of drug resistance among common respiratory pathogens, including *Streptococcus pneumoniae* and *Mycobacterium tuberculosis*, is an epidemic.

At the same time, MDR Gram-negative pathogens are also becoming increasingly prevalent in the community. One of the most worrisome and rapidly increasing community-acquired resistant diseases are found in *Neisseria gonorrhoeae*.[496] This bacterium causes gonorrhea, the second most commonly reported notifiable disease in the US. More than five hundred thousand cases of gonorrhea are isolated each year, yet CDC estimates 1.14 million new infections may occur. Half of these infections are resistant to at least one antibiotic that we use to treat them, a number that has never stopped rising since we first started studying these trends decades ago. Today, the US has only one recommended gonorrhea treatment option remaining.

With such beasts and a wide variety of ways to feed their monstrosity, the situation is becoming an overwhelming crisis. Humanity had a chance. We had the means to control bacteria and their way of infecting us. But not for long. This control blinded our search to destroy invisible enemies. We fought, but they fought back. Now, we face a time where

---

495 Akshay Shah, "Tackling the Crisis of Antibiotic Resistance," *South Asian Journal of Cancer* 2, no. 1 (January 2013): 3-4.

496 Takashi Deguchi et al., "Emergence and Spread of Drug Resistant Neisseria Gonorrhoeae," *Journal of Urology* 184, no. 3 (September 2010): 851–58.

bacterial diseases that were easily treated in the past; those to which we have developed immunity after centuries of suffering are coming back, carrying the powers of antibiotic resistance.

All questions have now turned into a single one: Do we have enough time to prepare for this future? We threw a stone over the sky and hoped it would never fall. However, it did. As we run out of effective drugs, understanding how antibiotic resistance works, the sources of this behavior, and how these pathogens behave becomes a pivotal activity and the last resource we might end up having in the near future. However, will that be enough?

CHAPTER 18

WHAT'S LEFT

"'Would you tell me, please, which way I ought to go from here?'
'That depends a good deal on where you want to get to,' said
the Cat.
'I don't much care where,' said Alice.
'Then it doesn't matter which way you go,' said the Cat."
—LEWIS CARROLL, ALICE IN WONDERLAND

Like me and any other human being on the planet, you are living trapped in a reality where antibiotics, the wonder drugs, do not work as we thought they would back in the last century. Still, my friend, we cling to this poisoned world while relying on what is killing us. Using a weapon whose time has been extended more than needed, we might end up involved in a future war in which our enemy is throwing nuclear bombs in response to our attacks with wooden sticks.

However, I am not saying that using those wooden sticks is useless. To completely abandon antibiotics and just focus on something else would be both worthless and insane. We still need them. As the road is coming to an end, we had better not rely too much on hope and start analyzing the crossroads ahead. Otherwise, we may end up in an abyss with no turning back.

Luckily, human beings possess bright minds and capable hands. We have mastered the power of science and became experts in fixing problems by finding alternatives. Decades of thoughtful research and keeping up with the challenges of the bacterial world have rendered results. Now it is time to harvest the apple tree and hope that the fruit we hold is the golden one.

The fight against AMR will be characterized by both a state of mind and art in which we need to change both our behavior and tools. Ironically, what might be the most efficient way to end this crisis involves changing ourselves. As such, the best way to fight AMR is to stop bacterial infections from reaching us.[497] *If there is no infection, there is no need to worry about one that cannot be treated.*

Nowadays, we all know that habits such as cleaning our hands with soap and warm water, making sure that our healthcare providers do the same, or avoiding contact when we are sick are things we all must do. They work in both theory and practice.[498] However, the reality is different, ranging from a simple "I forgot to do so" to the worst part of the spectrum found in an "*I do not care.*" Both answers and

---

497 Richard R. Yates, "New Intervention Strategies for Reducing Antibiotic Resistance," *Chest* 115, no. 3 SUPPL. (March 1999): 24S-27S.

498 Malene Plejdrup Hansen et al., "Antibiotic Resistance: What Are the Opportunities for Primary Care in Alleviating the Crisis?," *Frontiers in Public Health* 3 (February 2015): 35.

whatever comes within them impact society, with a weak equilibrium between those who make the rules and those who break them. We know that a world where everyone respected those practices would be ideal. However, can you even think about it?

So, let us assume that the simple fact of preventing all infections from happening is out of our league. Humanity is not yet prepared for that. So then, what do we do now? If we cannot change the minds of people, the best approach possible is to properly use the drug that is behind all this mess. That practice is called antibiotic stewardship, which aim to prescribe antibiotics only when necessary, while tailoring treatments as narrowly as possible.[499]

In parallel with all these approaches, some big pharmaceutical companies have continued innovating and producing our most valuable real resource: traditional antibiotics. Although it is true that the antibiotic pipeline, almost exhausted, is still releasing new compounds with different types of modifications, those can attack a fewer number of bacteria each time.[500]

As a consequence, science is slowly turning down the antibiotics path and looking elsewhere for solutions, hoping that whatever comes after becomes the new penicillin, just without all the associated problems. As such, over the last century,

---

499 Mary Lou Manning, Jeanne Pfeiffer, and Elaine L. Larson, "Combating Antibiotic Resistance: The Role of Nursing in Antibiotic Stewardship," *American Journal of Infection Control* 44, no. 12 (December 2016): 1454–57.

500 Bashar Hamad, "The Antibiotics Market," *Nature Reviews Drug Discovery* 9, no. 9 (September 2010): 675–76.

alternatives to antibiotics have been developed, tested, and deployed on the battlefield against AMR. So, what do we have out there?

One of the most promising therapies to fight AMR comes from nature itself: bacteriophages, which means "*bacteria eater*." Bacteriophages are a type of virus that infects bacteria.[501] The natural hunter of our hunter. These microorganisms are everywhere: on land, in water, and within all forms of life, including you, just as their prey. All of them are composed of a nucleic acid molecule surrounded by a protein structure, as happens in many types of viruses.

Bacteriophages can attach themselves to a susceptible bacterium and infect the host cell.[502] Following infection, the virus can hijack the bacterium's cellular machinery to prevent it from producing bacterial components that might interfere with its plans. Instead, the virus forces the cell to produce viral components. Eventually, new bacteriophages assemble inside, growing and spreading over time. Finally, they burst out of the bacterium in a process called lysis, which results in hundreds of them being released to the environment, ready to infect closer bacteria. Then, the process is repeated. All over again.

Although under debate, nowadays it is widely accepted that in 1915, the English bacteriologist Frederick Twort was the first

---

501 Donna H. Duckworth and Paul A. Gulig, "Bacteriophages: Potential Treatment for Bacterial Infections," *BioDrugs* 16, no. 1 (August 2002): 57–62.

502 Elizabeth Kutter and Alexander Sulakvelidze, *Bacteriophages: Biology and Applications* (Boca Raton, FL: CRC Press, 2004), 108.

to suggest that a virus was responsible for previous observations of a "*factor*" (as he called it) that killed bacteria.[503] A year before, Frederick plated some smallpox vaccines on nutrient agar and obtained large bacterial colonies of several colors.[504] He then took a closer look at what was growing on the plates and found small areas that would not grow when transferred to different plates. Surprised by this behavior, he quickly realized these areas were the result of the destruction of the bacterial cells.[505]

After several experiments, he discovered the essential features of bacteriophages. However, he seemed to favor the idea that the principle was not a separate form of life, but an enzyme secreted by the bacteria. He published these results in The Lancet in 1915 and called the mysterious element the *bacteriolytic agent*.[506] Unfortunately, his discovery was ignored by the scientific community, and when World War I erupted, he had to shut down his laboratory and research.

However, when something important is meant to see the light, it will, one way or another. In 1916, the French-Canadian microbiologist Felix d'Herelle, who was working at the Institute Pasteur in Paris, picked up where Twort left off. On September 3, 1917, he announced the discovery of "an invisible,

---

503 Forest Rowher, Merry Youle, Heather Maughan and Nao Hisakawa. *Life in Our Phage World* (Cincinnati, OH: Holon, 2014), 125-8.

504 Hongping Wei, "Bacteriophages, Revitalized after 100 Years in the Shadow of Antibiotics," *Virologica Sinica* 30, no. 1 (February 2015): 1–2.

505 Eric C. Keen, "A Century of Phage Research: Bacteriophages and the Shaping of Modern Biology," *BioEssays* 37, no. 1 (January 2015): 6–9.

506 F. W. Twort, "An Investigation on the Nature of Ultra-Microscopic Viruses," *The Lancet* 186, no. 4814 (December 1915): 1241–43.

antagonistic microbe of the dysentery bacillus." Two years after, Felix isolated phages from chicken feces, successfully treating a plague of chicken typhus with them.[507]

Shocked by this discovery, he first proposed phages as a therapy for human infections. That year, Felix and several hospital interns ingested a phage cocktail to check its safety. After a successful demonstration, they had to test its therapeutic effect. For the experiment, they used a twelve-year-old boy with severe dysentery.[508] Penicillin was still only a dream, so the expectations for the boy were pessimistic. With nothing to lose, they gave the cocktail of phages. Soon after, the kid's symptoms cleared up, and after only a single dose, and he was able to recover within a few days.

Despite this success, his work was under constant attack from critics, most of them closer to his field. Yet, he published his results in 1931, claiming the therapeutic effect of something that no one really understood. By that time, several articles reported that bacteria become resistant against a single phage, the reason why Felix suggested using "phage cocktails" containing different phage strains.[509] In 1930, the vast majority of his works were published in non-English journals. As a

---

507 Nina Chanishvili, "Phage Therapy-History from Twort and d'Herelle Through Soviet Experience to Current Approaches," *Advances in Virus Research* 83 (January 2012): 3–40.

508 Eric C. Keen, "Felix d'Herelle and Our Microbial Future," *Future Microbiology* 7, no. 12 (December 2012): 1337–39.

509 Benjamin K. Chan, Stephen T. Abedon, and Catherine Loc-Carrillo, "Phage Cocktails and the Future of Phage Therapy," *Future Microbiology* 8, no. 6 (June 2013): 769–83.

consequence, they did not immediately cause any impact in Western Europe and the US.

With the liberation of Europe on D-Day, his therapy's wonders were too late. Penicillin was already saving thousands and found its way into the hospitals in the West, filling the hopes and pockets of many alike. As it was more reliable and easier to use than phage therapy, the antibiotic soon became the method of choice.[510] It was not the right time.

Nowadays, with growing support over the past fifteen years from researchers and doctors, phage therapy has been gaining attention as an alternative to fight AMR.[511] Despite this, the main challenge that the therapy is facing is found in the regulatory pathway. Still, in February 2019, the US Food and Drug Administration (FDA) approved the first clinical trial of intravenously administered phage therapy in the US.[512]

However, bacteria do have something to say to all of this, which might be unavoidable due to the long-term relationship between the virus and the host. In a laboratory setting, bacterial resistance against phages has been widely reported, with a quick appearance.[513] However, just as bacteria can

---

510 A. Sulakvelidze and Jr Morris, "Bacteriophages as Therapeutic Agents," *Annals of Medicine* 33, no. 8 (November 2001): 507–9.

511 Meritxell García-Quintanilla et al., "Emerging Therapies for Multidrug Resistant Acinetobacter Baumannii," *Trends in Microbiology* 21, no. 3 (March 2013): 157–63.

512 Rebecca Voelker, "FDA Approves Bacteriophage Trial," *JAMA* 321, no. 7 (February 2019): 638.

513 Paul Hyman and Stephen T. Abedon, "Bacteriophage Host Range and Bacterial Resistance.," *Advances in Applied Microbiology* 70 (January 2010): 217–48.

evolve to show resistance, viruses can evolve to overcome it. Still, bacteriophages are very specific, meaning that they can target only one or a few bacteria strains. Therefore, this feature makes phage resistance a minor problem compared to the one found in antibiotics.[514]

So, viruses aside, what else do we have? The second group of relevant alternatives to antibiotics is antimicrobial peptides, also known as AMPs, defined as segments or portions of the innate immune response found among all life classes.[515] Over time, AMPs have demonstrated the ability to kill bacteria in a wide variety of settings, working both broadly and specifically and showing clinical promise.

Unlike most conventional antibiotics, AMPs have a defined composition, charge, and size that allows the molecules to attach to and insert into membrane bilayers to form pores by different mechanisms.[516] Alternately, they may penetrate the cell to bind intracellular molecules, which are crucial to cell living, inhibiting cell wall synthesis, alteration of the cytoplasmic membrane, or inhibition of DNA, RNA, and protein synthesis.[517] However, in many cases, the exact mechanism of killing is not known.

514 Clara Torres-Barceló, "Phage Therapy Faces Evolutionary Challenges," *Viruses* 10, no. 6 (June 2018): 323.

515 Ali Bahar and Dacheng Ren, "Antimicrobial Peptides," *Pharmaceuticals* 6, no. 12 (November 013): 1543–75.

516 Michael R. Yeaman and Nannette Y. Yount, "Mechanisms of Antimicrobial Peptide Action and Resistance," *Pharmacological Reviews* 55, no. 1 (March 2003): 27–55.

517 Richard M. Epand and Hans J. Vogel, "Diversity of Antimicrobial Peptides and Their Mechanisms of Action," *Biochimica et Biophysica Acta — Biomembranes* 1462, no. 1–2 (December 1999): 11–28.

The first report of the potential of AMPs as antimicrobial agents was done by Alexander Fleming himself when he discovered lysozyme in 1922 while treating bacterial cultures with nasal mucus from a patient suffering from a head cold.[518]

The next breakthrough came in 1939 with the isolation of Gramidicin A, B, and C, the first peptide family used clinically as antimicrobials, which was completed in 1942 thanks to the work of Georgyi Frantsevitch Gause and his wife Maria Brazhnikova, who isolated Gramidicin S from the bacterium *Bacillus brevis*.[519]

Rapidly after the discovery, Gramidicin S was used in the Soviet Union's military hospitals to treat infections. Due to the success of the clinical trials, the compound eventually found its way to the front lines of World War II by 1946. They were the first AMPs to be commercially manufactured as antibiotics.

Sadly, with the advent of penicillin and streptomycin in 1943 and the beginning of the "Golden Age of antibiotics," the general public and research suffered from a rapid loss of interest in the therapeutic potential of AMPs. Still, more and more AMPs were isolated. At the time these works

---

518 P. Jollès, "Relationship between Chemical Structure and Biological Activity of Hen Egg-White Lysozyme and Lysozymes of Different Species," *Proceedings of the Royal Society of London. Series B. Biological Sciences* 167, no. 1009 (April 1967): 350–64.

519 Yasha M. Gall and Mikhail B. Konashev, "The Discovery of Gramicidin S: The Intellectual Transformation of G.F. Gause from Biologist to Researcher of Antibiotics and on Its Meaning for the Fate of Russian Genetics," *History and Philosophy of the Life Sciences* 23, no. 1 (2001): 137–50.

were undertaken, the rise of multidrug-resistant microbial pathogens awakened interest in AMPs once again. It was this point in time that some sources consider the exact origin of research into these drugs.

However, just as they had learned to confront antibiotics and bacteriophages, bacteria also know how to defeat AMPs, and they know well. Bacteria use various resistance strategies to avoid being killed by these peptides. For instance, some bacterial species can alter their net surface charges, such as *Staphylococcus aureus*, reducing the net negative charge hence preventing the AMP from going inside.[520] Another brilliant case is found in *Haemophilus influenzae*, which can remodel its membranes completely. Doing so, the bacterium seems like it was already attacked by the AMPs.[521]

While laboratory studies show that resistance can evolve naturally, there is increasing concern over the use of synthetic copies of AMPs, which can lead to a faster resistance. Therefore, we might better find a different way to use them or isolate new ones, which likely will happen due to the wide variety of possibilities out there within the realm of mother nature.

Another alternative to antibiotics comes from a relatively small dimension: the nanoscale. Nanotechnology, which was

---

520 D. I. Andersson, D. Hughes, and J. Z. Kubicek-Sutherland, "Mechanisms and Consequences of Bacterial Resistance to Antimicrobial Peptides," *Drug Resistance Updates* 26 (May 2016): 43–57.

521 Timothy D. Starner et al., "Susceptibility of Nontypeable Haemophilus Influenzae to Human β-Defensins Is Influenced by Lipooligosaccharide Acylation," *Infection and Immunity* 70, no. 9 (September 2002): 5287–89.

released to society with a simple question, "Why can't we write the entire twenty-four volumes of the Encyclopedia Britannica on the head of a pen?" is nowadays called to revolutionize every single field of science in one way or another.

On December 29, 1959, at the American Physical Society's annual meeting, it was held at the California Institute of Technology (Caltech), the American theoretical physicist Richard P. Feynman gave his famous after-dinner lecture named "There's Plenty of Room at the Bottom" at the nearby Huntington-Sheraton Hotel. This was just the beginning.[522,523]

Soon after, nanotechnology met medicine, and the possibility of nanomedicine was presented. Since then, different nanomaterials have been used in various biomedical applications, finding a unique position in those involving the treatment of bacterial infections. From carbon-based nanostructures to polymeric particles or solid-lipid nanoparticles passing through liposomes, nanocrystals, and dendrimers, the list of nanomaterials with antibacterial properties is almost endless.

But why are nanomaterials suitable antibacterial agents? They may offer a promising solution as these nanosized materials can combat bacteria and act as carriers for antibiotics and natural antimicrobial compounds to achieve better delivery.

---

522 Richard P. Feynman, "There's Plenty of Room at the Bottom," (Transcript of a talk presented to the American Physical Society in Pasasena, CA, December 29, 1959).

523 J. E. Hulla, S. C. Sahu, and A. W. Hayes, "Nanotechnology: History and Future," *Human and Experimental Toxicology* 34, no. 12 (December 2015): 1318–21.

While various chemistries have been explored as nano-drug carriers, metallic vectors, such as gold nanoparticles, are attractive as core materials due to their substantially inert and nontoxic nature.[524]

Arguably, the most attractive aspect of nanoparticle-based drug delivery systems is their ability to introduce a wide range of drugs in different biological systems. For instance, antibiotics can be bound to the nanoparticles' large surface area or be contained within nanocages. Once functionalized, these nanomaterials are easily delivered to the site of infection in an effective and relatively safe manner by having a controlled rate of targeted delivery. While poor membrane transport limits antibiotic effectiveness, drug-loaded nanoparticles can enter host cells, facilitating their intracellular entry.[525]

Nevertheless, the most relevant therapeutic appeal of nanoparticles is enhanced by their ability to confer physical protection against bacterial resistance mechanisms. Therefore, different nanomaterials can be loaded with multiple drug combinations leading to the increasingly complex antimicrobial mechanism of action, to which bacteria are unlikely to develop resistance.[526]

---

524 Lev Dykman and Nikolai Khlebtsov, "Gold Nanoparticles in Biomedical Applications: Recent Advances and Perspectives," *Chemical Society Reviews* 41, no. 6 (February 2012): 2256–82.

525 Andrew L. Neal, "What Can Be Inferred from Bacterium-Nanoparticle Interactions about the Potential Consequences of Environmental Exposure to Nanoparticles?," *Ecotoxicology* 17, no. 5 (July 2008): 362–71.

526 Shariq Qayyum and Asad U. Khan, "Nanoparticles: Vs. Biofilms: A Battle against Another Paradigm of Antibiotic Resistance," *MedChemComm* 7, no. 8 (August 2016): 1479–98.

Nanomaterials, either combined with drugs or as sole therapeutics, can exert their antibacterial activity via a multitude of mechanisms, such as the direct interaction with the bacterial cell wall; triggering innate as well as adaptive host immune responses; generation of reactive oxygen species (ROS), well-known unstable molecules that contain oxygen and readily react with other molecules in a cell leading to damage; or the induction of intracellular effects linked with interactions with DNA and proteins.[527,528]

However, once more, *there is a "but."* This beneficial potential of nanomaterials is usually believed to be found often just in laboratory settings. As such, some studies report the development of bacterial resistance against nanoparticles made of silver, which have been extensively used for medical purposes.[529]

Now, as you may have noticed while reading to this point, there are plenty of good alternatives to fight the development of antibiotic resistance in bacteria. While we are learning from them, bacteria are quickly showing us that they know how to defeat our efforts. There is a crude reality behind this trend: It does not matter how many ways we find to fight bacteria—they will eventually find out how to counteract

527 Yael N. Slavin et al., "Metal Nanoparticles: Understanding the Mechanisms behind Antibacterial Activity," *Journal of Nanobiotechnology* 15, no. 1 (October 2017): 65.

528 Wen Ru Li et al., "Antibacterial Activity and Mechanism of Silver Nanoparticles on Escherichia Coli," *Applied Microbiology and Biotechnology* 85, no. 4 (January 2010): 1115–22.

529 Aleš Panáček et al., "Bacterial Resistance to Silver Nanoparticles and How to Overcome It," *Nature Nanotechnology* 13, no. 1 (January 2018): 65–71.

and fight back any treatment. They will adapt, because that is what they do; that is how bacteria survive.

The post-antibiotic era is like any other period in our history: it will have an end. When this time arrives, no antibiotic left nor an alternative to which the bacterial world has not developed resistance will be available for those who suffer. In the end, we live in their world, not the other way around. Does that mean that we have to stop fighting, give up, and stay still waiting for the inevitable to happen? No, it does not.

In the same way that they do, we will eventually find answers. Some of them will be far from current conceptions, strange to our present state of mind. However, it will be the time for those who will come after to decide. Choose between embracing the challenge and move forward, or do what we did, fight for a future where the choice is there, along with everything else.

CHAPTER 19

TO BE WHAT WE CHOOSE TO BECOME

"The future is there . . . looking back at us. Trying to make sense of the fiction we will have become."

—WILLIAM GIBSON, PATTERN RECOGNITION

By 2050, ten million people could die each year from bacterial diseases that have become resistant to the antibiotics we use today.[530] That means one person every three seconds. Superbugs will account for more deaths than any other diseases, even if you put them together. Now, if you just google *Antibiotic resistance* and *2050* and a few websites, including the WHO and the Smithsonian, reports will pop up with different messages whose outcomes are always the same. AMR is called to be the killer of the century, with numbers way more prominent than any other disease in the world.

---

530 Marc Mendelson and Malebona Precious Matsoso, "The World Health Organization Global Action Plan for Antimicrobial Resistance," *South African Medical Journal* 105, no. 5 (2015): 325.

Can you imagine living in a time like that? Everyone tends to look at the problems that they have to face in the present. Most of them are huge enough to not allow us to rise and look behind them to what is coming. Nowadays, in the middle of 2020, the COVID-19 crisis is peaking, altering every single aspect of society.

SARS-COVID-2 is striking us into the ground, reducing to ashes every conception we had about disease. We were supposed to be prepared, and clearly, we were not. Our whole society was shocked, and the scientific community started making the pandemic their primary focus: new policies, the establishment of funds, and monopolization of research.

We are all doing what we have to do. Thanks to that, there are more than a few vaccines in development and quite a handful of treatments worldwide for mild and severe cases. In one way or another, we quickly organized and responded to the challenge in front of us.

To date, the pandemic has caused the global social and economic disruption, including the most significant global recession since the Great Depression and global famines, effecting almost three hundred million people worldwide.[531] It has led to the total or partial shutdown of many countries for weeks and even months. Chaos and hysteria have led to widespread supply shortages and societal disturbance.[532]

---

531 Nuno Fernandes, "Economic Effects of Coronavirus Outbreak (COVID-19) on the World Economy," *SSRN Electronic Journal*, (March 2020).

532 A. Spinelli and G. Pellino, "COVID-19 Pandemic: Perspectives on an Unfolding Crisis," *British Journal of Surgery* 107, no. 7 (June 2020): 785–87.

Be witness, my dear reader, to the outcome, in just a few words, of a crisis that has killed over half a million people in the world. Can you imagine what would cause another one whose death toll will be ten times more significant? Honestly, I would not even dare to think about it.

Now, let me tell you something; this current catastrophe is not like any other that came before it. The COVID-19 pandemic is slowly dragging a second slow-motion pandemic behind, one that we already know too well: the AMR crisis. This combination has no precedents, and the outcome is far from desired. Let me explain why.

Even though SARS-CoV-2 is not affected by antibiotics, new data from hospitals worldwide reveals a crude reality. Their data shows that high proportions of patients—more than 90 percent in some countries—are being treated with antibiotics.[533] But why? Antibiotics do not work with viruses, and we know that. However, they can control whatever comes after, and this is often a secondary bacterial infection.

When a virus makes its appearance, there is always a struggle. If you catch the infection, your whole body enters an alarm setting, and fighting the parasite becomes the priority. A series of chained reactions end with the awakening of the owner's body defense system. Then, a fight starts from which you will recover if your immune system works as it is supposed to.

---

533 Julie L. Gerberding "Antibiotic Resistance: The Hidden Threat Lurking behind COVID-19," *STAT*, March 23, 2020.

Over the course or at the end of the infection, the immune system is entirely exhausted, getting weaker over time. Using this weakness to their advantage, opportunistic pathogenic bacteria take the chance and jump right into the system. Secondary bacterial infection is then developed, making the problem far worse than it was before.[534]

While we are still struggling to find the best drug or treatment for the virus, the only available resource to fight the bacteria passed through the use of antibiotics. Then, hospitals and clinicians do what they have to do to save a life, and they use antibiotics. There is no blame there. We use what we have available to save our kind.

Secondary bacterial infections are bound to viruses in ways that you would not even imagine. Several viral illnesses, such as the ones caused by influenza, respiratory syncytial, or parainfluenza viruses, can be extremely complicated by a secondary bacterial infection.[535]

Just imagine a bacterial population entering the body in stealth mode behind the virus. While the latter is causing the mess, rendering visible and painful symptoms, those bacteria have evolved to hide behind them and show symptoms similar to the virus to become almost impossible to

---

534 Michael J Cox et al., "Co-Infections: Potentially Lethal and Unexplored in COVID-19," *The Lancet Microbe* 1, no. 1 (May 2020): e11.

535 Denise E. Morris, David W. Cleary, and Stuart C. Clarke, "Secondary Bacterial Infections Associated with Influenza Pandemics," *Frontiers in Microbiology* 8, no. JUN (June 2017): 1041.

differentiate.[536] If you want to know these monsters, their names are *Streptococcus pneumoniae*, *Haemophilus influenzae*, and our well-known *Staphylococcus aureus*, among many others.

One of the worst bacterial complications behind viral infections is pneumonia, an old fellow-traveler to viral pandemics.[537] The relationship of the bacteria with the viral disease is well-linked and developed, appearing in up to 75 percent of those infected with influenza.[538]

In 2007, a group of scientists reviewed a raft of scientific literature from the 1918 flu, the most severe viral pandemic in recent history, with a third of the world's population becoming infected.[539] The scientists reexamined tissue samples stored from autopsies done during that outbreak. The conclusions were striking: the vast majority of the possibly one hundred million deaths during the pandemic were caused

536 John C. Kash and Jeffery K. Taubenberger, "The Role of Viral, Host, and Secondary Bacterial Factors in Influenza Pathogenesis," *American Journal of Pathology* 185, no. 6 (June 2015): 1528–36.

537 Chandini Raina MacIntyre et al., "The Role of Pneumonia and Secondary Bacterial Infection in Fatal and Serious Outcomes of Pandemic Influenza a(H1N1)Pdm09," *BMC Infectious Diseases* 18, no. 1 (December 2018): 1–20.

538 David M. Morens, Jeffery K. Taubenberger, and Anthony S. Fauci, "Predominant Role of Bacterial Pneumonia as a Cause of Death in Pandemic Influenza: Implications for Pandemic Influenza Preparedness," *The Journal of Infectious Diseases* 198, no. 7 (October 2008): 962–70.

539 Julie L. McAuley et al., "Expression of the 1918 Influenza A Virus PB1-F2 Enhances the Pathogenesis of Viral and Secondary Bacterial Pneumonia," *Cell Host and Microbe* 2, no. 4 (October 2007): 240–49.

not by the influenza virus.[540] The cause behind such a death toll was a bacterial infection affecting lung tissue traumatized by the virus.

One year after that analysis was published, the 2009 H1N1 epidemic began. That outbreak was initially considered mild by the WHO, with an estimated death toll of around two hundred eighty-four thousand people by the CDC. Once the pandemic started to disappear, data showed that up to 55 percent of the number of deaths were caused not by the initial assault of the flu, but by bacterial pneumonia coming along afterward.[541] Antibiotics were used to treat them, but they did not work.

In front of us, we now have a perfectly imbalanced equation accounting for necessity and misuse. When these are mixed in an infectious disease matter, we have a problem, a burden of AMR that is growing quicker than it should. Sadly, there is nothing we can do about it.

In the present, without the involvement of the COVID-19 crisis, seven hundred thousand people in the world die of drug-resistant diseases every year.[542] From those, two hundred thirty thousand deaths are caused by multidrug-resistant

---

540 John F. Brundage and G. Dennis Shanks, "What Really Happened during the 1918 Influenza Pandemic? The Importance of Bacterial Secondary Infections," *The Journal of Infectious Diseases* 196, no. 11 (December 2007): 1717–18.

541 John C. Kash et al., "Lethal Synergism of 2009 Pandemic H1N1 Influenza Virus and Streptococcus Pneumoniae Coinfection Is Associated with Loss of Murine Lung Repair Responses," *MBio* 2, no. 5 (September 2011).

542 World Health Organization "New Report Calls for Urgent Action to Avert Antimicrobial Resistance Crisis," April 29, 2019.

TB. Simultaneously, common problems like sexually transmitted diseases and urinary tract infections are also becoming resistant to treatments. Similarly, hospital procedures like C-sections or knee replacements are becoming more dangerous, with drug-resistant pathogens surviving the course of antibiotics that are often given to the patients before the operation.[543]

Antibiotics allowed modern medicine to set up and establish the standards we have today. These drugs enabled most of the techniques we use today to be done in a safe environment. Nowadays, they are also the cause of the slow destruction of these standards. Yet, doctors, farmers, and others continue to use too many antibiotics, more than we need, more than we should have, driving the resistance to levels that are off the charts.

A recent report from the United Nations added that drug resistance could severely mess up our economy by causing health care expenditures to skyrocket, prompting economic damage on par with the 2008–2009 financial crisis. One way or another, it will threaten everything that is part of our society.

Unfortunately, the AMR crisis is crossing medical boundaries and moving quickly toward making one of the medical practices that humanity relies most on impossible: cancer treatment. For instance, the UK's oncologists are extremely

543 Aude Teillant et al., "Potential Burden of Antibiotic Resistance on Surgery and Cancer Chemotherapy Antibiotic Prophylaxis in the USA: A Literature Review and Modelling Study," *The Lancet Infectious Diseases* 15, no. 12 (December 2015): 1429–37.

worried about the rise of antibiotic resistance and the consequences of this in their patients.[544] Forty-one percent of
the surveyed oncologists have seen a rise in drug-resistant
infections in the past year and almost all of them are worried
about the impact of superbugs on their patients. Moreover,
46 percent of cancer doctors polled say they believe drug-resistant infections could make chemotherapy unviable.

Can you imagine a world where almost twenty million
new cancer patients every year would be unable to receive
treatment? A current death toll of almost ten million deaths
worldwide would significantly grow to a rate that we cannot
even predict. Everyday cancer patients rely on antibiotics for
the prevention and treatment of infections. This is one of the
most common complications of their treatment. What would
happen if there is no antibiotic available?

Now, I have to be honest with you; a future dominated by
AMR does not seem like an excellent place to live. In a world
where going to a hospital is not safe, the privilege of health
will become an exception that not many will be able to have
within a continually changing world.

However, whether or not a reality like that becomes real, to
understand how the future will be, we have to look back to
the past, somewhere around the time the first chapter of this
book talked about. Something happened back then, an event
that was called to write the future of every other species on
the planet.

544 Kathy Talkington "Oncologists Fear Rising Antibiotic Resistance Will
    Make Cancer Treatments Less Effective" *The Pew Charitable Trusts*,
    March 11, 2020.

That *something*—let us call it "the incident"—might have gone unnoticed for many life forms, but it was a real revolution in the bacterial world. This event's roots deeply bury themselves into layers and layers of constant evolution. Nowadays, it is impossible to distinguish it from any other episode in the history of our planet. This incident has three main implications that I would like you to interiorize and keep once you close this book and put it back in your shelf:

- Firstly, bacteria created antibiotics billions of years ago; hence, resistance is primarily the result of bacterial adaptation to millions of years of antibiotic exposure without human intervention. Bacterial species have been using antibiotics as weapons to defeat and conquer other populations to reach new nutrient-rich environments. They have been doing this long before any eukaryotic cell was a reality, and doing so, they have developed resistance. The bacterial world has been breaking and creating new equilibria all throughout the history of the planet, regardless of any other species rising or falling around them. They did not care; all that mattered was to expand and consume, reaching the equilibrium again, and adapting until a new bacterium came along, starting all over again.

- Secondly, bacteria did not need a *superior* and intelligent species like us dumping antibiotics at them, claiming overuse and misuse of the drugs. We need to erase from our mind the concept that inappropriate antibiotic use is what selects for resistance. Microbial exposure to all antibiotics is what drives the speed of resistance, whether appropriately prescribed or not. Thus, even if all inappropriate antibiotic use was erased in the future, antibiotic-resistant infections would still occur, just at a slower rate.

- Thirdly, after billions of years of evolution, microbes have most likely produced and used antibiotics against every biochemical target that can be attacked; hence they have developed resistance mechanisms to protect all those bio-chemical targets. In 2016, a thousand feet under the New Mexico soil, in the deepest limestone cave in the country, researchers found an ancient bacterium that was resistant to many antibiotics used in human medicine nowadays. Surprisingly, the bacteria have not had any contact with humans or contaminated soil before after four million years of isolation.[545] Evolution gave this bacterium the ability to fight antibiotics, some of them not even dis-covered yet. These results underscore a critical reality: Antibiotic resistance already existed, widely disseminated in nature, to drugs we have not yet invented.

What are the obvious consequence of these three statements? Since their human discovery in 1928, the use of antibiotics has saved countless lives and changed medicine forever. At the same time, they have driven the resistance that threatens their very miracle.

Ultimately, humanity will run out of bacterial targets, and resistance mechanisms will become prevalent in most human pathogenic strains. There will be a moment when bacteria will show resistance to whatever we throw at them, antibiotics

---

545 J. H.(Han) van der Kolk, "Antibiotic Resistance from Prehistoric to Mod-ern Times," *Veterinary Quarterly* 35, no. 1 (January 2015): 1.

or not. Then, we will carry diseases with us for which no treatments are available, and just like our first ancestors, two options will arise: either we learn how to live with them or they will outlive us.

So, what is the solution? Find a way to fight bacteria without killing them.

But how? One possibility would be to disarm bacterial pathogens instead of showing them retribution for the damage they are causing. Doing so, these bacteria will not trigger any disease even when they are present. For instance, we can inhibit the synthesis of endotoxins (the compounds responsible for infections), so they can infect but cause no harm.

Another option would be to find a way to inhibit the biochemical signaling processes involved in the recognition of nutrients in wounds and other areas prompt to infection, so bacteria would lack interest in proliferating there. Alternatively, we could passively starve microbes of nutrients, so they cannot reproduce in the host. On the other hand, we could also protect our microbiota with probiotics, making native bacterial colonies so strong and well-prepared that they can efficiently deal with invasive species.

The possibilities are endless, and bacteria might develop resistance to all of them. Still, there is a chance, and where there is a will, there is a way: to adapt or perish. By adapting, we would have the potential to behave like those bacteria which eons ago started producing antibiotics to defeat others threatening their world.

Eventually, with enough time and resources, humankind will generate a short, narrowly focused, and customized treatment to control bacterial infections. This possible solution, whose shape I hope will be brought to reality, will allow for two pivotal behaviors: enhanced efficacy and reduced collateral damage. Why would bacteria develop resistance if there was no attack to defend against?

Whatever this potential solution is, it will need to be definitive. Or at least, for a while. The approach will pave the way for similar and alternative methods, whose collection will bring us closer to the brighter future that the dawn of antibiotics made us dream of.

Then, one day, we will simply have it, and within enough time, we will learn how to master its features. What then? I am a firm believer in the paradox of duality. I think that every aspect of life is created from a balanced interaction of competing forces that lean on an equilibrium that is never fully reached. Nonetheless, these forces are not just opposites; they are complementary. Therefore, they will bring us to a present where humanity will be granted with two choices. Either to widely use the solution and fail, as we did with antibiotics; or to pursue a complete reconceptualization of our relationship with bacteria.

Now, I do not know what the future will bring and what the final situation will be. Still, I believe that only the second path will lead to the best possible outcome: a long-term relationship where humanity will not seek the annihilation of the bacterial world, but instead to achieve peaceful coexistence. What might seem like a utopic claim may one day become an answer to a time that is yet to come, but not as far away as we would like to think.

APPENDIX

APPENDIX INTRODUCTION

Drexler, Madeleine and Institute of Medicine. *What You Need to Know About Infectious Disease*. Washington, DC: National Academies Press, 2010.

Sender, Ron, Shai Fuchs, and Ron Milo. "Revised Estimates for the Number of Human and Bacteria Cells in the Body." *PLOS Biology* 14, no. 8 (August 2016): e1002533. *https://doi.org/10.1371/journal.pbio.1002533*.

APPENDIX CHAPTER 1

Albertsson, T., D. Semenov, and Th. Henning. "Chemodynamical Deuterium Fractionation in the Early Solar Nebula: The Origin of Water on Earth and in Asteroids and Comets." *Astrophysical Journal* 784, no. 1 (March 2014): 39. *https://doi.org/10.1088/0004-637X/784/1/39*.

Baross, John A., and Sarah E. Hoffman. "Submarine Hydrothermal Vents and Associated Gradient Environments as Sites for the Origin and Evolution of Life." *Origins of Life and Evolution of the Biosphere* 15, no. 4 (December 1985): 327–45. *https://doi.org/10.1007/BF01808177*.

Baumgartner, Raphael J., Martin J. Van Kranendonk, David Wacey, Marco L. Fiorentini, Martin Saunders, Stefano Caruso, Anais Pages, Martin Homann, and Paul Guagliardo. "Nano-Porous Pyrite and Organic Matter in 3.5-Billion-Year-Old Stromatolites Record Primordial Life." *Geology* 47, no. 11 (November 2019): 1039–43. *https://doi.org/10.1130/G46365.1.*

Bryson, Bill. *In a Sunburned Country.* Portland: Broadway Books, 2000.

Canup, Robin M., and Erik Asphaug. "Origin of the Moon in a Giant Impact near the End of the Earth's Formation." *Nature* 412, no. 6848 (August 2001): 708–12. *https://doi.org/10.1038/35089010.*

Chalmers, J.A., and B. Chalmers. " XXXVII. The Expanding Universe—an Alternative View ." *The London, Edinburgh, and Dublin Philosophical Magazine and Journal of Science* 19, no. 126 (February 1935): 436–46. *https://doi.org/10.1080/14786443508561389.*

Ćuk, Matija, and Sarah T. Stewart. "Making the Moon from a Fast-Spinning Earth: A Giant Impact Followed by Resonant Despinning." *Science* 338, no. 6110 (November 2012): 1047–52. *https://doi.org/10.1126/science.1225542.*

Dauphas, Nicolas, Nicole L. Cates, Stephen J. Mojzsis, and Vincent Busigny. "Identification of Chemical Sedimentary Protoliths Using Iron Isotopes in the > 3750 Ma Nuvvuagittuq Supracrustal Belt, Canada." *Earth and Planetary Science Letters* 254, no. 3–4 (February 2007): 358–76. *https://doi.org/10.1016/j.epsl.2006.11.042.*

Delsemme, A. H. "Cometary Origin of Carbon, Nitrogen and Water on the Earth." *Origins of Life and Evolution of the Biosphere* 21, no. 5–6 (September 1991): 279–98. *https://doi.org/10.1007/BF01808303.*

Dodd, Matthew S., Dominic Papineau, Tor Grenne, John F. Slack, Martin Rittner, Franco Pirajno, Jonathan O'Neil, and Crispin T.S. Little. "Evidence for Early Life in Earth's Oldest Hydrothermal Vent Precipitates." *Nature* 543, no. 7643 (March 2017): 60–64. *https://doi.org/10.1038/nature21377.*

Feltman, Rachel "Stephen Hawking Thinks He Knows What Happened before the Beginning of Time," Popular Science, March 2, 2018 accessed October 24, 2020, *https://www.popsci.com/stephen-hawking-neil-degrasse-tyson-big-bang/.*

Ghosh, Pallab. "Earliest Evidence of Life on Earth 'found' — BBC News." Science & Environment, 2017. *https://www.bbc.com/news/science-environment-39117523.*

Gomes, R., H. F. Levison, K. Tsiganis, and A. Morbidelli. "Origin of the Cataclysmic Late Heavy Bombardment Period of the Terrestrial Planets." *Nature* 435, no. 7041 (May 2005): 466–69. *https://doi.org/10.1038/nature03676.*

Kasting, James F., and Janet L. Siefert. "Life and the Evolution of Earth's Atmosphere." *Science* 296, no. 5570 (May 2002): 1066–68. *https://doi.org/10.1126/science.1071184.*

Knoll, Andrew H. "Paleobiological Perspectives on Early Microbial Evolution." *Cold Spring Harbor Perspectives in Biology* 7, no. 7 (July 2015): 1–17. *https://doi.org/10.1101/cshperspect.a018093.*

Kuiper, G. P. "On the Origin of the Solar System." *Proceedings of the National Academy of Sciences* 37, no. 1 (January 1951): 1–14. *https://doi.org/10.1073/pnas.37.1.1.*

Lepot, Kevin, Karim Benzerara, Gordon E. Brown, and Pascal Philippot. "Microbially Influenced Formation of 2,724-Million-Year-Old Stromatolites." *Nature Geoscience* 1, no. 2 (February 2008): 118–21. *https://doi.org/10.1038/ngeo107.*

McMahon, Sean. "Earth's Earliest and Deepest Purported Fossils May Be Iron-Mineralized Chemical Gardens." *Proceedings of the Royal Society B: Biological Sciences* 286, no. 1916 (December 2019): 20192410. *https://doi.org/10.1098/rspb.2019.2410.*

Metzger, Brian D., Roman R. Rafikov, and Konstantin V. Bochkarev. "Global Models of Runaway Accretion in White Dwarf Debris Discs." *Monthly Notices of the Royal Astronomical Society* 423, no. 1 (June 2012): 505–28. *https://doi.org/10.1111/j.1365-2966.2012.20895.x.*

O'Neill, H. St C. "The Origin of the Moon and the Early History of the Earth-A Chemical Model. Part 2: The Earth." *Geochimica et Cosmochimica Acta* 55, no. 4 (April 1991): 1159–72. *https://doi.org/10.1016/0016-7037(91)90169-6.*

Titirici, Maria Magdalena, Axel Funke, and Andrea Kruse. "Hydrothermal Carbonization of Biomass." In *Recent Advances in Thermochemical Conversion of Biomass*, edited by Rajeev K. Sukumaran, 325–52. Amsterdam: Elsevier Inc., 2015. *https://doi.org/10.1016/B978-0-444-63289-0.00012-0.*

Tsiganis, K., R. Gomes, A. Morbidelli, and H. F. Levison. "Origin of the Orbital Architecture of the Giant Planets of the Solar System." *Nature* 435, no. 7041 (May 2005): 459–61. *https://doi.org/10.1038/nature03539.*

Wade, Jon, and B. J. Wood. "Core Formation and the Oxidation State of the Earth." *Earth and Planetary Science Letters* 236, no. 1–2 (July 2005): 78–95. *https://doi.org/10.1016/j.epsl.2005.05.017.*

Weinberg, Steven. *The First Three Minutes : A Modern View of the Origin of the Universe.* New York, NY: Basic Books, 1993.

Zimmer, Carl. "How and Where Did Life on Earth Arise." *Science* 309, no. 5731 (July 2005): 89. *https://doi.org/10.1126/science.309.5731.89.*

APPENDIX CHAPTER 2

Berkner, L. V., and L. C. Marshall. "Limitation on Oxygen Concentration in a Primitive Planetary Atmosphere." *Journal of the Atmospheric Sciences* 23, no. 2 (March 1966): 133–43. *https://doi.org/10.1175/1520-0469(1966)0232.0.co;2.*

Bindeman, I. N., A. Bekker, and D. O. Zakharov. "Oxygen Isotope Perspective on Crustal Evolution on Early Earth: A Record of Precambrian Shales with Emphasis on Paleoproterozoic Glaciations and Great Oxygenation Event." *Earth and Planetary Science Letters* 437 (March 2016): 101–13. *https://doi.org/10.1016/j.epsl.2015.12.029.*

Brinkmann, R. T. "Dissociation of Water Vapor and Evolution of Oxygen in the Terrestrial Atmosphere." *Journal of Geophysical Research* 74, no. 23 (October 1969): 5355–68. *https://doi.org/10.1029/JC074i023p05355.*

Castresana, Jose, and Matti Saraste. "Evolution of Energetic Metabolism: The Respiration-Early Hypothesis." *Trends in Biochemical Sciences* 20, no. 11 (November 1995): 443–48. *https://doi.org/10.1016/S0968-0004(00)89098-2.*

Cohen, Y., E. Padan, and M. Shilo. "Facultative Anoxygenic Photosynthesis in the Cyanobacterium Oscillatoria Limnetica." *Journal of Bacteriology* 123, no. 3 (September 1975): 855–61. *https://doi.org/10.1128/jb.123.3.855-861.1975.*

Doolittle, W. Ford. "The Nature of the Universal Ancestor and the Evolution of the Proteome." *Current Opinion in Structural Biology* 10, no. 3 (June 2000): 355–58. *https://doi.org/10.1016/S0959-440X(00)00096-8.*

Fischer, Woodward W., James Hemp, and Joan Selverstone Valentine. "How Did Life Survive Earth's Great Oxygenation?"

Current Opinion in Chemical Biology 31 (April 2016): 166–78. *https://doi.org/10.1016/j.cbpa.2016.03.013.*

Forterre, Patrick, Nadia Benachenhou-Lahfa, Fabrice Confalonieri, Michel Duguet, Christiane Elie, and Bernard Labedan. "The Nature of the Last Universal Ancestor and the Root of the Tree of Life, Still Open Questions." *BioSystems* 28, no. 1–3 (January 1992): 15–32. *https://doi.org/10.1016/0303-2647(92)90004-I.*

Garlick, S, A Oren, and E Padan. "Occurrence of Facultative Anoxygenic Photosynthesis among Filamentous and Unicellular Cyanobacteria." *Journal of Bacteriology* 129, no. 2 (February 1977): 623–29. *https://doi.org/10.1128/JB.129.2.623-629.1977.*

Gest, Howard. "Bicentenary Homage to Dr Jan Ingen-Housz, MD (1730-1799), Pioneer of Photosynthesis Research." *Photosynthesis Research* 63, no. 2 (February 2000): 183–90. *https://doi.org/10.1023/A:1006460024843.*

Giulio, Massimo Di. "The Universal Ancestor Lived in a Thermophilic or Hyperthermophilic Environment." *Journal of Theoretical Biology* 203, no. 3 (April 2000): 203–13. *https://doi.org/10.1006/jtbi.2000.1086.*

Jannasch, Holger W. "Microbial Processes at Deep Sea Hydrothermal Vents." In *Hydrothermal Processes at Seafloor Spreading Centers*, edited by Holger W. Jannasch, 677–709. New York: Springer US, 1983. *https://doi.org/10.1007/978-1-4899-0402-7_28.*

Kasting, James F., and Janet L. Siefert. "Life and the Evolution of Earth's Atmosphere." *Science* 296, no. 5570 (May 2002): 1066-68. *https://doi.org/10.1126/science.1071184.*

Kitadai, Norio, and Shigenori Maruyama. "Origins of Building Blocks of Life: A Review." *Geoscience Frontiers* 9, no. 4 (July 2018): 1117–53. *https://doi.org/10.1016/j.gsf.2017.07.007.*

Knight, Barry. "A Review of the Corrosion of Iron from Terrestrial Sites and the Problem of Post-excavation Corrosion." *The Conservator* 14, no. 1 (January 1990): 37–43. *https://doi.org/10.1080/01410096.1990.9995055.*

Koch, Arthur L. "Development and Diversification of the Last Universal Ancestor." *Journal of Theoretical Biology* 168, no. 3 (June 1994): 269–80. *https://doi.org/10.1006/jtbi.1994.1108.*

Kogelschatz, U., B. Eliasson, and M. Hirth. "Ozone Generation From Oxygen And Air: Discharge Physics And Reaction Mechanisms." *Ozone: Science & Engineering* 10, no. 4 (September 1988): 367–77. *https://doi.org/10.1080/01919518808552391.*

Luo, Genming, Shuhei Ono, Nicolas J. Beukes, David T. Wang, Shucheng Xie, and Roger E. Summons. "Rapid Oxygenation of Earth's Atmosphere 2.33 Billion Years Ago." *Science Advances* 2, no. 5 (May 2016): e1600134. *https://doi.org/10.1126/sciadv.1600134.*

Martin, William, John Baross, Deborah Kelley, and Michael J. Russell. "Hydrothermal Vents and the Origin of Life." *Nature Reviews Microbiology* 6, no. 11 (September 2008): 805–14. *https://doi.org/10.1038/nrmicro1991.*

Nelson, Nathan, and Adam Ben-Shem. "The Complex Architecture of Oxygenic Photosynthesis." *Nature Reviews Molecular Cell Biology* 5, no. 12 (December 2004): 971–82. *https://doi.org/10.1038/nrm1525.*

Olsen, G. J., C. R. Woese, and R. Overbeek. "The Winds of (Evolutionary) Change: Breathing New Life into Microbiology." *Journal of Bacteriology* 176, no. 1 (January 1994): 1–6. *https://doi.org/10.1128/jb.176.1.1-6.1994.*

Woese, Carl. "The Universal Ancestor." *Proceedings of the National Academy of Sciences of the United States of America* 95, no. 12 (June 1998): 6854–59. *https://doi.org/10.1073/pnas.95.12.6854.*

Young, Grant M. "Precambrian Supercontinents, Glaciations, Atmospheric Oxygenation, Metazoan Evolution and an Impact That May Have Changed the Second Half of Earth History." *Geoscience Frontiers* 4, no. 3 (May 2013): 247–61. *https://doi. org/10.1016/j.gsf.2012.07.003.*

Zahnle, Kevin, Laura Schaefer, and Bruce Fegley. "Earth's Earliest Atmospheres." *Cold Spring Harbor Perspectives in Biology* 2, no. 10 (October 2010): a004895. *https://doi.org/10.1101/cshperspect. a004895.*

APPENDIX CHAPTER 3

Akyurt, M., G. Zaki, and B. Habeebullah. "Freezing Phenomena in Ice-Water Systems." *Energy Conversion and Management* 43, no. 14 (October 1, 2002): 1773–89. *https://doi.org/10.1016/S0196- 8904(01)00129-7.*

Alvarez-Ponce, David, Philippe Lopez, Eric Bapteste, and James O. McInerney. "Gene Similarity Networks Provide Tools for Understanding Eukaryote Origins and Evolution." *Proceedings of the National Academy of Sciences of the United States of America* 110, no. 17 (April 2013): E1594–1603. *https://doi. org/10.1073/pnas.1211371110.*

Bendich, Arnold J. "Circular Chloroplast Chromosomes: The Grand Illusion." *Plant Cell* 16, no. 7 (July 2004): 1661–66. *https:// doi.org/10.1105/tpc.160771.*

Butterfield, Nicholas J. "Modes of Pre-Ediacaran Multicellularity." *Precambrian Research* 173, no. 1–4 (September 2009): 201–11. *https://doi.org/10.1016/j.precamres.2009.01.008.*

Gaidos, Eric, Brian Lanoil, Thorsteinn Thorsteinsson, Andrew Graham, Mark Skidmore, Suk Kyun Han, Terri Rust, and Brian Popp. "A Viable Microbial Community in a Subglacial

Volcanic Crater Lake, Iceland." *Astrobiology* 4, no. 3 (September 2004): 327–44. *https://doi.org/10.1089/ast.2004.4.327.*

Gould, Sven B., Ross F. Waller, and Geoffrey I. McFadden. "Plastid Evolution." *Annual Review of Plant Biology* 59, no. 1 (June 2008): 491–517. *https://doi.org/10.1146/annurev.arplant.59.032607.092915.*

Gray, Michael W., Gertraud Burger, and B. Franz Lang. "The Origin and Early Evolution of Mitochondria." *Genome Biology* 2, no. 6 (June 2001): 1–5. *https://doi.org/10.1186/gb-2001-2-6-reviews1018.*

Gray, Michael W., Gertraud Burger, and B. Franz Lang. "Mitochondrial Evolution." *Science* 282, no. 5407 (March 1999): 1476-81. *https://doi.org/10.1126/science.283.5407.1476.*

Gribaldo, Simonetta, and Celine Brochier-Armanet. "The Origin and Evolution of Archaea: A State of the Art." *Philosophical Transactions of the Royal Society B: Biological Sciences* 361, no. 1470 (June 2006): 1007–22. *https://doi.org/10.1098/rstb.2006.1841.*

Grosberg, Richard K., and Richard R. Strathmann. "The Evolution of Multicellularity: A Minor Major Transition?" *Annual Review of Ecology, Evolution, and Systematics* 38, no. 1 (December 2007): 621–54. *https://doi.org/10.1146/annurev.ecolsys.36.102403.114735.*

Grosberg, Rick K., and Richard R. Strathmann. "One Cell, Two Cell, Red Cell, Blue Cell: The Persistence of a Unicellular Stage in Multicellular Life Histories." *Trends in Ecology and Evolution* 13, no. 3 (March 1998): 112–16. *https://doi.org/10.1016/S0169-5347(97)01313-X.*

Hunter, Philip. "Molecular Fossils Probe Life's Origins." *EMBO Reports* 14, no. 11 (November 2013): 964–67. *https://doi.org/10.1038/embor.2013.162.*

Iwabe, N., K. Kuma, M. Hasegawa, S. Osawa, and T. Miyata. "Evolutionary Relationship of Archaebacteria, Eubacteria, and Eukaryotes Inferred from Phylogenetic Trees of Duplicated Genes." *Proceedings of the National Academy of Sciences of the United States of America* 86, no. 23 (December 1989): 9355–59. *https://doi.org/10.1073/pnas.86.23.9355.*

Jensen, R. G., and J. A. Bassham. "Photosynthesis by Isolated Chloroplasts." *Proceedings of the National Academy of Sciences of the United States of America* 56, no. 4 (October 1966): 1095–1101. *https://doi.org/10.1073/pnas.56.4.1095.*

Kuroiwa, Tsuneyoshi, Haruko Kuroiwa, Atsushi Sakai, Hidenori Takahashi, Kyoko Toda, and Ryuuichi Itoh. "The Division Apparatus of Plastids and Mitochondria." *International Review of Cytology* 181 (January 1998): 1–41. *https://doi.org/10.1016/s0074-7696(08)60415-5.*

Lynn Margulis. *Microcosmos: Four Billion Years of Microbial Evolution.* Berkeley: University of California Press, 1997.

Martin, William F., Sriram Garg, and Verena Zimorski. "Endosymbiotic Theories for Eukaryote Origin." *Philosophical Transactions of the Royal Society B: Biological Sciences* 370, no. 1678 (September 2015). *https://doi.org/10.1098/rstb.2014.0330.*

McFadden, Geoffrey Ian. "Primary and Secondary Endosymbiosis and the Origin of Plastids." *Journal of Phycology* 37, no. 6 (December 2001): 951–59. *https://doi.org/10.1046/j.1529-8817.2001.01126.x.*

Meyer, R. R., and M. V. Simpson. "DNA Biosynthesis in Mitochondria: Partial Purification of a Distinct DNA Polymerase from Isolated Rat Liver Mitochondria." *Proceedings of the National Academy of Sciences of the United States of America* 61, no. 1 (September 1968): 130–37. *https://doi.org/10.1073/pnas.61.1.130.*

Michod, R. E., and D. Roze. "Cooperation and Conflict in the Evolution of Multicellularity." *Heredity*. Nature Publishing Group, January 1, 2001. *https://doi.org/10.1046/j.1365-2540.2001.00808.x.*

Michod, Richard E., Yannick Viossat, Cristian A. Solari, Mathilde Hurand, and Aurora M. Nedelcu. "Life-History Evolution and the Origin of Multicellularity." *Journal of Theoretical Biology* 239, no. 2 (March 2006): 257–72. *https://doi.org/10.1016/j.jtbi.2005.08.043.*

Naftz, David L., and Mark E. Smith. "Ice Thickness, Ablation, and Other Glaciological Measurements on Upper Fremont Glacier, Wyoming." *Physical Geography* 14, no. 4 (1993): 404–14. *https://doi.org/10.1080/02723646.1993.10642488.*

Niklas, Karl J. "The Evolutionary-Developmental Origins of Multicellularity." *American Journal of Botany* 101, no. 1 (January 2014): 6–25. *https://doi.org/10.3732/ajb.1300314.*

Schirrmeister, Bettina E., Alexandre Antonelli, and Homayoun C. Bagheri. "The Origin of Multicellularity in Cyanobacteria." *BMC Evolutionary Biology* 11, no. 1 (February 2011): 1–21. *https://doi.org/10.1186/1471-2148-11-45.*

Sekine, Yasuhito, Eiichi Tajika, Ryuji Tada, Takemaru Hirai, Kosuke T. Goto, Tatsu Kuwatani, Kazuhisa Goto, et al. "Manganese Enrichment in the Gowganda Formation of the Huronian Supergroup: A Highly Oxidizing Shallow-Marine Environment after the Last Huronian Glaciation." *Earth and Planetary Science Letters* 307, no. 1–2 (July 2011): 201–10. *https://doi.org/10.1016/j.epsl.2011.05.001.*

Sojo, Víctor, Andrew Pomiankowski, and Nick Lane. "A Bioenergetic Basis for Membrane Divergence in Archaea and Bacteria." Edited by David Penny. *PLoS Biology* 12, no. 8 (August 2014): e1001926. *https://doi.org/10.1371/journal.pbio.1001926.*

Steven, Blaire, Richard Léveillé, Wayne H. Pollard, and Lyle G. Whyte. "Microbial Ecology and Biodiversity in Permafrost." *Extremophiles* 10, no. 4 (August 2006): 259–67. *https://doi.org/10.1007/s00792-006-0506-3.*

Tang, Haoshu, and Yanjing Chen. "Global Glaciations and Atmospheric Change at ca. 2.3 Ga." *Geoscience Frontiers* 4, no. 5 (September 2013): 583–96. *https://doi.org/10.1016/j.gsf.2013.02.003.*

Vopel, Kay, and Ian Hawes. "Photosynthetic Performance of Benthic Microbial Mats in Lake Hoare, Antarctica." *Limnology and Oceanography* 51, no. 4 (July 2006): 1801–12. *https://doi.org/10.4319/lo.2006.51.4.1801.*

Wächtershäuser, G. "From Pre-Cells to Eukarya — a Tale of Two Lipids." *Molecular Microbiology* 47, no. 1 (December 2002): 13–22. *https://doi.org/10.1046/j.1365-2958.2003.03267.x.*

Weiss, Madeline C., Filipa L. Sousa, Natalia Mrnjavac, Sinje Neukirchen, Mayo Roettger, Shijulal Nelson-Sathi, and William F. Martin. "The Physiology and Habitat of the Last Universal Common Ancestor." *Nature Microbiology* 1, no. 9 (July 2016): 1–8. *https://doi.org/10.1038/nmicrobiol.2016.116.*

Woese, C. R., O. Kandler, and M. L. Wheelis. "Towards a Natural System of Organisms: Proposal for the Domains Archaea, Bacteria, and Eucarya." *Proceedings of the National Academy of Sciences of the United States of America* 87, no. 12 (June 1990): 4576–79. *https://doi.org/10.1073/pnas.87.12.4576.*

Woese, Carl R. "On the Evolution of Cells." *Proceedings of the National Academy of Sciences of the United States of America* 99, no. 13 (June 2002): 8742–47. *https://doi.org/10.1073/pnas.132266999.*

Yamagishi, Jumpei F., Nen Saito, and Kunihiko Kaneko. "Symbiotic Cell Differentiation and Cooperative Growth in Multicellular

Aggregates." *PLoS Computational Biology* 12, no. 10 (October 2016): e1005042. *https://doi.org/10.1371/journal.pcbi.1005042*.

Zimorski, Verena, Chuan Ku, William F. Martin, and Sven B. Gould. "Endosymbiotic Theory for Organelle Origins." *Current Opinion in Microbiology* 22 (December 2014): 38–48. *https://doi.org/10.1016/j.mib.2014.09.008*.

APPENDIX CHAPTER 4

Abe, Francine R., and Bruce S. Lieberman. "Quantifying Morphological Change during an Evolutionary Radiation of Devonian Trilobites." *Paleobiology* 38, no. 2 (March 2012): 292–307. *https://doi.org/10.1666/10047.1*.

Alegado, Rosanna A., Steven Ferriera, Chad Nusbaum, Sarah K. Young, Qian Zeng, Alma Imamovic, Stephen R. Fairclough, and Nicole King. "Complete Genome Sequence of Algoriphagus Sp. PR1, Bacterial Prey of a Colony-Forming Choanoflagellate." *Journal of Bacteriology* 193, no. 6 (March 2011): 1485–86. *https://doi.org/10.1128/JB.01421-10*.

Cavalier-Smith, Thomas. "Origin of Animal Multicellularity: Precursors, Causes, Consequences—the Choanoflagellate/Sponge Transition, Neurogenesis and the Cambrian Explosion." *Philosophical Transactions of the Royal Society B: Biological Sciences* 372, no. 1713 (February 2017). *https://doi.org/10.1098/rstb.2015.0476*.

Dayel, Mark J., Rosanna A. Alegado, Stephen R. Fairclough, Tera C. Levin, Scott A. Nichols, Kent McDonald, and Nicole King. "Cell Differentiation and Morphogenesis in the Colony-Forming Choanoflagellate Salpingoeca Rosetta." *Developmental Biology* 357, no. 1 (September 2011): 73–82. *https://doi.org/10.1016/j.ydbio.2011.06.003*.

Dayel, Mark J., and Nicole King. "Prey Capture and Phagocytosis in the Choanoflagellate Salpingoeca Rosetta." *PLoS ONE* 9, no. 5 (May 7, 2014): e95577. *https://doi.org/10.1371/journal.pone.0095577.*

Dirks, Ulrich, Harald R. Gruber-Vodicka, Nikolaus Leisch, Silvia Bulgheresi, Bernhard Egger, Peter Ladurner, and Jörg A. Ott. "Bacterial Symbiosis Maintenance in the Asexually Reproducing and Regenerating Flatworm Paracatenula Galateia." *PLoS ONE* 7, no. 4 (April 2012): e34709. *https://doi.org/10.1371/journal.pone.0034709.*

Fairclough, Stephen R., Zehua Chen, Eric Kramer, Qiandong Zeng, Sarah Young, Hugh M. Robertson, Emina Begovic, et al. "Premetazoan Genome Evolution and the Regulation of Cell Differentiation in the Choanoflagellate Salpingoeca Rosetta." *Genome Biology* 14, no. 2 (February 2013): 1–15. *https://doi.org/10.1186/gb-2013-14-2-r15.*

Fairclough, Stephen R., Mark J. Dayel, and Nicole King. "Multicellular Development in a Choanoflagellate." *Current Biology* 20, no. 20 (October 2010): R875–76. *https://doi.org/10.1016/j.cub.2010.09.014.*

Fraune, Sebastian, and Thomas C.G. Bosch. "Why Bacteria Matter in Animal Development and Evolution." *BioEssays* 32, no. 7 (July 2010): 571–80. *https://doi.org/10.1002/bies.200900192.*

Galluzzi, Luca, Aurora Diotallevi, and Mauro Magnani. "Endoplasmic Reticulum Stress and Unfolded Protein Response in Infection by Intracellular Parasites." *Future Science OA* 3, no. 3 (August 2017): FSO198. *https://doi.org/10.4155/fsoa-2017-0020.*

Grazhdankin, Dmitriy V., Uwe Balthasar, Konstantin E. Nagovitsin, and Boris B. Kochnev. "Carbonate-Hosted Avalon-Type Fossils in Arctic Siberia." *Geology* 36, no. 10 (October 2008): 803–6. *https://doi.org/10.1130/G24946A.1.*

Gruber-Vodicka, Harald R., Nikolaus Leisch, Manuel Kleiner, Tjorven Hinzke, Manuel Liebeke, Margaret McFall-Ngai, Michael G. Hadfield, and Nicole Dubilier. "Two Intracellular and Cell Type-Specific Bacterial Symbionts in the Placozoan Trichoplax H2." *Nature Microbiology* 4, no. 9 (September 2019): 1465–74. *https://doi.org/10.1038/s41564-019-0475-9.*

Gruber-Vodicka, Harald Ronald, Ulrich Dirks, Nikolaus Leisch, Christian Baranyi, Kilian Stoecker, Silvia Bulgheresi, Niels Robert Heindl, et al. "Paracatenula, an Ancient Symbiosis between Thiotrophic Alphaproteobacteria and Catenulid Flatworms." *Proceedings of the National Academy of Sciences of the United States of America* 108, no. 29 (July 2011): 12078–83. *https://doi.org/10.1073/pnas.1105347108.*

Hazen, Robert M. *The Story of Earth : The First 4.5 Billion Years, from Stardust to Living Planet.* London: Penguin Books, 2013.

iBiology. "Choanoflagellates and the Origin of Animal Multicellularity." Accessed July 12, 2020. *https://www.ibiology.org/ecology/choanoflagellates/.*

Jäckle, Oliver, Brandon K.B. Seah, Målin Tietjen, Nikolaus Leisch, Manuel Liebeke, Manuel Kleiner, Jasmine S. Berg, and Harald R. Gruber-Vodicka. "Chemosynthetic Symbiont with a Drastically Reduced Genome Serves as Primary Energy Storage in the Marine Flatworm Paracatenula." *Proceedings of the National Academy of Sciences of the United States of America* 116, no. 17 (April 2019): 8505–14. *https://doi.org/10.1073/pnas.1818995116.*

Kat McGowan. "How Life Made the Leap From Single Cells to Multicellular Animals" WIRED, August 1, 2014. *https://www.wired.com/2014/08/where-animals-come-from/.*

Knoll, Andrew H. "The Multiple Origins of Complex Multicellularity." *Annual Review of Earth and Planetary Sciences*

39, no. 1 (May 2011): 217–39. *https://doi.org/10.1146/annurev. earth.031208.100209.*

Kumler, William E., Justin Jorge, Paul M. Kim, Noama Iftekhar, and M.A.R. Koehl. "Does Formation of Multicellular Colonies by Choanoflagellates Affect Their Susceptibility to Capture by Passive Protozoan Predators?" *Journal of Eukaryotic Microbiology* 67, no. 5 (May 2020): 555–65. *https://doi.org/10.1111/jeu.12808.*

Landing, Ed, Gerd Geyer, Martin D. Brasier, and Samuel A. Bowring. "Cambrian Evolutionary Radiation: Context, Correlation, and Chronostratigraphy-Overcoming Deficiencies of the First Appearance Datum (FAD) Concept." *Earth-Science Reviews* 123 (August 2013): 133–72. *https://doi.org/10.1016/j.earscirev.2013.03.008.*

Lok, Corie. "Mining the Microbial Dark Matter." *Nature* 522, no. 7556 (June 2015): 270–73. *https://doi.org/10.1038/522270a.*

Mángano, M. Gabriela, Luis A. Buatois, Ricardo Astini, and Andrew K. Rindsberg. "Trilobites in Early Cambrian Tidal Flats and the Landward Expansion of the Cambrian Explosion." *Geology* 42, no. 2 (February 2014): 143–46. *https://doi.org/10.1130/G34980.1.*

Margulis, and L. *Symbiosis in Cell Evolution: Life and Its Environment on the Early Earth.* New York: W. H. Freeman & Co, 1981.

McFall-Ngai, Margaret J. "Unseen Forces: The Influence of Bacteria on Animal Development." *Developmental Biology* 242, no. 1 (February 2002): 1–14. *https://doi.org/10.1006/dbio.2001.0522.*

Shen, Bing, Lin Dong, Shuhai Xiao, and Michał Kowalewski. "The Avalon Explosion: Evolution of Ediacara Morphospace." *Science* 319, no. 5859 (January 2008): 81–84. *https://doi.org/10.1126/science.1150279.*

Stoupin, Daniel, Aron K. Kiss, Hartmut Arndt, Anastasia V. Shatilovich, David A. Gilichinsky, and Frank Nitsche. "Cryptic Diversity within the Choanoflagellate Morphospecies Complex Codosiga Botrytis — Phylogeny and Morphology of Ancient and Modern Isolates." *European Journal of Protistology* 48, no. 4 (November 2012): 263–73. *https://doi.org/10.1016/j.ejop.2012.01.004.*

Streelman, J. Todd, and Patrick D. Danley. "The Stages of Vertebrate Evolutionary Radiation." *Trends in Ecology and Evolution* 18, no. 3 (March 2003): 126–31. *https://doi.org/10.1016/S0169-5347(02)00036-8.*

Tanghe, Koen B. "On *The Origin of Species* : The Story of Darwin's Title." *Notes and Records: The Royal Society Journal of the History of Science* 73, no. 1 (March 2019): 83–100. *https://doi.org/10.1098/rsnr.2018.0015.*

Thomsen, Helge Abildhauge. "External Morphology of the Choanoflagellate Salpingoeca Gracilis James-Clark." *Journal of the Marine Biological Association of the United Kingdom* 57, no. 3 (August 1977): 629–34. *https://doi.org/10.1017/S0025315400025078.*

Woznica, Arielle, Alexandra M. Cantley, Christine Beemelmanns, Elizaveta Freinkman, Jon Clardy, and Nicole King. "Bacterial Lipids Activate, Synergize, and Inhibit a Developmental Switch in Choanoflagellates." *Proceedings of the National Academy of Sciences of the United States of America* 113, no. 28 (July 2016): 7894–99. *https://doi.org/10.1073/pnas.1605015113.*

APPENDIX CHAPTER 5

Ambrose, S. H. "Paleolithic Technology and Human Evolution." *Science* 291, no. 5509 (March 2001): 1748–53. *https://doi.org/10.1126/science.1059487.*

Atherton, John C., and Martin J. Blaser. "Coadaptation of Helicobacter Pylori and Humans: Ancient History, Modern Implications." *Journal of Clinical Investigation* 119, no. 9 (September 2009): 2475–87. *https://doi.org/10.1172/JCI38605.*

Blaser, Martin J. "Disappearing Microbiota: Helicobacter Pylori Protection against Esophageal Adenocarcinoma." *Cancer Prevention Research* 1, no. 5 (October 2008): 308–11. *https://doi.org/10.1158/1940-6207.CAPR-08-0170.*

Blaser, Martin J. "Who Are We?" *EMBO Reports* 7, no. 10 (August 2006): 956–60. *https://doi.org/10.1038/sj.embor.7400812.*

Bowles, Samuel. "Warriors, Levelers, and the Role of Conflict in Human Social Evolution." *Science* 336, no. 6083 (May 2012): 876–79. *https://doi.org/10.1126/science.1217336.*

Braun, David R. "Palaeoanthropology: Australopithecine Butchers." *Nature* 466, no. 7308 (August 2010): 828. *https://doi.org/10.1038/466828a.*

D'Anastasio, R., T. Staniscia, M. L. Milia, L. Manzoli, and L. Capasso. "Origin, Evolution and Paleoepidemiology of Brucellosis." *Epidemiology and Infection* 139, no. 1 (January 2011): 149–56. *https://doi.org/10.1017/S095026881000097X.*

Dagosto, Marian, Daniel Gebo, Xijun Ni, and Thierry Smith. "Estimating Body Size in Early Primates: The Case of Archicebus and Teilhardina." *Journal of Human Evolution* 115 (February 2018): 8–19. *https://doi.org/10.1016/j.jhevol.2017.02.005.*

Dehority, Burk A. "Protozoa of the Digestive Tract of Herbivorous Mammals." *International Journal of Tropical Insect Science* 7, no. 03 (June 1986): 279–96. *https://doi.org/10.1017/s1742758400009346.*

Du, Andrew, John Rowan, Steve C. Wang, Bernard A. Wood, and Zeresenay Alemseged. "Statistical Estimates of Hominin Origination and Extinction Dates: A Case Study Examining the Australopithecus Anamensis–Afarensis Lineage." *Journal of Human Evolution* 138 (January 2020): 102688. *https://doi.org/10.1016/j.jhevol.2019.102688.*

Guerra-Doce, Elisa. "The Origins of Inebriation: Archaeological Evidence of the Consumption of Fermented Beverages and Drugs in Prehistoric Eurasia." *Journal of Archaeological Method and Theory* 22, no. 3 (September 2015): 751–82. *https://doi.org/10.1007/s10816-014-9205-z.*

Kaplan, Hillard, Kim Hill, Jane Lancaster, and A. Magdalena Hurtado. "A Theory of Human Life History Evolution: Diet, Intelligence, and Longevity." *Evolutionary Anthropology: Issues, News, and Reviews* 9, no. 4 (January 2000): 156–85. *https://doi.org/10.1002/1520-6505(2000)9:43.0.CO;2-7.*

Krause, David W. "Paleocene Primates from Western Canada." *Canadian Journal of Earth Sciences* 15, no. 8 (August 1978): 1250–71. *https://doi.org/10.1139/e78-133.*

Leonard, William R., and Marcia L. Robertson. "Evolutionary Perspectives on Human Nutrition: The Influence of Brain and Body Size on Diet and Metabolism." *American Journal of Human Biology* 6, no. 1 (January 1994): 77–88. *https://doi.org/10.1002/ajhb.1310060111.*

Moeller, Andrew H., Yingying Li, Eitel Mpoudi Ngole, Steve Ahuka-Mundeke, Elizabeth V. Lonsdorf, Anne E. Pusey, Martine Peeters, Beatrice H. Hahn, and Howard Ochman. "Rapid Changes in the Gut Microbiome during Human Evolution." *Proceedings of the National Academy of Sciences of the United States of America* 111, no. 46 (November 2014): 16431–35. *https://doi.org/10.1073/pnas.1419136111.*

Neubauer, Simon, Jean Jacques Hublin, and Philipp Gunz. "The Evolution of Modern Human Brain Shape." *Science Advances* 4, no. 1 (January 2018): eaao5961. *https://doi.org/10.1126/sciadv. aao5961.*

Olson, Maynard V., and Ajit Varki. "Sequencing the Chimpanzee Genome: Insights into Human Evolution and Disease." *Nature Reviews Genetics* 4, no. 1 (January 2003): 20–28. *https://doi. org/10.1038/nrg981.*

Sayers, Ken, and C. Owen Lovejoy. "Blood, Bulbs, and Bunodonts: On Evolutionary Ecology and the Diets of Ardipithecus, Australopithecus, and Early Homo." *Quarterly Review of Biology* 89, no. 4 (December 2014): 319–57. *https://doi.org/10.1086/678568.*

Schnorr, Stephanie L., Krithivasan Sankaranarayanan, Cecil M. Lewis, and Christina Warinner. "Insights into Human Evolution from Ancient and Contemporary Microbiome Studies." *Current Opinion in Genetics and Development* 41 (December 2016): 14–26. *https://doi.org/10.1016/j.gde.2016.07.003.*

Shear, William A., and Jarmila Kukalová-Peck. "The Ecology of Paleozoic Terrestrial Arthropods: The Fossil Evidence." *Canadian Journal of Zoology* 68, no. 9 (September 1990): 1807–34. *https://doi.org/10.1139/z90-262.*

Skinner, Matthew M., Nicholas B. Stephens, Zewdi J. Tsegai, Alexandra C. Foote, N. Huynh Nguyen, Thomas Gross, Dieter H. Pahr, Jean Jacques Hublin, and Tracy L. Kivell. "Human-like Hand Use in Australopithecus Africanus." *Science* 347, no. 6220 (January 2015): 395–99. *https://doi.org/10.1126/science.1261735.*

Sponheimer, Matt, and Julia A. Lee-Thorp. "Isotopic Evidence for the Diet of an Early Hominid, Australopithecus Africanus." *Science* 283, no. 5400 (January 1999): 368–70. *https:// doi.org/10.1126/science.283.5400.368.*

Tobias, Phillip V. "The Discovery of the Taung Skull of Australopithecus Africanus Dart and the Neglected Role of Professor R.B. Young." *Transactions of the Royal Society of South Africa* 61, no. 2 (January 2006): 131–38. *https://doi.org/10.1080/00359190609519963.*

Ewen Callaway. "Ancient Bones Show Earliest 'human' Infection" *New Scientist*, August 5, 2009. *https://institutions.newscientist.com/article/dn17559-ancient-bones-show-earliest-human-infection/.*

White, T. D., D. C. Johanson, and W. H. Kimbel. "Australopithecus Africanus." In *New Interpretations of Ape and Human Ancestry*, edited by Russell L. Ciochon and Robert S. Corruccini, 721–80. New York: US Springer, 1983. *https://doi.org/10.1007/978-1-4684-8854-8_29.*

Wood, Bernard. "Origin and Evolution of the Genus Homo." *Nature* 355, no. 6363 (February 1992): 783–90. *https://doi.org/10.1038/355783a0.*

Worthy, Trevor H., Suzanne J. Hand, Michael Archer, R. Paul Scofield, and Vanesa L. De Pietri. "Evidence for a Giant Parrot from the Early Miocene of New Zealand." *Biology Letters* 15, no. 8 (August 2019): 20190467. *https://doi.org/10.1098/rsbl.2019.0467.*

APPENDIX CHAPTER 6

Allentoft, Morten E., Martin Sikora, Karl Göran Sjögren, Simon Rasmussen, Morten Rasmussen, Jesper Stenderup, Peter B. Damgaard, et al. "Population Genomics of Bronze Age Eurasia." *Nature* 522, no. 7555 (June 10, 2015): 167–72. *https://doi.org/10.1038/nature14507.*

Bar-Yosef, Ofer. "The Natufian Culture in the Levant, Threshold to the Origins of Agriculture." *Evolutionary Anthropology: Issues,*

News, and Reviews 6, no. 5 (January 1998): 159–77. *https://doi. org/10.1002/(SICI)1520-6505(1998)6:53.0.CO;2-7.*

Barros Damgaard, Peter de, Rui Martiniano, Jack Kamm, J. Víctor Moreno-Mayar, Guus Kroonen, Michaël Peyrot, Gojko Barjamovic, et al. "The First Horse Herders and the Impact of Early Bronze Age Steppe Expansions into Asia." *Science* 360, no. 6396 (June 2018): eaar7711. *https://doi.org/10.1126/science.aar7711.*

Cardona, Pere Joan, Martí Català, and Clara Prats. "Origin of Tuberculosis in the Paleolithic Predicts Unprecedented Population Growth and Female Resistance." *Scientific Reports* 10, no. 1 (December 2020): 1–20. *https://doi.org/10.1038/s41598-019-56769-1.*

Cole, Stewart T. "Comparative and Functional Genomics of the Mycobacterium Tuberculosis Complex." *Microbiology* 148, no. 10 (October 2002): 2919–28. *https://doi.org/10.1099/00221287-148-10-2919.*

Gengenbacher, Martin, and Stefan H.E. Kaufmann. "Mycobacterium Tuberculosis: Success through Dormancy." *FEMS Microbiology Reviews* 36, no. 3 (May 2012): 514–32. *https://doi. org/10.1111/j.1574-6976.2012.00331.x.*

Han, Xiang Y., and Francisco J. Silva. "On the Age of Leprosy." *PLoS Neglected Tropical Diseases* 8, no. 2 (February 2014): e2544. *https://doi.org/10.1371/journal.pntd.0002544.*

King, Anthony. "How Did the Plague Reshape Bronze Age Europe?" *Horizon: The EU Research & Innovation*, December 3, 2019. *https://horizon-magazine.eu/article/how-did-plague-reshape-bronze-age-europe.html.*

Larsen, Clark Spencer, Simon W. Hillson, Başak Boz, Marin A. Pilloud, Joshua W. Sadvari, Sabrina C. Agarwal, Bonnie Glencross, et al. "Bioarchaeology of Neolithic Çatalhöyük: Lives and Lifestyles of an Early Farming Society in Transition." *Journal of World Prehistory* 28, no. 1 (March 2015): 27–68. *https://doi.org/10.1007/s10963-015-9084-6.*

Larsen, Clark Spencer, Christopher J. Knüsel, Scott D. Haddow, Marin A. Pilloud, Marco Milella, Joshua W. Sadvari, Jessica Pearson, et al. "Bioarchaeology of Neolithic Çatalhöyük Reveals Fundamental Transitions in Health, Mobility, and Lifestyle in Early Farmers." *Proceedings of the National Academy of Sciences of the United States of America* 116, no. 26 (June 2019): 12615–23. *https://doi.org/10.1073/pnas.1904345116.*

Ledger, Marissa L., Evilena Anastasiou, Lisa-Marie Shillito, Helen Mackay, Ian D. Bull, Scott D. Haddow, Christopher J. Knüsel, and Piers D. Mitchell. "Parasite Infection at the Early Farming Community of Çatalhöyük." *Antiquity* 93, no. 369 (June 2019): 573–87. *https://doi.org/10.15184/aqy.2019.61.*

Mira, Alex, Ravindra Pushker, and Francisco Rodríguez-Valera. "The Neolithic Revolution of Bacterial Genomes." *Trends in Microbiology* 14, no. 5 (May 2006): 200–206. *https://doi.org/10.1016/j.tim.2006.03.001.*

Rascovan, Nicolás, Karl Göran Sjögren, Kristian Kristiansen, Rasmus Nielsen, Eske Willerslev, Christelle Desnues, and Simon Rasmussen. "Emergence and Spread of Basal Lineages of Yersinia Pestis during the Neolithic Decline." *Cell* 176, no. 1–2 (January 2019): 295-305.e10. *https://doi.org/10.1016/j.cell.2018.11.005.*

Rasmussen, Simon, Morten Erik Allentoft, Kasper Nielsen, Ludovic Orlando, Martin Sikora, Karl Göran Sjögren, Anders Gorm Pedersen, et al. "Early Divergent Strains of Yersinia Pestis in Eurasia 5,000 Years Ago." *Cell* 163, no. 3 (October 2015): 571–82. *https://doi.org/10.1016/j.cell.2015.10.009.*

Rock, Daniel. "Tuberculosis: A Global Emergency." *Work* 8, no. 1 (January 1997): 93–105. *https://doi.org/10.3233/wor-1997-8111.*

Schiermeier, Q., and K. Stehle. "Frozen Body Offers Chance to Travel Back in Time." *Nature* 407, no. 6804 (October 2000): 550. *https://doi.org/10.1038/35036727.*

Stiner, Mary C., and Steven L. Kuhn. "Changes in the 'connectedness' and Resilience of Paleolithic Societies in Mediterranean Ecosystems." *Human Ecology* 34, no. 5 (October 2006): 693–712. *https://doi.org/10.1007/s10745-006-9041-1.*

Trueba, Gabriel. "The Origin of Human Pathogens." In *Confronting Emerging Zoonoses: The One Health Paradigm*, edited by Lisa Conti, 3–11. Tokyo: Springer Japan, 2014. *https://doi.org/10.1007/978-4-431-55120-1_1.*

Trueba, Gabriel, and Micah Dunthorn. "Many Neglected Tropical Diseases May Have Originated in the Paleolithic or before: New Insights from Genetics." *PLoS Neglected Tropical Diseases* 6, no. 3 (March 2012): e1393. *https://doi.org/10.1371/journal.pntd.0001393.*

Weber, J., and J. Wahl. "Neurosurgical Aspects of Trepanations from Neolithic Times." *International Journal of Osteoarchaeology* 16, no. 6 (November 2006): 536–45. *https://doi.org/10.1002/oa.844.*

Weisdorf, Jacob L. "From Foraging To Farming: Explaining The Neolithic Revolution." *Journal of Economic Surveys* 19, no. 4 (September 2005): 561–86. *https://doi.org/10.1111/j.0950-0804.2005.00259.x.*

Weyrich, Laura S. "Evolution of the Human Microbiome and Impacts on Human Health, Infectious Disease, and Hominid Evolution," In *Reticulate Evolution*, edited by Nathalie Gontier,

231–53. New York: Springer, 2015. *https://doi.org/10.1007/978-3-319-16345-1_9.*

APPENDIX CHAPTER 7

Brandt-Rauf, P. W., and S. I. Brandt-Rauf. "History of Occupational Medicine: Relevance of Imhotep and the Edwin Smith Papyrus." *British Journal of Industrial Medicine* 44, no. 1 (January 1987): 68–70. *https://doi.org/10.1136/oem.44.1.68.*

Carol Clark. "Ancient Brewers Tapped Antibiotic Secrets," eScienceCommons (blog) Emory University, August 30, 2010. *http://esciencecommons.blogspot.com/2010/08/ancient-brew-masters-tapped-drug.html.*

Crissey, John Thorne, and Lawrence Charles Parish. "Wound Healing: Development of the Basic Concepts." *Clinics in Dermatology* 2, no. 3 (July 1984): 1–7. *https://doi.org/10.1016/0738-081X(84)90021-X.*

Edmund S. Meltzer, and Gonzalo M. Sanchez. *The Edwin Smith Papyrus: Updated Translation of the Trauma Treatise and Modern Medical Commentaries.* London: Lockwood Press, 2012.

Feldman, Robert P, and James T Goodrich. "The Edwin Smith Surgical Papyrus." *Child's Nervous System* 15, no. 6–7 (July 1999): 281–84. *https://doi.org/10.1007/s003810050395.*

Hamburger, Walter W. "The Earliest Known Reference to the Heart and Circulation. The Edwin Smith Surgical Papyrus, circa 3,000 B.C." *American Heart Journal* 17, no. 3 (March 1939): 259–74. *https://doi.org/10.1016/S0002-8703(39)90001-3.*

Johnson, Paul. *The Civilization Of Ancient Egypt.* London: Weidenfeld & Nicholson, 1978.

Kirkham, P. "Oxidative Stress and Macrophage Function: A Failure to Resolve the Inflammatory Response." *Biochemical Society Transactions* 35, no. 2 (April 2007): 284–87. *https://doi.org/10.1042/BST0350284.*

Loriaux, D Lynn. "Diabetes and The Ebers Papyrus." *The Endocrinologist* 16, no. 2 (March 2006): 55–56. *https://doi.org/10.1097/01.ten.0000202534.83446.69.*

Maggiano, Corey, Tosha Dupras, Michael Schultz, and John Biggerstaff. "Spectral and Photobleaching Analysis Using Confocal Laser Scanning Microscopy: A Comparison of Modern and Archaeological Bone Fluorescence." *Molecular and Cellular Probes* 20, no. 3–4 (June 2006): 154–62. *https://doi.org/10.1016/j.mcp.2005.11.009.*

Mahmood, Zafar A., Iqbal Azhar, and S. W. Ahmed. "Kohl Use in Antiquity: Effects on the Eye." In *Toxicology in Antiquity*, edited by Philip Wexler, 93–103. Amsterdam: Elsevier, 2018. *https://doi.org/10.1016/B978-0-12-815339-0.00005-6.*

Malcolm Moore. "Hittites 'used Germ Warfare 3,500 Years Ago' " *Telegraph*, December 8, 2007. *https://www.telegraph.co.uk/news/worldnews/1571927/Hittites-used-germ-warfare-3500-years-ago.html.*

Mandal, Santi M., Suman Saha, Jayangshu Sengupta, and Sanjay Pratihar. "Kaajal Fights against Eye Pathogens and Is Safe for Eye Make-up: A Reinvestigation of an Ancient Practice." *Analyst* 138, no. 18 (September 2013): 5197–99. *https://doi.org/10.1039/c3an01085f.*

Martino, Stefano de. "Some Questions on the Political History and Chronology of the Early Hittite Empire." *Altorientalische Forschungen* 37, no. 2 (December 2010): 186–97. *https://doi.org/10.1524/aofo.2010.0016.*

Metcalfe, Ryan. "Bread and Beer in Ancient Egyptian Medicine." In *Mummies, Magic and Medicine in Ancient Egypt*, edited by Campbell Price, 157–68. Manchester: Manchester University Press, 2016. *https://doi.org/10.7765/9781784997502.00025.*

Nelson, Mark L., Andrew Dinardo, Jeffery Hochberg, and George J. Armelagos. "Brief Communication: Mass Spectroscopic Characterization of Tetracycline in the Skeletal Remains of an Ancient Population from Sudanese Nubia 350-550 CE." *American Journal of Physical Anthropology* 143, no. 1 (September 2010): 151–54. *https://doi.org/10.1002/ajpa.21340.*

Norrie, Philip, and Philip Norrie. "How Disease Affected the History of the Hittite Empire." In *A History of Disease in Ancient Times*, 37–59. New Work: Springer, 2016. *https://doi.org/10.1007/978-3-319-28937-3_4.*

Panagiotakopulu, Eva. "Pharaonic Egypt and the Origins of Plague." *Journal of Biogeography* 31, no. 2 (February 2004): 269–75. *https://doi.org/10.1046/j.0305-0270.2003.01009.x.*

Reeves, Carole. "Egyptian Medicine," London: Shire Books, 2008.

Rosso, Ana María. "Beer and Wine in Antiquity: Beneficial Remedy or Punishment Imposed by the Gods?" *Acta Medico-Historica Adriatica : AMHA* 10, no. 2 (December 2012): 237–62.

Seidlitz, Eric, Zeina Saikali, and Gurmit Singh. "Use of Tetracyclines for Bone Metastases." In *Bone Metastasis*, edited by Gurmit SinghShafaat and A. Rabbani, 293–303. Totowa, Humana Press, 2005. *https://doi.org/10.1385/1-59259-892-7:293.*

Stiefel, Marc, Arlene Shaner, and Steven D. Schaefer. "The Edwin Smith Papyrus: The Birth of Analytical Thinking in Medicine and Otolaryngology." *The Laryngoscope* 116, no. 2 (February 2006): 182–88. *https://doi.org/10.1097/01.mlg.0000191461.08542.a3.*

Takamiya, Izumi H. "Egyptian Pottery Distribution in A-Group Cemeteries, Lower Nubia: Towards an Understanding of Exchange Systems between the Naqada Culture and the A-Group Culture." *The Journal of Egyptian Archaeology* 90, no. 1 (December 2004): 35–62. *https://doi.org/10.1177/030751330409000103.*

Tapsoba, Issa, Stéphane Arbault, Philippe Walter, and Christian Amatore. "Finding out Egyptian Gods' Secret Using Analytical Chemistry: Biomedical Properties of Egyptian Black Makeup Revealed by Amperometry at Single Cells." *Analytical Chemistry* 82, no. 2 (January 2010): 457–60. *https://doi.org/10.1021/ac902348g.*

Trevisanato, Siro I. "Did an Epidemic of Tularemia in Ancient Egypt Affect the Course of World History?" *Medical Hypotheses* 63, no. 5 (January 2004): 905–10. *https://doi.org/10.1016/j.mehy.2004.05.015.*

Trevisanato, Siro Igino. "The 'Hittite Plague', an Epidemic of Tularemia and the First Record of Biological Warfare." *Medical Hypotheses* 69, no. 6 (January 2007): 1371–74. *https://doi.org/10.1016/j.mehy.2007.03.012.*

Wenke, Robert J. "The Evolution of Early Egyptian Civilization: Issues and Evidence." *Journal of World Prehistory* 5, no. 3 (September 1991): 279–329. *https://doi.org/10.1007/BF00974992.*

Whitaker, Iain S., Richard O. Karoo, George Spyrou, and Oliver M. Fenton. "The Birth of Plastic Surgery: The Story of Nasal Reconstruction from the Edwin Smith Papyrus to the Twenty-First Century." *Plastic and Reconstructive Surgery* 120, no. 1 (July 2007): 327–36. *https://doi.org/10.1097/01.prs.0000264445.76315.6d.*

Zink, A. R., W. Grabner, U. Reischl, H. Wolf, and A. G. Nerlich. "Molecular Study on Human Tuberculosis in Three Geographically Distinct and Time Delineated Populations from Ancient

Egypt." *Epidemiology and Infection* 130, no. 2 (April 2003): 239–49. *https://doi.org/10.1017/S0950268802008257.*

Ziskind, B, and B Halioua. "Tuberculosis in Ancient Egypt." *Revue Des Maladies Respiratoires* 24, no. 10 (December 2007): 1277–83. *https://doi.org/10.1016/s0761-8425(07)78506-6.*

APPENDIX CHAPTER 8

Achtman, Mark, Giovanna Morelli, Peixuan Zhu, Thierry Wirth, Ines Diehl, Barica Kusecek, Amy J. Vogler, et al. "Microevolution and History of the Plague Bacillus, Yersinia Pestis." *Proceedings of the National Academy of Sciences of the United States of America* 101, no. 51 (December 2004): 17837–42. *https://doi.org/10.1073/pnas.0408026101.*

Barros Damgaard, Peter De, Nina Marchi, Simon Rasmussen, Michaël Peyrot, Gabriel Renaud, Thorfinn Korneliussen, J. Víctor Moreno-Mayar, et al. "137 Ancient Human Genomes from across the Eurasian Steppes." *Nature* 557, no. 7705 (May 2018): 369–74. *https://doi.org/10.1038/s41586-018-0094-2.*

Burki, Talha. "Justinian's Flea: Plague, Empire and the Birth of Europe." *The Lancet Infectious Diseases* 7, no. 12 (December 2007): 774. *https://doi.org/10.1016/s1473-3099(07)70285-2.*

Carter, K. Codell. "The Germ Theory, Beriberi, and the Deficiency Theory of Disease." *Medical History* 21, no. 2 (April 1977): 119–36. *https://doi.org/10.1017/S0025727300037662.*

Colin Michael Wells. *The Roman Empire*. Cambridge: Harvard University Press, 2004.

Dirckx, J H. "Pestilence Narratives in Classical Literature: A Study in Creative Imitation: I. Homer, Sophocles, Thucydides, and Lucretius." *The American Journal of Dermatopathology* 22, no. 2 (April 2000): 197–202. *https://doi.org/10.1097/00000372-200004000-00021.*

Eddy, Jared J. "The Ancient City of Rome, Its Empire, and the Spread of Tuberculosis in Europe." *Tuberculosis* 95, no. S1 (June 2015): S23–28. *https://doi.org/10.1016/j.tube.2015.02.005.*

Evans, J. A. S. "Procopius of Caesarea and the Emperor Justinian." *Historical Papers* 3, no. 1 (July 2012): 126. *https://doi.org/10.7202/030693ar.*

Findlay, Ronald, Mats Lundahl, Ronald Findlay, and Mats Lundahl. "Demographic Shocks and the Factor Proportions Model: From the Plague of Justinian to the Black Death." In *The Economics of the Frontier: Conquest and Settlement*, 125–72. London: Palgrave Macmillan, 2017. *https://doi.org/10.1057/978-1-137-60237-4_5.*

Joe Pinkstone. "Ancient Romans to Blame for the Spread of Tuberculosis from Africa" *Daily Mail Online*, July 4, 2018. *https://www.dailymail.co.uk/sciencetech/article-5917749/Ancient-Romans-blame-spread-tuberculosis-Africa.html.*

Jonathan M. Hall. *A History of the Archaic Greek World, ca. 1200-479 BCE* Hoboken: Wiley-Blackwell, 2006.

Keller, Marcel, Maria A. Spyrou, Christiana L. Scheib, Gunnar U. Neumann, Andreas Kröpelin, Brigitte Haas-Gebhard, Bernd Päffgen, et al. "Ancient Yersinia Pestis Genomes from across Western Europe Reveal Early Diversification during the First Pandemic (541–750)." *Proceedings of the National Academy of Sciences of the United States of America* 116, no. 25 (June 2019): 12363–72. *https://doi.org/10.1073/pnas.1820447116.*

Kyle Harper. *The Fate of Rome: Climate, Disease, and the End of an Empire.* Princeton: Princeton University Press, 2017.

Langmuir, Alexander D., Thomas D. Worthen, Jon Solomon, C. George Ray, and Eskild Petersen. "The Thucydides Syndrome: A New Hypothesis for the Cause of the Plague of Athens." *New England Journal of Medicine* 313, no. 16 (October 1985): 1027–30. *https://doi.org/10.1056/NEJM198510173131618.*

Littman, R. J., and M. L. Littman. "Galen and the Antonine Plague." *American Journal of Philology* 94 (1973): 243–55. *https://doi. org/10.2307/293979.*

Littman, Robert J. "The Plague of Athens: Epidemiology and Paleopathology." *Mount Sinai Journal of Medicine: A Journal of Translational and Personalized Medicine* 76, no. 5 (October 2009): 456–67. *https://doi.org/10.1002/msj.20137.*

McSherry, J, and R Kilpatrick. "The Plague of Athens." *Journal of the Royal Society of Medicine* 85, no. 11 (November 1992): 713. *http://www.ncbi.nlm.nih.gov/pubmed/1474568.*

Mitchell, Piers D. "Human Parasites in the Roman World: Health Consequences of Conquering an Empire." *Parasitology* 144, no. 1 (January 2017): 48–58. *https://doi.org/10.1017/S0031182015001651.*

Morens, David M., and Robert J. Littman. "Epidemiology of the Plague of Athens." *Transactions of the American Philological Association (1974-2014)* 122 (1992): 271. *https://doi. org/10.2307/284374.*

Nutton, Vivian. "The Seeds of Disease: An Explanation of Contagion and Infection from the Greeks to the Renaissance." *Medical History* 27, no. 1 (January 1983): 1–34. *https://doi.org/10.1017/ S0025727300042241.*

O'Neill, Mary B., Abigail Shockey, Alex Zarley, William Aylward, Vegard Eldholm, Andrew Kitchen, and Caitlin S. Pepperell. "Lineage Specific Histories of *Mycobacterium Tuberculosis* Dispersal in Africa and Eurasia." *Molecular Ecology* 28, no. 13 (July 2019): mec.15120. *https://doi.org/10.1111/mec.15120.*

Page, D. L. "Thucydides' Description of the Great Plague at Athens." *The Classical Quarterly* 3, no. 3–4 (1953): 97–119. *https://doi.org/10.1017/S0009838800003050.*

Papagrigorakis, Manolis J., Christos Yapijakis, and Philippos N. Synodinos. "Typhoid Fever Epidemic in Ancient Athens." In *Paleomicrobiology: Past Human Infections*, edited by Didier Raoult and Michel Drancourt, 161–73. Berlin, Springer Berlin Heidelberg, 2008. *https://doi.org/10.1007/978-3-540-75855-6_10.*

Papagrigorakis, Manolis J., Christos Yapijakis, Philippos N. Synodinos, and Effie Baziotopoulou-Valavani. "DNA Examination of Ancient Dental Pulp Incriminates Typhoid Fever as a Probable Cause of the Plague of Athens." *International Journal of Infectious Diseases* 10, no. 3 (May 2006): 206–14. *https://doi.org/10.1016/j.ijid.2005.09.001.*

Pirages, Dennis C. "Nature, Disease, and Globalization: An Evolutionary Perspective." *International Studies Review* 9, no. 4 (December 2007): 616–28. *https://doi.org/10.1111/j.1468-2486.2007.00726.x.*

Saxonhouse, Arlene W. "Nature & Convention in Thucydides' History." *Polity* 10, no. 4 (June 1978): 461–87. *https://doi.org/10.2307/3234401.*

Stubbs, H. W. "The Plague of Athens: 430–428 B.C. Epidemic and Epizoötic." *The Classical Quarterly* 33, no. 1 (January1983): 6–11. *https://doi.org/10.1017/S0009838800034224.*

Wagner, David M., Jennifer Klunk, Michaela Harbeck, Alison Devault, Nicholas Waglechner, Jason W. Sahl, Jacob Enk, et al. "Yersinia Pestis and the Plague of Justinian 541-543 AD: A

Genomic Analysis." *The Lancet Infectious Diseases* 14, no. 4 (April 2014): 319–26. *https://doi.org/10.1016/S1473-3099(13)70323-2.*

William Rosen. *Justinian's Flea: The First Great Plague and the End of the Roman Empire.* London: Penguin Books, 2007.

Yannopoulos, Stavros, Christos Yapijakis, Asimina Kaiafa-Saropoulou, George Antoniou, and Andreas N. Angelakis. "History of Sanitation and Hygiene Technologies in the Hellenic World." *Journal of Water Sanitation and Hygiene for Development* 7, no. 2 (June 2017): 163–80. *https://doi.org/10.2166/washdev.2017.178.*

APPENDIX CHAPTER 9

Belcastro, Giovanna, Elisa Rastelli, Valentina Mariotti, Chiara Consiglio, Fiorenzo Facchini, and Benedetta Bonfiglioli. "Continuity or Discontinuity of the Life-Style in Central Italy during the Roman Imperial Age-Early Middle Ages Transition: Diet, Health, and Behavior." *American Journal of Physical Anthropology* 132, no. 3 (March 2007): 381–94. *https://doi.org/10.1002/ajpa.20530.*

Cohn, Samuel. "After the Black Death: Labour Legislation and Attitudes towards Labour in Late-Medieval Western Europe." *The Economic History Review* 60, no. 3 (August 2007): 457–85. *https://doi.org/10.1111/j.1468-0289.2006.00368.x.*

David Herlihy. *The Black Death and the Transformation of the West.* Cambridge: Harvard University Press, 1997.

DeWitte, Sharon N., and James W. Wood. "Selectivity of Black Death Mortality with Respect to Preexisting Health." *Proceedings of the National Academy of Sciences of the United States of America* 105, no. 5 (February 2008): 1436–41. *https://doi.org/10.1073/pnas.0705460105.*

Dunnell, Ruth W. *China among Equals: The Middle Kingdom and Its Neighbors, 10th–14th Centuries.* Berkeley: University of California Press, 1983. *https://doi.org/10.2307/2056775.*

Dyer, Alan. "The English Sweating Sickness of 1551: An Epidemic Anatomized." *Medical History* 41, no. 3 (July 1997): 362–84. *https://doi.org/10.1017/s0025727300062724.*

Ell, Stephen R. "Immunity as a Factor in the Epidemiology of Medieval Plague." *Reviews of Infectious Diseases* 6, no. 6 (November 1984): 866–79. *https://doi.org/10.1093/CLINIDS/6.6.866.*

Evans, Elizabeth C. "Galen the Physician as Physiognomist." *Transactions and Proceedings of the American Philological Association* 76 (1945): 287. *https://doi.org/10.2307/283342.*

Flood, John L. "'Safer on the Battlefield than in the City': England, the 'Sweating Sickness', and the Continent." *Renaissance Studies* 17, no. 2 (June 2003): 147–76. *https://doi.org/10.1111/1477-4658.00015.*

Gensini, Gian Franco, Magdi H. Yacoub, and Andrea A. Conti. "The Concept of Quarantine in History: From Plague to SARS." *Journal of Infection* 49, no. 4 (November 2004): 257–61. *https://doi.org/10.1016/j.jinf.2004.03.002.*

Gottfried, R. S. "Population, Plague, and the Sweating Sickness: Demographic Movements in Late Fifteenth-Century England." *Journal of British Studies* 17 (Autumn 1977): 12–37. *https://doi.org/10.2307/175690.*

Haensch, Stephanie, Raffaella Bianucci, Michel Signoli, Minoarisoa Rajerison, Michael Schultz, Sacha Kacki, Marco Vermunt, et al. "Distinct Clones of Yersinia Pestis Caused the Black Death." Edited by Nora J. Besansky. *PLoS Pathogens* 6, no. 10 (October 2010): e1001134. *https://doi.org/10.1371/journal.ppat.1001134.*

Hunter, Paul R. "The English Sweating Sickness, with Particular Reference to the 1551 Outbreak in Chester." *Reviews of Infectious Diseases* 13, no. 2 (March 1991): 303–6. *https://doi.org/10.1093/CLINIDS/13.2.303.*

Irwin, Robert. "Toynbee and Ibn Khaldun." *Middle Eastern Studies* 33, no. 3 (July 1997): 461–79. *https://doi.org/10.1080/00263209708701164.*

Khan, Iqbal Akhtar. "Plague: The Dreadful Visitation Occupying the Human Mind for Centuries." *Transactions of the Royal Society of Tropical Medicine and Hygiene* 98, no. 5 (May 2004): 270–77. *https://doi.org/10.1016/S0035-9203(03)00059-2.*

Leah DeVun. *Prophecy, Alchemy, and the End of Time.* New York: Columbia University Press, 2009.

Matus, Zachary A. "Alchemy and Christianity in the Middle Ages." *History Compass* 10, no. 12 (December 2012): 934–45. *https://doi.org/10.1111/hic3.12013.*

McSweegan, Edward. "Anthrax and the Etiology of the English Sweating Sickness." *Medical Hypotheses* 62, no. 1 (January 2004): 155–57. *https://doi.org/10.1016/S0306-9877(03)00303-7.*

Nohl, Johannes, and C. H Clarke. *The Black Death. A Chronicle of the Plague.* Yardley: Westholme Publishing, 1924.

Norris, John. "East or West? The Geographic Origin of the Black Death." *Bulletin of the History of Medicine* 51, no. 0 (Spring 1977): 1–24. *https://doi.org/10.2307/44450388.*

Ole J. Benedictow. "Yersinia Pestis, the Bacterium of Plague, Arose in East Asia. Did It Spread Westwards via the Silk Roads, the Chinese Maritime Expeditions of Zheng He or over the Vast Eurasian Populations of Sylvatic (Wild) Rodents?" *Journal of*

Asian History 47, no. 1-31 (2013): 1. *https://doi.org/10.13173/jasi-ahist.47.1.0001.*

Ole Jørgen Benedictow, and Ole L. Benedictow. *The Black Death, 1346-1353: The Complete History.* Woodbridge: Boydell Press, 2004.

Pamuk, Şevket. "The Black Death and the Origins of the 'great Divergence' across Europe, 1300-1600." *European Review of Economic History* 11, no. 3 (December 2007): 289–317. *https://doi.org/10.1017/S1361491607002031.*

Payne, J. F. "On an Unpublished English Anatomical Treatise of the Fourteenth Century; and Its Relation to the 'Anatomy' of Thomas Vicary." *British Medical Journal* 1, no. 1830 (January1896): 200–203. *https://doi.org/10.1136/bmj.1.1830.200.*

Plinio Prioreschi. *A History of Medicine: Medieval Medicine.* Omaha: Horatius Press, 1996.

Robert S. Gottfried. *The Black Death: Natural and Human Disaster in Medieval Europe.* New York: Free Press, 1985.

Samuel K. Cohn, Jr. *The Black Death Transformed: Disease and Culture in Early Renaissance Europe.* London: Bloomsbury Academic, 2003.

Schammoglu, Uli. "Preliminary Remarks on the Role of Disease in the History of the Golden Horde." *Central Asian Survey* 12, no. 4 (January 1993): 447–57. *https://doi.org/10.1080/02634939308400830.*

Sehdev, Paul S. "The Origin of Quarantine." *Clinical Infectious Diseases* 35, no. 9 (November 2002): 1071–72. *https://doi.org/10.1086/344062.*

Slack, Paul. "The Black Death Past and Present. 2. Some Historical Problems." *Transactions of the Royal Society of Tropical*

Medicine and Hygiene 83, no. 4 (July 1989): 461–63. *https://doi. org/10.1016/0035-9203(89)90247-2.*

Smail, Daniel Lord. "Accommodating Plague in Medieval Marseille." *Continuity and Change* 11, no. 1 (May 1996): 11–41. *https:// doi.org/10.1017/s0268416000003076.*

Wheelis, Mark. "Biological Warfare at the 1346 Siege of Caffa." *Emerging Infectious Diseases* 8, no. 9 (September 2002): 971–75. *https://doi.org/10.3201/eid0809.010536.*

APPENDIX CHAPTER 10

Acuna-Soto, Rodolfo, David W. Stahle, Matthew D. Therrell, Sergio Gomez Chavez, and Malcolm K. Cleaveland. "Drought, Epidemic Disease, and the Fall of Classic Period Cultures in Mesoamerica (AD 750-950). Hemorrhagic Fevers as a Cause of Massive Population Loss." *Medical Hypotheses* 65, no. 2 (January 2005): 405–9. *https://doi.org/10.1016/j.mehy.2005.02.025.*

Alfred W. Crosby. *The Columbian Exchange: Biological and Cultural Consequences of 1492.* Westport: Praeger, 2003.

Angela Herren Rajagopalan. *Portraying the Aztec Past: The Codices Boturini, Azcatitlan, and Aubin.* Texas: University of Texas Press, 2018.

Armelagos, George J., Molly K. Zuckerman, and Kristin N. Harper. "The Science Behind Pre-Columbian Evidence of Syphilis in Europe: Research by Documentary." *Evolutionary Anthropology: Issues, News, and Reviews* 21, no. 2 (March 2012): 50–57. *https://doi.org/10.1002/evan.20340.*

Baker, B. J., and G. J. Armelagos. "The Origin and Antiquity of Syphilis: Paleopathological Diagnosis and Interpretation." *Current Anthropology* 29, no. 5 (October 1988): 703–38. *https:// doi.org/10.1086/203691.*

Black, Francis L. "An Explanation of High Death Rates among New World Peoples When in Contact with Old World Diseases." *Perspectives in Biology and Medicine* 37, no. 2 (Winter 1994): 292–307. *https://doi.org/10.1353/pbm.1994.0030.*

Charles Q. Choi. "Case Closed? Columbus Introduced Syphilis to Europe," Scientific American, December 27, 2011. *https://www.scientificamerican.com/article/case-closed-columbus/.*

Chen, Angus. "One of History's Worst Epidemics May Have Been Caused by a Common Food Poisoning Microbe," Science, January 16, 2018. *https://doi.org/10.1126/science.aato253.*

Childs, Wendy R. "1492-1494: Columbus and the Discovery of America." *The Economic History Review* 48, no. 4 (November 1995): 754. *https://doi.org/10.2307/2598134.*

Crosby, A. W. "Virgin Soil Epidemics as a Factor in the Aboriginal Depopulation in America." *The William and Mary Quarterly* 33 (April 1976): 289–99. *https://doi.org/10.2307/1922166.*

Deagan, Kathleen. "Reconsidering Taíno Social Dynamics after Spanish Conquest: Gender and Class in Culture Contact Studies." *American Antiquity* 69, no. 4 (October 2004): 597–626. *https://doi.org/10.2307/4128440.*

Fleming, William L. "Syphilis Through the Ages." *Medical Clinics of North America* 48, no. 3 (May 1964): 587–612. *https://doi.org/10.1016/s0025-7125(16)33444-7.*

Greg Elwell. "Oklahoma Scientists Still Study Explorers' Impact on Disease," The Oklahoman, October 12, 2013. *http://oklahoman.com/article/3892221/oklahoma-scientists-still-study-explorers-impact-on-disease.*

Grieco, M. H. "The Voyage of Columbus Led to the Spread of Syphilis to Europe." *Allergy Proceedings* 13, no. 5 (September-October 1992): 233–35. *https://doi.org/10.2500/108854192778817130.*

Kathleen A. Deagan, and José María Cruxent. *Columbus's Outpost Among the Taínos: Spain and America at La Isabela, 1493-1498.* London: Yale University Press, 2002.

Knell, Robert J. "Syphilis in Renaissance Europe: Rapid Evolution of an Introduced Sexually Transmitted Disease?" *Proceedings of the Royal Society of London. Series B: Biological Sciences* 271, no. suppl 4 (May 2004): S174–S176. *https://doi.org/10.1098/rsbl.2003.0131.*

Koch, Alexander, Chris Brierley, Mark M. Maslin, and Simon L. Lewis. "Earth System Impacts of the European Arrival and Great Dying in the Americas after 1492." *Quaternary Science Reviews* 207 (March 2019): 13–36. *https://doi.org/10.1016/j.quascirev.2018.12.004.*

Lester Bivens. *Basic Health Care Series: Sexually Transmitted Diseases (STD)* (New Delhi: Alpha Editions, 2017).

McCaa, Robert. "Spanish and Nahuatl Views on Smallpox and Demographic Catastrophe in Mexico." *Journal of Interdisciplinary History* 25, no. 3 (Winter 1995): 397. *https://doi.org/10.2307/205693.*

Noble David Cook. *Born to Die: Disease and New World Conquest, 1492-1650.* Cambridge: Cambridge University Press, 1998.

———. *Demographic Collapse: Indian Peru, 1520-1620.* Cambridge: Cambridge University Press, 1982.

Nunn, Nathan, and Nancy Qian. "The Columbian Exchange: A History of Disease, Food, and Ideas." *Journal of Economic Per-*

spectives 24, no. 2 (March 2010): 163–88. *https://doi.org/10.1257/ jep.24.2.163.*

O'Rourke, Kevin H., and Jeffrey G. Williamson. "After Columbus: Explaining Europe's Overseas Trade Boom, 1500-1800." *Journal of Economic History* 62, no. 2 (June 2002): 417–56. *https://doi. org/10.1017/s0022050702000554.*

Patterson, Kristine B., and Thomas Runge. "Smallpox and the Native American." *American Journal of the Medical Sciences* 323, no. 4 (April 2002): 216–22. *https://doi.org/10.1097/00000441- 200204000-00009.*

Puente, José Luis, and Edmundo Calva. "The One Health Concept-the Aztec Empire and Beyond." *Pathogens and Disease* 75, no. 6 (August2017): 62. *https://doi.org/10.1093/femspd/ftx062.*

Rothschild, B. M. "History of Syphilis." *Clinical Infectious Diseases* 40, no. 10 (May 2005): 1454–63. *https://doi.org/10.1086/429626.*

Rothschild, Bruce M., Fernando Luna Calderon, Alfredo Coppa, and Christine Rothschild. "First European Exposure to Syphilis: The Dominican Republic at the Time of Columbian Contact." *Clinical Infectious Diseases* 31, no. 4 (October 2000): 936–41. *https://doi.org/10.1086/318158.*

Vågene, Åshild J., Alexander Herbig, Michael G. Campana, Nelly M. Robles García, Christina Warinner, Susanna Sabin, Maria A. Spyrou, et al. "Salmonella Enterica Genomes from Victims of a Major Sixteenth-Century Epidemic in Mexico." *Nature Ecology and Evolution* 2, no. 3 (March 2018): 520–28. *https:// doi.org/10.1038/s41559-017-0446-6.*

William McNeill. *Plagues and Peoples.* New York: Anchor, 1976.

APPENDIX CHAPTER 11

Ash, C. "Hooke's Microscope." *Trends in Microbiology* 6, no. 10 (October 1998): 391. *https://doi.org/10.1016/s0966-842x(98)01380-8.*

Atallah, S. "Some Observations on the Great Fire of London, 1666." *Nature* 211, no. 5044 (July 1966): 105–6. *https://doi.org/10.1038/211105b0.*

Bardell, D. "The Roles of the Sense of Taste and Clean Teeth in the Discovery of Bacteria by Antoni van Leeuwenhoek." *Microbiological Reviews* 47, no. 1 (March 1983): 121–26. *http://www.ncbi.nlm.nih.gov/pubmed/6343826.*

Bell, W. G. *The Great Plague in London in 1665.* London: Random House UK Ltd, 1995.

Boulton, Jeremy. "Wage Labour in Seventeenth-Century London." *The Economic History Review* 49, no. 2 (May 1996): 268-290. *https://doi.org/10.2307/2597916.*

Corliss, John O. "Three Centuries of Protozoology: A Brief Tribute to Its Founding Father, A. van Leeuwenhoek of Delft*." *The Journal of Protozoology* 22, no. 1 (February 1975): 3–7. *https://doi.org/10.1111/j.1550-7408.1975.tb00934.x.*

Dennis, Michael Aaron. "Graphic Understanding: Instruments and Interpretation in Robert Hooke's Micrographia." *Science in Context* 3, no. 2 (Autumn 1989): 309–64. *https://doi.org/10.1017/S0269889700000855.*

Ford, B. J. "Bacteria and Cells of Human Origin on van Leeuwenhoek's Sections of 16741,2." *Transactions of the American Microscopical Society* 101, no. 1 (January 1982): 1–9. *https://doi.org/10.2307/3225566.*

Gest, H. "The Discovery of Microorganisms by Robert Hooke and Antoni van Leeuwenhoek, Fellows of The Royal Society." *Notes and Records of the Royal Society of London* 58, no. 2 (May 2004): 187–201. *https://doi.org/10.1098/rsnr.2004.0055.*

Greenberg, Stephen. "Plague, the Printing Press, and Public Health in Seventeenth-Century London." *Huntington Library Quarterly* 67, no. 4 (December 2004): 508–27. *https://doi.org/10.1525/hlq.2004.67.4.508.*

Hollingsworth, Mary F., and T. H. Hollingsworth. "Plague Mortality Rates by Age and Sex in the Parish of St. Botolph's without Bishopsgate, London, 1603." *Population Studies* 25, no. 1 (March 1971): 131–46. *https://doi.org/10.1080/00324728.1971.10405789.*

Jones, P. E., and A. V. Judges. "London Population in the Late Seventeenth Century." *The Economic History Review* 6, no. 1 (October 1935): 45. *https://doi.org/10.2307/2590030.*

Karamanou, M, E Poulakou-Rebelakou, M Tzetis, and G Androutsos. "Anton van Leeuwenhoek (1632-1723): Father of Micromorphology and Discoverer of Spermatozoa." *Rev Argent Microbiol* 42, no. 4 (October-December 2010): 311–14.

Larner, Andrew J. "Antony van Leeuwenhoek and the Description of Diaphragmatic Flutter (Respiratory Myoclonus)." *Movement Disorders* 20, no. 8 (August 2005): 917–18. *https://doi.org/10.1002/mds.20614.*

Lawson, Ian. "Crafting The Microworld: How Robert Hooke Constructed Knowledge about Small Things." *Notes and Records* 70, no. 1 (2016): 23–44. *https://doi.org/10.1098/rsnr.2015.0057.*

O'Mara, Joseph G. "On Leeuwenhoek's Magnifications." *Antonie van Leeuwenhoek* 45, no. 2 (June 1979): 161–64. *https://doi.org/10.1007/BF00418580.*

Palmer, Richard. "The Church, Leprosy and Plague in Medieval and Early Modern Europe." *Studies in Church History* 19 (1982): 79–99. *https://doi.org/10.1017/s0424208400009311*.

Pearl, Valerie. "Change and Stability in Seventeenth-Century London." *The London Journal* 5, no. 1 (July 2013): 3–34. *https://doi.org/10.1179/ldn.1979.5.1.3*.

Porter, J. R. "Antony Van Leeuwenhoek. Tercentenary of His Discovery of Bacteria." *Bacteriological Reviews* 40, no. 2 (June 1976): 260–69. *https://doi.org/10.1128/mmbr.40.2.260-269.1976*.

Robert Hooke. *Micrographia*. Scotts Valley, CreateSpace Independent Publishing Platform, 2014.

Roberts, R. S. "Tercentenary of the Plague of London 1665: The Place of Plague in English History." *Journal of the Royal Society of Medicine* 59, no. 2 (February 1966): 101–5. *https://doi.org/10.1177/003591576605900209*.

Rosen, Alan. "Plague, Fire, and Typology in Defoe's A Journal of the Plague Year" 1, no. 3 (July 1991). *https://doi.org/10.25623/conn001.3-rosen-1*.

Zuylen, J. "The Microscopes of Antoni van Leeuwenhoek." *Journal of Microscopy* 121, no. 3 (March 1981): 309–28. *https://doi.org/10.1111/j.1365-2818.1981.tb01227.x*.

Zwick, Rachel K., and Barbara A. Schmidt. "When Anton van Leeuwenhoek Looked through His Early Microscopes in the 1600s, He Realized That the World Was Teeming with Microbial Organisms. Introduction." *The Yale Journal of Biology and Medicine* 87, no. 1 (March 2014): 1. *https://www.ncbi.nlm.nih.gov/pmc/articles/PMC3941459/*.

APPENDIX CHAPTER 12

Alexander, J. T. "Plague in Russia and Danilo Samoilovich: An Historiographical Comment and Research Note." *Canadian-American Slavic Studies. Revue Canadienne-Americaine d"etudes Slaves* VIII, no. 4 (December 1974): 525–31. *https://doi.org/10.1163/221023974x00145.*

Anderson, Gaylord W. "The Conquest of Epidemic Disease: A Chapter in the History of Ideas." *The American Historical Review* 49, no. 2 (January 1944): 272–73. *https://doi.org/10.1086/ahr/49.2.272.*

Best, M., and D. Neuhauser. "Ignaz Semmelweis and the Birth of Infection Control." *Quality and Safety in Health Care* 13, no. 3 (June 2004): 233–34. *https://doi.org/10.1136/qshc.2004.010918.*

Borodi, N. K. "The History of the Plague Epidemic in the Ukraine in 1770-74." *Soviet Studies in History* 25, no. 4 (1987): 33–43. *https://doi.org/10.2753/rsh1061-1983250433.*

Bradley, Richard, Benjamin Marten, Jean-Baptiste Goiffon, and Raymond Williamson. "The Germ Theory of Disease. Neglected Precursors of Louis Pasteur." *Annals of Science* 11, no. 1 (June 2006): 44–57. *https://doi.org/10.1080/00033795500200035.*

Bramanti, Barbara, Nils Chr Stenseth, Lars Walløe, and Xu Lei. "Plague: A Disease Which Changed the Path of Human Civilization," in *Advances in Experimental Medicine and Biology*, edited by John D. Lambris, 1-26. New York: Springer New York LLC, 2016. *https://doi.org/10.1007/978-94-024-0890-4_1.*

Carter, K. Codell. "Ignaz Semmelweis, Carl Mayrhofer, and the Rise of Germ Theory." *Medical History* 29, no. 1 (January 1985): 33–53. *https://doi.org/10.1017/S0025727300043738.*

Charles de Mertens. *An Account of the Plague Which Raged at Moscow in 1771*. Scotts Valley, CreateSpace Independent Publishing Platform, 2015.

Devaux, Christian A. "Small Oversights That Led to the Great Plague of Marseille (1720-1723): Lessons from the Past." *Infection, Genetics and Evolution* 14, no. 1 (March 2013): 169–85. *https://doi.org/10.1016/j.meegid.2012.11.016.*

Hashemi Shahraki, Abdolrazagh, Elizabeth Carniel, and Ehsan Mostafavi. "Plague in Iran: Its History and Current Status." *Epidemiology and Health* 38 (July 2016): e2016033. *https://doi.org/10.4178/epih.e2016033.*

John T. Alexander. *Bubonic Plague in Early Modern Russia: Public Health and Urban Disaster*. Oxford: Oxford University Press, 2002.

K. Codell Carter and Barbara R. Carter, Childbed Fever: A Scientific Biography of Ignaz Semmelweis. Abingdon: Routledge, 2005.

Karamanou, Marianna, George Panayiotakopoulos, Gregory Tsoucalas, Antonis A Kousoulis, and George Androutsos. "From Miasmas to Germs: A Historical Approach to Theories of Infectious Disease Transmission." *Le Infezioni in Medicina* 20, no. 1 (March 2012): 58–62. *https://pubmed.ncbi.nlm.nih.gov/22475662/*

Leonetti, Georges, Michel Signoli, Anne Laure Pelissier, Pierre Champsaur, Israel Hershkovitz, Christian Brunet, and Olivier Dutour. "Evidence of Pin Implantation as a Means of Verifying Death During the Great Plague of Marseilles (1722)." *Journal of Forensic Sciences* 42, no. 4 (July 1997): 14197J. *https://doi.org/10.1520/jfs14197j.*

Manor, Joshua, Nava Blum, and Yoav Lurie. "'No Good Deed Goes Unpunished': Ignaz Semmelweis and the Story of Puerperal Fever." *Infection Control and Hospital Epidemiology* 37, no. 8 (August 2016): 881–87. *https://doi.org/10.1017/ice.2016.100.*

Meagan Flynn. "The Man Who Discovered That Unwashed Hands Could Kill — and Was Ridiculed for It," *The Washington Post*, March 23, 2020. *https://www.washingtonpost.com/nation/2020/03/23/ignaz-semmelweis-handwashing-coronavirus/.*

Prokhorov, M. F. "The Moscow Uprising of September 1771." *Soviet Studies in History* 25, no. 4 (1987): 44–78. *https://doi.org/10.2753/rsh1061-1983250444.*

Raemer, Daniel B. "Ignaz Semmelweis Redux?" *Simulation in Healthcare: The Journal of the Society for Simulation in Healthcare* 9, no. 3 (June 2014): 153–55. *https://doi.org/10.1097/SIH.0000000000000016.*

Rochelle, Pierre La, and Anne-Sophie Julien. "How Dramatic Were the Effects of Handwashing on Maternal Mortality Observed by Ignaz Semmelweis?" *Journal of the Royal Society of Medicine* 106, no. 11 (November 2013): 459–60. *https://doi.org/10.1177/0141076813507843.*

Schmid, Boris V., Ulf Büntgen, W. Ryan Easterday, Christian Ginzler, Lars Walløe, Barbara Bramanti, and Nils Chr Stenseth. "Climate-Driven Introduction of the Black Death and Successive Plague Reintroductions into Europe." *Proceedings of the National Academy of Sciences of the United States of America* 112, no. 10 (March 2015): 3020–25. *https://doi.org/10.1073/pnas.1412887112.*

Semmelweis, Ignaz. *The Etiology, Concept, and Prophylaxis of Childbed Fever*, translated by K. Codell Carter. Madison: University of Wisconsin Press, 1983.

Signoli, M. "La Rechute Epidemique de La Grande Peste de Marseille [Mai-Juillet 1722] : Le Charnier de l'observance." *Medecine Tropicale* 58, no. 2 SUPPL. 1 (January 1998): 7–13. *https://europepmc.org/article/med/9812303*.

W. F. Bynum, *Science and the Practice of Medicine in the Nineteenth Century.* Cambridge: Cambridge University Press, 1990.

Wenger, Alexandre. "[Regulations in the Struggle against the Plague. Geneva Facing the Great Plague of Marseille (1720-1723)]." *Gesnerus* 60, no. 1–2 (January 2003): 62–82. *http://www.ncbi.nlm.nih.gov/pubmed/12918298*.

APPENDIX CHAPTER 13

Azizi, Mh, and F Azizi. "History of Cholera Outbreaks in Iran during the 19(Th) and 20(Th) Centuries." *Middle East Journal of Digestive Diseases* 2, no. 1 (January 2010): 51–55. *https://doi.org/10.15171/middleeastjdi.v2i1.426*.

Bairoch, Paul, and Gary Goertz. "Factors of Urbanisation in the Nineteenth Century Developed Countries." *Urban Studies* 23, no. 4 (August 1986): 285–305. *https://doi.org/10.1080/00420988620080351*.

Barbara Bates. *Bargaining for Life: A Social History of Tuberculosis, 1876-1938.* Philadelphia: University of Pennsylvania Press, 1992.

Barua, Dhiman. "History of Cholera." In *Cholera* edited by Dhiman Barua William and B. Greenough III, 1–36. New York: Springer US, 1992. *https://doi.org/10.1007/978-1-4757-9688-9_1*.

Blevins, Steve M., and Michael S. Bronze. "Robert Koch and the 'golden Age' of Bacteriology." *International Journal of Infectious Diseases* 14, no. 9 (September 2010): e744–51. *https://doi.org/10.1016/j.ijid.2009.12.003*.

Cohn, Samuel. "Fear and the Corpse: Cholera and Plague Riots Compared." In *Histories of Post-Mortem Contagion*, edited by Christos Lynteris and Nicholas H. A. Evans, 55–81. New York: Springer International Publishing, 2018. *https://doi.org/10.1007/978-3-319-62929-2_3*.

Daniel, Thomas M. "The History of Tuberculosis." *Respiratory Medicine* 100, no. 11 (November 2006): 1862–70. *https://doi.org/10.1016/j.rmed.2006.08.006*.

Devault, Alison M., G. Brian Golding, Nicholas Waglechner, Jacob M. Enk, Melanie Kuch, Joseph H. Tien, Mang Shi, et al. "Second-Pandemic Strain of *Vibrio Cholerae* from the Philadelphia Cholera Outbreak of 1849." *New England Journal of Medicine* 370, no. 4 (January 2014): 334–40. *https://doi.org/10.1056/NEJMoa1308663*.

Donoghue, Helen D., Mark Spigelman, Charles L. Greenblatt, Galit Lev-Maor, Gila Kahila Bar-Gal, Carney Matheson, Kim Vernon, Andreas G. Nerlich, and Albert R. Zink. "Tuberculosis: From Prehistory to Robert Koch, as Revealed by Ancient DNA." *Lancet Infectious Diseases* 4, no. 9 (September 2004): 584–92. *https://doi.org/10.1016/S1473-3099(04)01133-8*.

Friedlander, A. M. "Microbiology: Tackling Anthrax." *Nature* 414, no. 6860 (November 2001): 160–61. *https://doi.org/10.1038/35102660*.

Gill, Geoffrey, Sean Burrell, and Jody Brown. "Fear and Frustration — The Liverpool Cholera Riots of 1832." *Lancet* 358, no. 9277 (July 2001): 233–37. *https://doi.org/10.1016/S0140-6736(01)05463-0*.

Hardy, Anne. "Cholera, Quarantine and the English Preventive System, 1850–1895." *Medical History* 37, no. 3 (July 1993): 250–69. *https://doi.org/10.1017/S0025727300058440*.

Howard-Jones, N. "Robert Koch and the Cholera Vibrio: A Centenary." *British Medical Journal (Clinical Research Ed.)* 288, no. 6414 (February 1984): 379–81. *https://doi.org/10.1136/bmj.288.6414.379.*

Howard-Jones, Norman. "Cholera Nomenclature and Nosology: A Historical Note." *Bulletin of the World Health Organization* 51, no. 3 (1974): 317. /pmc/articles/PMC2366284/?report=abstract.

John Snow. *On the Mode of Communication of Cholera.* London: Wilson and Ogilvy for John Churchill, 1849.

Kobarfard, F. "Tuberculosis and Traditional Medicine: Fighting the Oldest Infectious Disease Using the Oldest Source of Medicines." *Iranian Journal of Pharmaceutical Research*, vol. 0 (November 2004): 182-87. *https://doi.org/10.22037/IJPR.2010.578.*

Koch, Tom, and Kenneth Denike. "Crediting His Critics' Concerns: Remaking John Snow's Map of Broad Street Cholera, 1854." *Social Science and Medicine* 69, no. 8 (October 2009): 1246–51. *https://doi.org/10.1016/j.socscimed.2009.07.046.*

McGrew, R. E. "The First Cholera Epidemic and Social History." *Bulletin of the History of Medicine* 34, no. 1 (1960): 61–73. *https://www.jstor.org/stable/44446659.*

Münch, Ragnhild. "Robert Koch." *Microbes and Infection* 5, no. 1 (January 2003): 69–74. *https://doi.org/10.1016/S1286-4579(02)00053-9.*

Murray, John F., Dean E. Schraufnagel, and Philip C. Hopewell. "Treatment of Tuberculosis: A Historical Perspective." *Annals of the American Thoracic Society* 12, no. 12 (December 2015): 1749–59. *https://doi.org/10.1513/AnnalsATS.201509-632PS.*

Myron Echenberg. "Pestis Redux: The Initial Years of the Third Bubonic Plague Pandemic, 1894-1901." *Journal of World History*

13, no. 2 (Fall 2002). *https://www.jstor.org/stable/20078978?se-q=1#metadata_info_tab_contents*.

Pasteur, M. "An Address on Vaccination in Relation to Chicken Cholera and Splenic Fever." *British Medical Journal* 2, no. 1076 (August 1881): 283–84. *https://doi.org/10.1136/bmj.2.1076.283*.

Perry, Robert D., and Jacqueline D. Fetherston. "Yersinia Pestis — Etiologic Agent of Plague." *Clinical Microbiology Reviews* 10, no. 1 (January 1997): 35–66. *https://doi.org/10.1128/cmr.10.1.35*.

Pollitzer, R, and George Williams Hooper Foundation. "Cholera Studies." *Bull. Org. Mond. Sante* 10, no. 3 (1954): 421–61. /pmc/articles/PMC2542143/?report=abstract.

René Jules Dubos, and Jean Dubos. *The White Plague: Tuberculosis, Man, and Society.* New Brunswick: Rutgers University Press, 1987.

Richard K. Riegelman. *Public Health 101: Healthy People-Healthy Populations.* Burlington: Jones & Bartlett Learning, 2010.

Ryan, Edward T. "The Cholera Pandemic, Still with Us after Half a Century: Time to Rethink." *PLoS Neglected Tropical Diseases* 5, no. 1 (January 2011): e1003. *https://doi.org/10.1371/journal.pntd.0001003*.

Sandra Hempel. *The Strange Case of the Broad Street Pump: John Snow and the Mystery of Cholera.* Berkeley: University of California Press, 2007.

Schwartz, Maxime. "Dr. Jekyll and Mr. Hyde: A Short History of Anthrax." *Molecular Aspects of Medicine* 30, no. 6 (December 2009): 347–55. *https://doi.org/10.1016/j.mam.2009.06.004*.

Scorpio, A., T. E. Blank, W. A. Day, and D. J. Chabot. "Anthrax Vaccines: Pasteur to the Present." *Cellular and Molecular Life*

Sciences 63, no. 19–20 (January 2006): 2237–48. *https://doi. org/10.1007/s00018-006-6312-3.*

Seas, Carlos, and Eduarde Gotuzzo. "Cholera: Overview of Epidemiologic, Therapeutic, and Preventive Issues Learned from Recent Epidemics." *International Journal of Infectious Diseases* 1, no. 1 (July 1996): 37–46. *https://doi.org/10.1016/S1201-9712(96)90076-4.*

Sepulveda, J., H. Gomez-Dantes, and M. Bronfman. "Cholera in the Americas: An Overview." *Infection* 20, no. 5 (September 1992): 243–48. *https://doi.org/10.1007/BF01710787.*

Siddique, A. K., and Richard Cash. "Cholera Outbreaks in the Classical Biotype Era." *Current Topics in Microbiology and Immunology*, no. 379 (2014): 1–16. *https://doi.org/10.1007/82_2013_361.*

Spyrou, Maria A., Rezeda I. Tukhbatova, Michal Feldman, Joanna Drath, Sacha Kacki, Julia Beltrán De Heredia, Susanne Arnold, et al. "Historical Y. Pestis Genomes Reveal the European Black Death as the Source of Ancient and Modern Plague Pandemics." *Cell Host and Microbe* 19, no. 6 (June 2016): 874–81. *https://doi. org/10.1016/j.chom.2016.05.012.*

Thomas Butler. "Yersinia Infections: Centennial of the Discovery of the Plague Bacillus." *Clinical Infectious Diseases* 19, no. 4 (October 1994). *https://www.jstor.org/stable/4458084?seq=1#metadata_info_tab_contents.*

Witkowski, Joseph A., and Lawrence Charles Parish. "The Story of Anthrax from Antiquity to the Present: A Biological Weapon of Nature and Humans." *Clinics in Dermatology* 20, no. 4 (July 2002): 336–42. *https://doi.org/10.1016/S0738-081X(02)00250-X.*

Xu, Lei, Qiyong Liu, Leif Chr Stige, Tamara Ben Ari, Xiye Fang, Kung Sik Chan, Shuchun Wang, Nils Chr Stenseth, and Zhibin Zhang. "Nonlinear Effect of Climate on Plague during the

Third Pandemic in China." *Proceedings of the National Academy of Sciences of the United States of America* 108, no. 25 (June 2011): 10214–19. *https://doi.org/10.1073/pnas.1019486108.*

Zajaczkowski, Thaddaeus. "Genitourinary Tuberculosis: Historical and Basic Science Review: Past and Present." *Central European Journal of Urology* 65, no. 4 (December 2012): 182–87. *https://doi.org/10.5173/ceju.2012.04.art1.*

APPENDIX CHAPTER 14

Bennett, Joan W., and King Thom Chung. "Alexander Fleming and the Discovery of Penicillin." *Advances in Applied Microbiology* 49 (January 2001): 163–84. *https://doi.org/10.1016/S0065-2164(01)49013-7.*

Brennan, S. S., M. E. Foster, and D. J. Leaper. "Antiseptic Toxicity in Wounds Healing by Secondary Intention." *Journal of Hospital Infection* 8, no. 3 (November 1986): 263–67. *https://doi.org/10.1016/0195-6701(86)90122-2.*

Chain, Ernst. "The Early Years of the Penicillin Discovery." *Trends in Pharmacological Sciences* 1, no. 1 (January 1979): 6–11. *https://doi.org/10.1016/0165-6147(79)90004-X.*

Cooper, R. D.G. "The Enzymes Involved in Biosynthesis of Penicillin and Cephalosporin; Their Structure and Function." *Bioorganic and Medicinal Chemistry* 1, no. 1 (July 1993): 1–17. *https://doi.org/10.1016/S0968-0896(00)82098-2.*

Faxon, N. W., and E. D. Churchill. "The Cocoanut Grove Disaster in Boston: A Preliminary Account." *Journal of the American Medical Association* 120, no. 17 (December 1942): 1385–88. *https://doi.org/10.1001/jama.1942.82830520005010.*

Fleming, Alexander. "A Comparison of the Activities Antiseptics on Bacteria and on Leucocytes." *Proceedings of the Royal Soci-*

ety of London. Series B, Containing Papers of a Biological Character* 96, no. 674 (April 1924): 171–80. *https://doi.org/10.1098/rspb.1924.0019.*

———. "On the Antibacterial Action of Cultures of a Penicillium, with Special Reference to Their Use in the Isolation of B. Influenzæ." *British Journal of Experimental Pathology* 10, no. 3 (June 1929): 226. *https://www.ncbi.nlm.nih.gov/pmc/articles/PMC2048009/.*

———. "Penicillin." *British Medical Journal* 2, no. 4210 (September 1941): 386. *https://www.ncbi.nlm.nih.gov/pmc/articles/PMC2162878/.*

Grossman, Charles M. "The First Use of Penicillin in the United States." *Annals of Internal Medicine* 149, no. 2 (July 2008): 135. *https://doi.org/10.7326/0003-4819-149-2-200807150-00009.*

Hans T. Clarke. *Chemistry of Penicillin.* Princeton: Princeton University Press, 1949.

Harris, H. "Howard Florey and the Development of Penicillin." *Notes and Records of the Royal Society of London* 53, no. 2 (May 1999): 243–52. *https://doi.org/10.1098/rsnr.1999.0078.*

Henderson, John Warren. "The Yellow Brick Road to Penicillin: A Story of Serendipity." *Mayo Clinic Proceedings* 72, no. 7 (July 1997): 683–87. *https://doi.org/10.4065/72.7.683.*

Jollès, Pierre, and Jacqueline Jollès. "What's New in Lysozyme Research? — Always a Model System, Today as Yesterday." *Molecular and Cellular Biochemistry* 63, no. 2 (September 1984): 165–89. *https://doi.org/10.1007/BF00285225.*

Judith Walzer Leavitt, and Ronald L. *Sickness and Health in America: Readings in the History of Medicine and Public Health.* Madison: University of Wisconsin Press, 1997.

Kardos, Nelson, and Arnold L. Demain. "Penicillin: The Medicine with the Greatest Impact on Therapeutic Outcomes." *Applied Microbiology and Biotechnology* 92, no. 4 (November 2011): 677–87. *https://doi.org/10.1007/s00253-011-3587-6.*

Levy, Stuart B., and Stuart B. Levy. "From Tragedy the Antibiotic Age Is Born." In *The Antibiotic Paradox*, 1–12. Cambridge: Da Capo Press, 2002. *https://doi.org/10.1007/978-1-4899-6042-9_1.*

Ligon, B. Lee. "Penicillin: Its Discovery and Early Development." *Seminars in Pediatric Infectious Diseases* 15, no. 1 (January 2004): 52–57. *https://doi.org/10.1053/j.spid.2004.02.001.*

———. "Sir Alexander Fleming: Scottish Researcher Who Discovered Penicillin." *Seminars in Pediatric Infectious Diseases* 15, no. 1 (January 2004): 58–64. *https://doi.org/10.1053/j.spid.2004.02.002.*

Mark Jackson. *The History of Medicine: A Beginner's Guide.* London: Oneworld Publications, 2014.

Moberg, Carol L. "Penicillin's Forgotten Man: Norman Heatley; Although He's Been Overlooked, His Skills in Growing Penicillin Were a Key to Florey and Chain's Clinical Trials." *Science* 253, no. 5021 (August 1991): 734–36.

Neushul, Peter. "Science, Government, and the Mass Production of Penicillin." *Journal of the History of Medicine and Allied Sciences* 48, no. 3 (October 1993): 371–95. *https://doi.org/10.1093/jhmas/48.4.371.*

Oxford, John, Herman Goossens, Michael Schedler, Armine Sefton, Aurelio Sessa, and Alike Van Der Velden. "Factors Influencing Inappropriate Antibiotic Prescription in Europe." *Education for Primary Care* 24, no. 4 (July 2013): 291–93. *https://doi.org/10.1080/14739879.2013.11494187.*

American Chemical Society "Penicillin Production through Deep-Tank Fermentation — National Historic Chemical Landmark" Accessed July 7, 2020. *https://www.acs.org/content/acs/en/education/whatischemistry/landmarks/penicillin.html.*

Raja, Kavita. "Editorial on Penicillin-Sensitive Bacteria." *Journal of The Academy of Clinical Microbiologists* 16, no. 1 (2014): 17. *https://doi.org/10.4103/0972-1282.134457.*

Robert Bud. *Penicillin: Triumph and Tragedy.* Oxford: Oxford University Press, 2007.

Schmidt, W H, and A J Moyer. "Penicillin: I. Methods of Assay." *Journal of Bacteriology* 47, no. 2 (February 1944): 199–209. *https://doi.org/10.1042/bjo380061.*

Sykes, R. "Penicillin: From Discovery to Product." *Bulletin of the World Health Organization* 79, no. 8 (2001): 778–79. *https://doi.org/10.1590/S0042-96862001000800016.*

Tan, Siang Yong, and Yvonne Tatsumura. "Alexander Fleming (1881–1955): Discoverer of Penicillin." *Singapore Medical Journal* 56, no. 7 (July 2015): 366–67. *https://doi.org/10.11622/smedj.2015105.*

Weisse, A. B. "The Long Pause: The Discovery and Rediscovery of Penicillin." *Hospital Practice* 26, no. 8 (August 1991): 93–118. *https://doi.org/10.1080/21548331.1991.11705281.*

APPENDIX CHAPTER 15

Aminov, Rustam. "History of Antimicrobial Drug Discovery: Major Classes and Health Impact." *Biochemical Pharmacology* 133 (June 1, 2017): 4–19. *https://doi.org/10.1016/j.bcp.2016.10.001.*

Barber, Mary. "Staphylococcal Infection Due to Penicillin-Resistant Strains." *British Medical Journal* 2, no. 4534 (November 1947): 863–65. *https://doi.org/10.1136/bmj.2.4534.863.*

Barber, Mary, A. A.C. Dutton, M. A. Beard, P. C. Elmes, and Roger Williams. "Reversal of Antibiotic Resistance in Hospital Staphylococcal Infection." *British Medical Journal* 1, no. 5165 (January 1960): 11–17. *https://doi.org/10.1136/bmj.1.5165.11.*

Boucher, Helen W., and G. Ralph Corey. "Epidemiology of Methicillin-Resistant *Staphylococcus Aureus.*" *Clinical Infectious Diseases* 46, no. S5 (June 2008): S344–49. *https://doi.org/10.1086/533590.*

National Academies of Sciences, Engineering, and Medicine. *"Combating Antimicrobial Resistance: A One Health Approach to a Global Threat,"* Proceedings of a Workshop. Washington, DC: The National Academies Press, 2017. *https://doi.org/10.17226/24914.*

Crawford, Paul, Brian Brown, Brigitte Nerlich, and Nelya Koteyko. "The 'Moral Careers' of Microbes and the Rise of the Matrons: An Analysis of UK National Press Coverage of Methicillin-Resistant *Staphylococcus Aureus* (MRSA) 1995–2006." *Health, Risk & Society* 10, no. 4 (August 2008): 331–47. *https://doi.org/10.1080/13698570802167397.*

Dahle, Ulf R., Charlotte Ulstad, and Sophie Berg. "Norwegian Public Health Investigation Shows That Antibiotic Resistance Concerns Us All." *BMJ (Online)* 351 (July 2015). *https://doi.org/10.1136/bmj.h4055.*

Frederick R. Falkiner, "Antibiotics in Plant Tissue Culture and Micropropagation — What Are We Aiming At?" In *Pathogen and Microbial Contamination Management in Micropropagation,* edited by A. C. Cassells, 155–60. New York, Springer, 1997. *https://doi.org/10.1007/978-94-015-8951-2_18.*

Herbst, Christine, Frauke Naumann, Eva Brigitta Kruse, Ina Monsef, Julia Bohlius, Holger Schulz, and Andreas Engert. "Prophylactic Antibiotics or G-CSF for the Prevention of Infections and Improvement of Survival in Cancer Patients Undergoing Chemotherapy," *Cochrane Database of Systematic Reviews* 21, no. 1 (January 2009): CD007107. *https://doi.org/10.1002/14651858. CD007107.pub2.*

Higgins, N. Patrick, and Alexander V. Vologodskii. "Topological Behavior of Plasmid DNA." *Microbiology Spectrum* 3, no. 2 (April 2015). https://doi.org/10.1128/microbiolspec.plas-0036-2014.

Hiramatsu, Keiichi. "The Emergence of Staphylococcus Aureus with Reduced Susceptibility to Vancomycin in Japan." *American Journal of Medicine* 104, no. 5 A (May 1998): 7S-10S. *https:// doi.org/10.1016/S0002-9343(98)00149-1.*

Hooton, Thomas M., and Stuart B. Levy. "Antimicrobial Resistence: A Plan of Action for Community Practice." *American Family Physician* 63, no. 6 (March 2001): 1087. *www.aafp.org/ afpAMERICANFAMILYPHYSICIAN1087.*

Jacoby, George A. "History of Drug-Resistant Microbes." In *Antimicrobial Drug Resistance*, edited by Douglas L. Mayers, 3-8. New York: Springer International Publishing, 2017. *https://doi. org/10.1007/978-3-319-46718-4_1.*

Claas Kirchhelle, Picking One's Poisons. New Brunswick: Rutgers University Press, 2020. *https://www.ncbi.nlm.nih.gov/books/ NBK554194/.*

Kurosu, Michio, Shajila Siricilla, and Katsuhiko Mitachi. "Advances in MRSA Drug Discovery: Where Are We and Where Do We Need to Be?" *Expert Opinion on Drug Discovery* 8, no. 9 (September 2013): 1095–1116. *https://doi.org/10.1517/ 17460441.2013.807246.*

Laskin, Daniel M., C. Daniel Dent, Harold F. Morris, Shigeru Ochi, and John W. Olson. "The Influence of Preoperative Antibiotics on Success of Endosseous Implants at 36 Months." *Annals of Periodontology* 5, no. 1 (December 2000): 166–74. *https://doi. org/10.1902/annals.2000.5.1.166.*

Lederberg, Joshua. "Cell Genetics and Hereditary Symbiosis." *Physiological Reviews* 32, no. 4 (October 1952): 403–30. *https:// doi.org/10.1152/physrev.1952.32.4.403.*

Levy, Stuart B. "Antibiotic Resistance: Consequences of Inaction." *Clinical Infectious Diseases* 33, no. s3 (September 2001): S124–29. *https://doi.org/10.1086/321837.*

Levy, Stuart B. "Antibiotic Resistance — The Problem Intensifies." *Advanced Drug Delivery Reviews* 57, no. 10 (July 2005): 1446–50. *https://doi.org/10.1016/j.addr.2005.04.001.*

Lyddiard, Dane, Graham L. Jones, and Ben W. Greatrex. "Keeping It Simple: Lessons from the Golden Era of Antibiotic Discovery." *FEMS Microbiology Letters* 363, no. 8 (March 2016): fnw084. *https://doi.org/10.1093/femsle/fnw084.*

National Academies of Sciences, Engineering, and Medicine. "Combating Antimicrobial Resistance: A One Health Approach to a Global Threat, " Proceedings of a Workshop. Washington, DC: The National Academies Press, 2017.

Patrick Guilfoile, I., and Edward Alcamo. *Antibiotic-Resistant Bacteria.* New York: Chelsea House Publications, 2006.

Peeters, Michael J., and Juan C. Sarria. "Clinical Characteristics of Linezolid-Resistant Staphylococcus Aureus Infections." *American Journal of the Medical Sciences* 330, no. 2 (August 2005): 102–4. *https://doi.org/10.1097/00000441-200508000-00007.*

Ridley, Mark, Dinah Barrie, R. Lynn, and K. C. Stead. "Antibiotic-Resistant Staphylococcus Aureus and Hospital Antibiotic Policies." *The Lancet* 295, no. 7640 (January 1970): 230–33. *https://doi.org/10.1016/S0140-6736(70)90585-4.*

Scott H. Podolsky. *The Antibiotic Era: Reform, Resistance, and the Pursuit of a Rational Therapeutics.* Baltimore: Johns Hopkins University Press, 2015.

Sievert, D. M., J. T. Rudrik, J. B. Patel, L. C. McDonald, M. J. Wilkins, and J. C. Hageman. "Vancomycin-Resistant Staphylococcus Aureus in the United States, 2002-2006." *Clinical Infectious Diseases* 46, no. 5 (March 2008): 668–74. *https://doi. org/10.1086/527392.*

Silver, L. L., and K. A. Bostian. "Discovery and Development of New Antibiotics: The Problem of Antibiotic Resistance." *Antimicrobial Agents and Chemotherapy* 37, no. 3 (March 1993): 377–83. *https://doi.org/10.1128/AAC.37.3.377.*

Simon, David M., and Stuart Levin. "Infectious Complications of Solid Organ Transplantations." *Infectious Disease Clinics of North America* 15, no. 2 (June 2001): 521–49. *https://doi. org/10.1016/S0891-5520(05)70158-6.*

Spellberg, B., R. Guidos, D. Gilbert, J. Bradley, H. W. Boucher, W. M. Scheld, J. G. Bartlett, and J. Edwards. "The Epidemic of Antibiotic-Resistant Infections: A Call to Action for the Medical Community from the Infectious Diseases Society of America." *Clinical Infectious Diseases* 46, no. 2 (January 2008): 155–64. *https://doi.org/10.1086/524891.*

Vandenesch, François, Timothy Naimi, Mark C. Enright, Gerard Lina, Graeme R. Nimmo, Helen Heffernan, Nadia Liassine, et al. "Community-Acquired Methicillin-Resistant Staphylococcus Aureus Carrying Panton-Valentine Leukocidin Genes:

Worldwide Emergence." *Emerging Infectious Diseases* 9, no. 8 (August 2003): 978–84. *https://doi.org/10.3201/eid0908.030089.*

Watts, Geoff. "Ephraim Saul Anderson." *The Lancet* 367, no. 9520 (April 2006): 1392. *https://doi.org/10.1016/s0140-6736(06)68603-0.*

Wintersdorff, Christian J.H. Von, John Penders, Julius M. Van Niekerk, Nathan D. Mills, Snehali Majumder, Lieke B. Van Alphen, Paul H.M. Savelkoul, and Petra F.G. Wolffs. "Dissemination of Antimicrobial Resistance in Microbial Ecosystems through Horizontal Gene Transfer." *Frontiers in Microbiology* 7 (February 2016): 173. *https://doi.org/10.3389/fmicb.2016.00173.*

World Health Organization "Antimicrobial Resistance." Accessed July 8, 2020. *https://www.who.int/health-topics/antimicrobial-resistance.*

Young, Kathleen T., and Thomas F. O'Brien. "Alliance for the Prudent Use of Antibiotics: Scientific Vision and Public Health Mission." In *Frontiers in Antimicrobial Resistance: A Tribute to Stuart B. Levy,* edited by David G. White, Michael N. Alekshun and Patrick F. McDermott, 519-27. Washington, D.C.:American Society of Microbiology, 2014. *https://doi.org/10.1128/9781555817572.ch38.*

APPENDIX CHAPTER 16

Andersson, Dan I. "Persistence of Antibiotic Resistant Bacteria." *Current Opinion in Microbiology* 6, no. 5 (October 2003): 452–56. *https://doi.org/10.1016/j.mib.2003.09.001.*

Bennett, P. M. "Plasmid Encoded Antibiotic Resistance: Acquisition and Transfer of Antibiotic Resistance Genes in Bacteria." *British Journal of Pharmacology* 153, no. SUPPL. 1 (March 2008): S347–57. *https://doi.org/10.1038/sj.bjp.0707607.*

Calfee, David P. "Recent Advances in the Understanding and Management of Klebsiella Pneumoniae." *F1000Research* 6 (September 2017): 1760. *https://doi.org/10.12688/f1000research.11532.1.*

Costerton, J. W., J. M. Ingram, and K. J. Cheng. "Structure and Function of the Cell Envelope of Gram Negative Bacteria." *Bacteriological Reviews* 38, no. 1 (March 1974): 87–110. *https://doi.org/10.1128/mmbr.38.1.87-110.1974.*

Cox, Georgina, and Gerard D. Wright. "Intrinsic Antibiotic Resistance: Mechanisms, Origins, Challenges and Solutions." *International Journal of Medical Microbiology* 303, no. 6–7 (August 2013): 287–92. *https://doi.org/10.1016/j.ijmm.2013.02.009.*

Duin, David van, and David L. Paterson. "Multidrug-Resistant Bacteria in the Community: Trends and Lessons Learned." *Infectious Disease Clinics of North America* 30, no. 2 (June 2016): 377–90. *https://doi.org/10.1016/j.idc.2016.02.004.*

Freire-Moran, Laura, Bo Aronsson, Chris Manz, Inge C. Gyssens, Anthony D. So, Dominique L. Monnet, and Otto Cars. "Critical Shortage of New Antibiotics in Development against Multidrug-Resistant Bacteria — Time to React Is Now." *Drug Resistance Updates* 14, no. 2 (April 2011): 118–24. *https://doi.org/10.1016/j.drup.2011.02.003.*

Friedrich, Carol L., Dianne Moyles, Terry J. Beveridge, and Robert E.W. Hancock. "Antibacterial Action of Structurally Diverse Cationic Peptides on Gram- Positive Bacteria." *Antimicrobial Agents and Chemotherapy* 44, no. 8 (August 2000): 2086–92. *https://doi.org/10.1128/AAC.44.8.2086-2092.2000.*

Girgis, Hany S., Alison K. Hottes, and Saeed Tavazoie. "Genetic Architecture of Intrinsic Antibiotic Susceptibility." Edited by Christophe Herman. *PLoS ONE* 4, no. 5 (May 2009): e5629. *https://doi.org/10.1371/journal.pone.0005629.*

Huang, Susan S., Rupak Datta, and Richard Platt. "Risk of Acquiring Antibiotic-Resistant Bacteria from Prior Room Occupants." *Archives of Internal Medicine* 166, no. 18 (October 2006): 1945–51. *https://doi.org/10.1001/archinte.166.18.1945*.

Josey, D. P., J. L. Neynon, A. W.B. Johnston, and J. E. Beringer. "Strain Identification in Rhizobium Using Intrinsic Antibiotic Resistance." *Journal of Applied Bacteriology* 46, no. 2 (April 1979): 343–50. *https://doi.org/10.1111/j.1365-2672.1979.tb00830.x*.

Levy, Stuart B., George B. Fitzgerald, and Ann B. Macone. "Spread of Antibiotic-Resistant Plasmids from Chicken to Chicken and from Chicken to Man." *Nature* 260, no. 5546 (March 1976): 40–42. *https://doi.org/10.1038/260040a0*.

Lown, J. William. "The Mechanism of Action of Quinone Antibiotics." *Molecular and Cellular Biochemistry* 55, no. 1 (March 1983): 17–40. *https://doi.org/10.1007/BF00229240*.

Moura, Alexandra, Carolina Pereira, Isabel Henriques, and António Correia. "Novel Gene Cassettes and Integrons in Antibiotic-Resistant Bacteria Isolated from Urban Wastewaters." *Research in Microbiology* 163, no. 2 (February 2012): 92–100. *https://doi.org/10.1016/j.resmic.2011.10.010*.

Olaitan, Abiola O., Serge Morand, and Jean Marc Rolain. "Mechanisms of Polymyxin Resistance: Acquired and Intrinsic Resistance in Bacteria." *Frontiers in Microbiology* 5 (November 2014): 643. *https://doi.org/10.3389/fmicb.2014.00643*.

Reynolds, P. E. "Structure, Biochemistry and Mechanism of Action of Glycopeptide Antibiotics." *European Journal of Clinical Microbiology & Infectious Diseases* 8, no. 11 (November 1989): 943–50. *https://doi.org/10.1007/BF01967563*.

Sizemore, R. K., and R. R. Colwell. "Plasmids Carried by Antibiotic Resistant Marine Bacteria." *Antimicrobial Agents and*

Chemotherapy 12, no. 3 (September 1977): 373–82. *https://doi. org/10.1128/AAC.12.3.373.*

Souli, M., I. Galani, and H. Giamarellou. "Emergence of Extensively Drug-Resistant and Pandrug-Resistant Gram-Negative Bacilli in Europe." *Euro Surveillance : Bulletin Européen Sur Les Maladies Transmissibles = European Communicable Disease Bulletin* 13, no. 47 (November 2008): 19045. *https://doi. org/10.2807/ese.13.47.19045-en.*

Stalder, Thibault, Olivier Barraud, Magali Casellas, Christophe Dagot, and Marie Cécile Ploy. "Integron Involvement in Environmental Spread of Antibiotic Resistance." *Frontiers in Microbiology* 3, no. APR (April 2012): 119. *https://doi.org/10.3389/ fmicb.2012.00119.*

Teuber, Michael, Leo Meile, and Franziska Schwarz. "Acquired Antibiotic Resistance in Lactic Acid Bacteria from Food." *Antonie van Leeuwenhoek, International Journal of General and Molecular Microbiology* 76, no. 1–4 (November 1999): 115–37. *https://doi.org/10.1023/A:1002035622988.*

Ubeda, Carles, and Eric G. Pamer. "Antibiotics, Microbiota, and Immune Defense." *Trends in Immunology* 33, no. 9 (September 2012): 459–66. *https://doi.org/10.1016/j.it.2012.05.003.*

Wang, C. Y., J. S. Jerng, K. Y. Cheng, L. N. Lee, C. J. Yu, P. R. Hsueh, and P. C. Yang. "Pandrug-Resistant Pseudomonas Aeruginosa among Hospitalised Patients: Clinical Features, Risk-Factors and Outcomes." *Clinical Microbiology and Infection* 12, no. 1 (January 2006): 63–68. *https://doi.org/10.1111/j.1469- 0691.2005.01305.x.*

APPENDIX CHAPTER 17

Aiello, Allison E., Bonnie Marshall, Stuart B. Levy, Phyllis Della-Latta, Susan X. Lin, and Elaine Larson. "Antibacterial

Cleaning Products and Drug Resistance." *Emerging Infectious Diseases* 11, no. 10 (2005): 1565–70. *https://doi.org/10.3201/ eid1110.041276.*

Alonso, Ana, Patricia Sa, Â Nchez, and Jose Â L Martõ Ânez. "Environmental Selection of Antibiotic Resistance Genes." *Environmental Microbiology* 3, no. 1 (2001): 1–9. *https://doi. org/10.1046/j.1462-2920.2001.00161.x.*

Bartlett, John G, David N Gilbert, and Brad Spellberg. "Seven Ways to Preserve the Miracle of Antibiotics." *Clinical Infectious Diseases* 56, no. 10 (May 2013): 1445–50. *https://doi.org/10.1093/ cid/cit070.*

Bengtsson-Palme, Johan, and D. G.Joakim Larsson. "Concentrations of Antibiotics Predicted to Select for Resistant Bacteria: Proposed Limits for Environmental Regulation." *Environment International* 86 (January 2016): 140–49. *https://doi.org/10.1016/j. envint.2015.10.015.*

Birošová, Lucia, and Mária Mikulášová. "Development of Triclosan and Antibiotic Resistance in Salmonella Enterica Serovar Typhimurium." *Journal of Medical Microbiology* 58, no. 4 (April 2009): 436–41. *https://doi.org/10.1099/jmm.0.003657-0.*

Boeckel, Thomas P. Van, Sumanth Gandra, Ashvin Ashok, Quentin Caudron, Bryan T. Grenfell, Simon A. Levin, and Ramanan Laxminarayan. "Global Antibiotic Consumption 2000 to 2010: An Analysis of National Pharmaceutical Sales Data." *The Lancet Infectious Diseases* 14, no. 8 (August 2014): 742–50. *https:// doi.org/10.1016/S1473-3099(14)70780-7.*

Boeckel, Thomas P. Van, João Pires, Reshma Silvester, Cheng Zhao, Julia Song, Nicola G. Criscuolo, Marius Gilbert, Sebastian Bonhoeffer, and Ramanan Laxminarayan. "Global Trends in Antimicrobial Resistance in Animals in Low- And Middle-Income

Countries." *Science* 365, no. 6459 (September 2019). *https://doi. org/10.1126/science.aaw1944.*

Bogaard, Anthony E. Van Den, and Ellen E. Stobberingh. "Antibiotic Usage in Animals. Impact on Bacterial Resistance and Public Health." *Drugs* 58, no. 4 (November 1999): 589–607. *https://doi.org/10.2165/00003495-199958040-00002.*

Capita, Rosa, and Carlos Alonso-Calleja. "Antibiotic-Resistant Bacteria: A Challenge for the Food Industry." *Critical Reviews in Food Science and Nutrition* 53, no. 1 (January 2013): 11–48. *https://doi.org/10.1080/10408398.2010.519837.*

Carey, Daniel E., and Patrick J. McNamara. "The Impact of Triclosan on the Spread of Antibiotic Resistance in the Environment." *Frontiers in Microbiology* 5 (January 2014): 780. *https:// doi.org/10.3389/fmicb.2014.00780.*

Centers for Disease Control and Prevention, "Antibiotic Use in Outpatient Settings, 2017 | Antibiotic Use." Accessed July 9, 2020. *https://www.cdc.gov/antibiotic-use/stewardship-report/ outpatient.html.*

Centers for Disease Control and Prevention "Biggest Threats and Data | Antibiotic/Antimicrobial Resistance." Accessed July 10, 2020. *https://www.cdc.gov/drugresistance/biggest-threats.html.*

Deguchi, Takashi, Keita Nakane, Mitsuru Yasuda, and Shin Ichi Maeda. "Emergence and Spread of Drug Resistant Neisseria Gonorrhoeae." *Journal of Urology* 184, no. 3 (September 2010): 851–58. *https://doi.org/10.1016/j.juro.2010.04.078.*

Falkow, Stanley, and Donald Kennedy. "Antibiotics, Animals, and People—Again!" *Science* 291, no. 5503 (January 2001): 397–397. *https://doi.org/10.1126/science.1058907.*

Graham, Jay P., John J. Boland, and Ellen Silbergeld. "Growth Promoting Antibiotics in Food Animal Production: An Economic Analysis." *Public Health Reports* 122, no. 1 (January 2007): 79–87. *https://doi.org/10.1177/003335490712200111.*

Kotwani, Anita, and Kathleen Holloway. "Trends in Antibiotic Use among Outpatients in New Delhi, India." *BMC Infectious Diseases* 11, no. 1 (April 2011): 1–9. *https://doi.org/10.1186/1471-2334-11-99.*

Larsson, D. G. Joakim. "Pollution from Drug Manufacturing: Review and Perspectives." *Philosophical Transactions of the Royal Society B: Biological Sciences* 369, no. 1656 (November 2014): 20130571. *https://doi.org/10.1098/rstb.2013.0571.*

Liu, Xiaohui, Shaoyong Lu, Wei Guo, Beidou Xi, and Weiliang Wang. "Antibiotics in the Aquatic Environments: A Review of Lakes, China." *Science of the Total Environment* 627 (June 2018): 1195–1208. *https://doi.org/10.1016/j.scitotenv.2018.01.271.*

Maillard, Jean-Yves, Sally Bloomfield, Joana Rosado Coelho, Phillip Collier, Barry Cookson, Séamus Fanning, Andrew Hill, et al. "Does Microbicide Use in Consumer Products Promote Antimicrobial Resistance? A Critical Review and Recommendations for a Cohesive Approach to Risk Assessment." *Microbial Drug Resistance* 19, no. 5 (October 2013): 344–54. *https://doi.org/10.1089/mdr.2013.0039.*

Marshall, Bonnie M., Eduardo Robleto, Theresa Dumont, and Stuart B. Levy. "The Frequency of Antibiotic-Resistant Bacteria in Homes Differing in Their Use of Surface Antibacterial Agents." *Current Microbiology* 65, no. 4 (October 2012): 407–15. *https://doi.org/10.1007/s00284-012-0172-x.*

Martin J. Blaser. *Missing Microbes: How the Overuse of Antibiotics Is Fueling Our Modern Plagues.* New York: Henry Holt and Co, 2014.

Mathew, Alan G., Robin Cissell, and S. Liamthong. "Antibiotic Resistance in Bacteria Associated with Food Animals: A United States Perspective of Livestock Production." *Foodborne Pathogens and Disease* 4, no. 2 (June 2007): 115–33. *https://doi.org/10.1089/fpd.2006.0066.*

McManus, Patricia S., and Virginia O. Stockwell. "Antibiotic Use for Plant Disease Management in the United States." *Plant Health Progress* 2, no. 1 (January 2001): 14. *https://doi.org/10.1094/php-2001-0327-01-rv.*

McManus, Patricia S., Virginia O. Stockwell, George W. Sundin, and Alan L. Jones. "Antibiotic Use in Plant Agriculture." *Annual Review of Phytopathology* 40, no. 1 (September 2002): 443–65. *https://doi.org/10.1146/annurev.phyto.40.120301.093927.*

Nathan, Carl, and Otto Cars. "Antibiotic Resistance — Problems, Progress, and Prospects." *New England Journal of Medicine* 371, no. 19 (November 2014): 1761–63. *https://doi.org/10.1056/NEJMp1408040.*

Okerman, Lieve, and Jan Van Hoof. "Evaluation of the European Four-Plate Test as a Tool for Screening Antibiotic Residues in Meat Samples from Retail Outlets." *Journal of AOAC INTERNATIONAL* 81, no. 1 (January 1998): 51–56. *https://doi.org/10.1093/JAOAC/81.1.51.*

Sanchez, Wilfried, William Sremski, Benjamin Piccini, Olivier Palluel, Emmanuelle Maillot-Maréchal, Stéphane Betoulle, Ali Jaffal, et al. "Adverse Effects in Wild Fish Living Downstream from Pharmaceutical Manufacture Discharges." *Environment International* 37, no. 8 (November 2011): 1342–48. *https://doi.org/10.1016/j.envint.2011.06.002.*

Shah, Akshay. "Tackling the Crisis of Antibiotic Resistance." *South Asian Journal of Cancer* 2, no. 1 (January 2013): 3. *https://doi.org/10.4103/2278-330x.105859.*

Shallcross, Laura J. "Editorials: Antibiotic Overuse: A Key Driver of Antimicrobial Resistance." *British Journal of General Practice* 64, no. 629 (December 2014): 604–5. *https://doi.org/10.3399/bjgp14X682561.*

Ventola, C Lee. "The Antibiotic Resistance Crisis: Causes and Threats." *P & T Journal* 40, no. 4 (April 2015): 277–83. *https://www.ncbi.nlm.nih.gov/pmc/articles/PMC4378521/.*

Walther, S. M., M. Erlandsson, L. G. Burman, O. Cars, H. Gill, M. Hoffman, B. Isaksson, et al. "Antibiotic Prescription Practices, Consumption and Bacterial Resistance in a Cross Section of Swedish Intensive Care Units." *Acta Anaesthesiologica Scandinavica* 46, no. 9 (October 2002): 1075–81. *https://doi.org/10.1034/j.1399-6576.2002.460904.x.*

Wang, Jin, Pan Wang, Xinghe Wang, Yingdong Zheng, and Yonghong Xiao. "Use and Prescription of Antibiotics in Primary Health Care Settings in China." *JAMA Internal Medicine* 174, no. 12 (December 2014): 1914–20. *https://doi.org/10.1001/jamainternmed.2014.5214.*

Witte, Wolfgang. "Selective Pressure by Antibiotic Use in Livestock." *International Journal of Antimicrobial Agents* 16, no. SUPPL. 1 (November 2000): 19–24. *https://doi.org/10.1016/s0924-8579(00)00301-0.*

Wright, Elli A., Joanne L. Fothergill, Steve Paterson, Michael A. Brockhurst, and Craig Winstanley. "Sub-Inhibitory Concentrations of Some Antibiotics Can Drive Diversification of Pseudomonas Aeruginosa Populations in Artificial Sputum Medium." *BMC Microbiology* 13, no. 1 (July 2013): 1–12. *https://doi.org/10.1186/1471-2180-13-170.*

APPENDIX CHAPTER 18

Andersson, D. I., D. Hughes, and J. Z. Kubicek-Sutherland. "Mechanisms and Consequences of Bacterial Resistance to Antimicrobial Peptides." *Drug Resistance Updates* 26 (May 2016): 43–57. *https://doi.org/10.1016/j.drup.2016.04.002.*

Bahar, Ali, and Dacheng Ren. "Antimicrobial Peptides." *Pharmaceuticals* 6, no. 12 (November 2013): 1543–75. *https://doi.org/10.3390/ph6121543.*

Chan, Benjamin K., Stephen T. Abedon, and Catherine Loc-Carrillo. "Phage Cocktails and the Future of Phage Therapy." *Future Microbiology* 8, no. 6 (June 2013): 769–83. *https://doi.org/10.2217/fmb.13.47.*

Chanishvili, Nina. "Phage Therapy-History from Twort and d'Herelle Through Soviet Experience to Current Approaches." *Advances in Virus Research* 83 (January 2012): 3–40. *https://doi.org/10.1016/B978-0-12-394438-2.00001-3.*

Duckworth, Donna H., and Paul A. Gulig. "Bacteriophages: Potential Treatment for Bacterial Infections." *BioDrugs* 16, no. 1 (August 2002): 57–62. *https://doi.org/10.2165/00063030-200216010-00006.*

Dykman, Lev, and Nikolai Khlebtsov. "Gold Nanoparticles in Biomedical Applications: Recent Advances and Perspectives." *Chemical Society Reviews* 41, no. 6 (February 2012): 2256–82. *https://doi.org/10.1039/c1cs15166e.*

Elizabeth Kutter and Alexander Sulakvelidze, Bacteriophages: Biology and Applications. Boca Raton, FL: CRC Press, 2004.

Epand, Richard M., and Hans J. Vogel. "Diversity of Antimicrobial Peptides and Their Mechanisms of Action." *Biochimica et Bio-*

physica Acta — Biomembranes 1462, no. 1–2 (December 1999): 11–28. *https://doi.org/10.1016/S0005-2736(99)00198-4.*

FForest Rowher, Merry Youle, Heather Maughan and Nao Hisakawa. Life in Our Phage World. Cincinnati, OH: Holon, 2014.

Gall, Yasha M., and Mikhail B. Konashev. "The Discovery of Gramicidin S: The Intellectual Transformation of G.F. Gause from Biologist to Researcher of Antibiotics and on Its Meaning for the Fate of Russian Genetics." *History and Philosophy of the Life Sciences* 23, no. 1 (2001): 137–50. *https://doi.org/10.2307/23332264.*

García-Quintanilla, Meritxell, Marina R. Pulido, Rafael López-Rojas, Jerónimo Pachón, and Michael J. McConnell. "Emerging Therapies for Multidrug Resistant Acinetobacter Baumannii." *Trends in Microbiology* 21, no. 3 (March 2013): 157–63. *https://doi.org/10.1016/j.tim.2012.12.002.*

Hamad, Bashar. "The Antibiotics Market." *Nature Reviews Drug Discovery* 9, no. 9 (September 2010): 675–76. *https://doi.org/10.1038/nrd3267.*

Hansen, Malene Plejdrup, Tammy C. Hoffmann, Amanda R. McCullough, Mieke L. van Drie, and Chris B. Del Mar. "Antibiotic Resistance: What Are the Opportunities for Primary Care in Alleviating the Crisis?" *Frontiers in Public Health* 3 (February 2015): 35. *https://doi.org/10.3389/fpubh.2015.00035.*

Hulla, J. E., S. C. Sahu, and A. W. Hayes. "Nanotechnology: History and Future." *Human and Experimental Toxicology* 34, no. 12 (December 2015): 1318–21. *https://doi.org/10.1177/0960327115603588.*

Hyman, Paul, and Stephen T. Abedon. "Bacteriophage Host Range and Bacterial Resistance." *Advances in Applied Microbiol-*

ogy 70 (January 2010): 217–48. *https://doi.org/10.1016/S0065-2164(10)70007-1.*

Jollès, P. "Relationship between Chemical Structure and Biological Activity of Hen Egg-White Lysozyme and Lysozymes of Different Species." *Proceedings of the Royal Society of London. Series B. Biological Sciences* 167, no. 1009 (April 1967): 350–64. *https://doi.org/10.1098/rspb.1967.0033.*

Keen, Eric C. "A Century of Phage Research: Bacteriophages and the Shaping of Modern Biology." *BioEssays* 37, no. 1 (January 2015): 6–9. *https://doi.org/10.1002/bies.201400152.*

———. "Felix d'Herelle and Our Microbial Future." *Future Microbiology* 7, no. 12 (December 2012): 1337–39. *https://doi.org/10.2217/fmb.12.115.*

Li, Wen Ru, Xiao Bao Xie, Qing Shan Shi, Hai Yan Zeng, You Sheng Ou-Yang, and Yi Ben Chen. "Antibacterial Activity and Mechanism of Silver Nanoparticles on Escherichia Coli." *Applied Microbiology and Biotechnology* 85, no. 4 (January 2010): 1115–22. *https://doi.org/10.1007/s00253-009-2159-5.*

Manning, Mary Lou, Jeanne Pfeiffer, and Elaine L. Larson. "Combating Antibiotic Resistance: The Role of Nursing in Antibiotic Stewardship." *American Journal of Infection Control* 44, no. 12 (December 2016): 1454–57. *https://doi.org/10.1016/j.ajic.2016.06.023.*

Neal, Andrew L. "What Can Be Inferred from Bacterium-Nanoparticle Interactions about the Potential Consequences of Environmental Exposure to Nanoparticles?" *Ecotoxicology* 17, no. 5 (July 2008): 362–71. *https://doi.org/10.1007/s10646-008-0217-x.*

Panáček, Aleš, Libor Kvítek, Monika Smékalová, Renata Večeřová, Milan Kolář, Magdalena Röderová, Filip Dyčka, et al. "Bacterial Resistance to Silver Nanoparticles and How to Overcome It." *Nature Nanotechnology* 13, no. 1 (January 2018): 65–71. *https://doi.org/10.1038/s41565-017-0013-y.*

Qayyum, Shariq, and Asad U. Khan. "Nanoparticles: Vs. Biofilms: A Battle against Another Paradigm of Antibiotic Resistance." *MedChemComm* 7, no. 8 (August 2016): 1479–98. *https://doi. org/10.1039/c6md00124f.*

Richard P. Feynman, "There's Plenty of Room at the Bottom." Transcript of a talk presented to the American Physical Society in Pasasena, CA, December 29, 1959. *https://www2.cs.duke.edu/ courses/cps296.5/spring06/papers/Feynman59.pdf.*

Slavin, Yael N., Jason Asnis, Urs O. Häfeli, and Horacio Bach. "Metal Nanoparticles: Understanding the Mechanisms behind Antibacterial Activity." *Journal of Nanobiotechnology* 15, no. 1 (October 2017): 65. *https://doi.org/10.1186/s12951-017-0308-z.*

Starner, Timothy D., W. Edward Swords, Michael A. Apicella, and Paul B. McCray. "Susceptibility of Nontypeable Haemophilus Influenzae to Human β-Defensins Is Influenced by Lipooli-gosaccharide Acylation." *Infection and Immunity* 70, no. 9 (September 2002): 5287–89. *https://doi.org/10.1128/IAI.70.9.5287-5289.2002.*

Sulakvelidze, A., and Jr Morris. "Bacteriophages as Therapeutic Agents." *Annals of Medicine* 33, no. 8 (November 2001): 507–9. *https://doi.org/10.3109/07853890108995959.*

Torres-Barceló, Clara. "Phage Therapy Faces Evolutionary Chal-lenges." *Viruses* 10, no. 6 (June 2018): 323. *https://doi.org/10.3390/ v10060323.*

Twort, F. W. "An Investigation on the Nature of Ultra-Microscopic Viruses." *The Lancet* 186, no. 4814 (December 1915): 1241–43. *https://doi.org/10.1016/S0140-6736(01)20383-3.*

Voelker, Rebecca. "FDA Approves Bacteriophage Trial." *JAMA* 321, no. 7 (February 2019): 638. *https://doi.org/10.1001/jama.2019.0510.*

Wei, Hongping. "Bacteriophages, Revitalized after 100 Years in the Shadow of Antibiotics." *Virologica Sinica* 30, no. 1 (February 2015): 1–2. *https://doi.org/10.1007/s12250-014-3562-y.*

Yates, Richard R. "New Intervention Strategies for Reducing Antibiotic Resistance." *Chest* 115, no. 3 SUPPL. (March 1999): 24S-27S. *https://doi.org/10.1378/chest.115.suppl_1.24S.*

Yeaman, Michael R., and Nannette Y. Yount. "Mechanisms of Antimicrobial Peptide Action and Resistance." *Pharmacological Reviews* 55, no. 1 (March 2003): 27–55. *https://doi.org/10.1124/pr.55.1.2.*

APPENDIX CHAPTER 19

Brundage, John F., and G. Dennis Shanks. "What Really Happened during the 1918 Influenza Pandemic? The Importance of Bacterial Secondary Infections." *The Journal of Infectious Diseases* 196, no. 11 (December 2007): 1717–18. *https://doi.org/10.1086/522355.*

Cox, Michael J, Nicholas Loman, Debby Bogaert, and Justin O'Grady. "Co-Infections: Potentially Lethal and Unexplored in COVID-19." *The Lancet Microbe* 1, no. 1 (May 2020): e11. *https://doi.org/10.1016/s2666-5247(20)30009-4.*

Fernandes, Nuno. "Economic Effects of Coronavirus Outbreak (COVID-19) on the World Economy," SSRN Electronic Journal, (March 2020). *https://doi.org/10.2139/ssrn.3557504.*

Julie L. Gerberding "Antibiotic Resistance: The Hidden Threat Lurking behind COVID-19," STAT, March 23, 2020.

Kash, John C., and Jeffery K. Taubenberger. "The Role of Viral, Host, and Secondary Bacterial Factors in Influenza Pathogenesis." *American Journal of Pathology* 185, no. 6 (June 2015): 1528–36. *https://doi.org/10.1016/j.ajpath.2014.08.030.*

Kash, John C., Kathie Anne Walters, A. Sally Davis, Aline Sandouk, Louis M. Schwartzman, Brett W. Jagger, Daniel S. Chertow, et al. "Lethal Synergism of 2009 Pandemic H1n1 Influenza Virus and Streptococcus Pneumoniae Coinfection Is Associated with Loss of Murine Lung Repair Responses." *MBio* 2, no. 5 (September 2011). *https://doi.org/10.1128/mBio.00172-11.*

Kathy Talkington "Oncologists Fear Rising Antibiotic Resistance Will Make Cancer Treatments Less Effective" The Pew Charitable Trusts, March 11, 2020. *https://www.pewtrusts.org/en/research-and-analysis/articles/2020/03/11/oncologists-fear-rising-antibiotic-resistance-will-make-cancer-treatments-less-effective.*

Kolk, J. H.(Han) van der. "Antibiotic Resistance from Prehistoric to Modern Times." *Veterinary Quarterly* 35, no. 1 (January 2015): 1. *https://doi.org/10.1080/01652176.2015.1008215.*

MacIntyre, Chandini Raina, Abrar Ahmad Chughtai, Michelle Barnes, Iman Ridda, Holly Seale, Renin Toms, and Anita Heywood. "The Role of Pneumonia and Secondary Bacterial Infection in Fatal and Serious Outcomes of Pandemic Influenza a(H1N1)Pdm09." *BMC Infectious Diseases* 18, no. 1 (December 2018): 1–20. *https://doi.org/10.1186/s12879-018-3548-0.*

McAuley, Julie L., Felicita Hornung, Kelli L. Boyd, Amber M. Smith, Raelene McKeon, Jack Bennink, Jonathan W. Yewdell, and Jonathan A. McCullers. "Expression of the 1918 Influenza A Virus PB1-F2 Enhances the Pathogenesis of Viral and Secondary Bacterial Pneumonia." *Cell Host and Microbe* 2, no. 4 (October 2007): 240–49. *https://doi.org/10.1016/j.chom.2007.09.001.*

Mendelson, Marc, and Malebona Precious Matsoso. "The World Health Organization Global Action Plan for Antimicrobial Resistance." *South African Medical Journal* 105, no. 5 (2015): 325. *https://doi.org/10.7196/SAMJ.9644.*

Morens, David M., Jeffery K. Taubenberger, and Anthony S. Fauci. "Predominant Role of Bacterial Pneumonia as a Cause of Death in Pandemic Influenza: Implications for Pandemic Influenza Preparedness." *The Journal of Infectious Diseases* 198, no. 7 (October 2008): 962–70. *https://doi.org/10.1086/591708.*

Morris, Denise E., David W. Cleary, and Stuart C. Clarke. "Secondary Bacterial Infections Associated with Influenza Pandemics." *Frontiers in Microbiology* 8, no. JUN (June 2017): 1041. *https://doi.org/10.3389/fmicb.2017.01041.*

Spinelli, A., and G. Pellino. "COVID-19 Pandemic: Perspectives on an Unfolding Crisis." *British Journal of Surgery* 107, no. 7 (June 2020): 785–87. *https://doi.org/10.1002/bjs.11627.*

Teillant, Aude, Sumanth Gandra, Devra Barter, Daniel J. Morgan, and Ramanan Laxminarayan. "Potential Burden of Antibiotic Resistance on Surgery and Cancer Chemotherapy Antibiotic Prophylaxis in the USA: A Literature Review and Modelling Study." *The Lancet Infectious Diseases* 15, no. 12 (December 2015): 1429–37. *https://doi.org/10.1016/S1473-3099(15)00270-4.*

World Health Organization "New Report Calls for Urgent Action to Avert Antimicrobial Resistance Crisis," April 29, 2019.. *https://www.who.int/news-room/detail/29-04-2019-new-report-calls-for-urgent-action-to-avert-antimicrobial-resistance-crisis.*